Water Sprite Emerging

Awakening the Master Feminine

Published by Grand Trine Productions
Atlanta, Georgia

Library of Congress Catalog Card Number:

ISBN 978-0-9643263-4-5

Table of Contents

CHAPTER 1 THE HOUSE OF THE WOMAN 5

THE FOUR FEMININE ARCHETYPES...5
THE MOON ARCHETYPE 7
THE SEATED HAWK 9
THE ELEGANT ROSE 10

CHAPTER 2 THE DECLINE OF THE FEMININE WOMAN....................22

THE CONCEPT OF NATURAL SEXUALITY 23

CHAPTER 3 THE MASTER FEMININE FACULTY 26

SECOND PUBERTY MOON EDITION...29
THE AWAKENING CIRCLE 30
AWAKENING EXERCISES 30
THE AWAKENING REGIMEN 30

CHAPTER 4 MONEY, POWER AND RELIGION 36

THE SCARCITY MODEL 44

CHAPTER 5 TOXIC WOMB SYNDROME 51

THE WOMB IMPRINT..53
REPRODUCTIVE SYSTEM ISSUES 55
FIBROID TUMORS...58
CANCER 58

CHAPTER 6 AWAKENING THE MOON..63

SECOND PUBERTY MOON EDITION...64
ERASING BAD MEMORIES 67

CHAPTER 7 AWAKENING THE ROSE..70

ABOUT TANTRA..72
ABOUT NATURAL SEXUAL IDEOLOGY 73
GENITAL REFLEXOLOGY..74
ACHIEVING THE ORGASMIC PLATEAU 81
HER BREASTS 85
TANTRIC MANTRA..88
SECOND PUBERTY ROSE EDITION 90
THE NON ORGASMIC FEMALE 95
FEMALE BEAUTY AS EROTIC ART..97
TANTRA ENERGY HEALING 100
THE SEXUAL RENAISSANCE...102
AWAKENING EXERCISE 103
CASE EXAMPLE- JENNIFER 107

Awakening the Master Feminine

The House of the Woman

Chapter 1   The House of the Woman

The house of the woman is a metaphor for the attributes in nature which define the distinction of female from the male. The 'House of the Woman' contains ALL of these possible traits and attributes. In other words all of the possible feminine attributes that any woman has ever had. For the spirit of each woman contains a composite of the spirits of every ancestor of that woman, going back 10,000 years. And on the physical side, in her DNA all of these physical attributes are stored and she can bring forward any one of them. In other words, any female born today has the potential to manifest any trait that any woman in her bloodline has had. Thus the house of the woman is like a bank of potential attributes. These attributes are stored there in her storehouse. But they do not do anything or cause anything to happen unless they are activated. There are tens of thousands of these attributes which make a woman feminine and make her different from a man. Any woman can manifest any one of these attributes.

The Four Feminine Archetypes

There are four sets of these feminine attributes. The traits or attributes we describe above in the house of the woman fit naturally into four categories. We can say these are archetypes of the feminine energy. They derive from the elemental nature of energy. We name the four archetypes as:

1. The Moon
2. The Seated Hawk
3. The Elegant Rose
4. The   Treasure   Chest

These four archetypes of feminine energy correspond to the most common life tasks of the female.
1. Maternal instinct.
2. Right-brain orientation and leaning.
3. Pleasure attributes.
4. Nesting instinct.

Each archetype is not one attribute, but a bank or category of attributes which have similar functions. These four archetypes of feminine energy define what we call a feminine woman, or a woman with natural feminine energy. If a female brought forward all 100% of the possible attributes from all four archetypes, she would become the highest and best version of a woman she is capable of becoming. She would almost be a goddess, an embodiment of divinity. The more she is able to awaken these traits out of the dormant and latent state and infuse them into her actual physical and spiritual being, the more perfect will be her expression of womanhood. The less of these traits and attributes she is able to develop, then the more she will resemble a juvenile or an animal or an artificial human.

Now in the table that follows we show the key words for each feminine archetype and contrast them with each other. As we move through the book, we will be exploring each aspect of the feminine nature in some detail. Not every woman is expressing all four archetypes, and part of the job of the awakening circles is to uncover for each woman in a healing program, which archetypes she has brought forward, and which archetypes are still asleep in her subconscious. This information will be very helpful in changing her relationships, changing her sexual life and improving her reproductive health.   And a female can change her feminine profile. That is what this book is all about!

The House of the Woman
The Four Archetypes of Feminine Attributes

The Moon	The Seated Hawk
Nurturing, Caring, Generous, Submissive, Maternal. Nurture What is Growing. Constructing Family.	Synergistic, Imposing, Intuitive Right Brain Thinking Intuit the Plan
The Elegant Rose	**The Treasure Chest**
Joyous, beautiful, sensual, artistic, carefree, arousing. Giving and Generating Pleasure Redesigning reality.	Unifying, Prosperous, Social, Earthy, And Matriarchal. Constructing Community. The Harvest, Abundance

The Moon Archetype

Icon: The icon of the Moon archetype is the moon, and inside the moon are a clutch of eggs.
Image: The image for purposes of visualization is a young mother with her baby to her breasts.

It is an intuitive faculty of nurturing others. It is to supply the need implied by a growing thing. It is the capacity to give, and the desire to give, without a sense of loss. It generates an unending supply, based on the need to give unceasingly. It is the cornucopia for the starving. It is the well in the desert.

We use the icon of the moon to denote the component or archetype of feminine energy that is associated with the abstract concept of an egg. This type of feminine energy is designed to bring forth new life, or support existing life. The attributes of the moon archetype are:

- Receptiveness,
- Instinct to nurture,
- Devotion,
- Attention to detail,
- Maternal,

When the woman's master feminine faculty has awakened this archetype in the woman, she becomes fertile. And more than this, she gains the capacity to give, without a sense of loss. Normally this is a contradiction. When you subtract a quantity from a thing, it should logically become less. But in this case the woman actually becomes more. She gives, and yet she increases. This faculty is special, and different from any other component of the feminine energy. The mechanism within this energy is such that it reorders the woman's spirit and body to compensate for her giving. Her body takes in extra nutrients, so that she always has more than what is needed to give and yet retain the balance. Her spirit takes in extra energy so that she distributes energy, but never runs low. The perfect example of the moon icon is the mother breastfeeding her baby. Women gain weight during pregnancy and as they breastfeed the baby they gradually lose weight. But when they reach their ideal weight, continued feeding of the baby causes her to gain muscle mass. And when the baby is done with the breasts, and converts to table food, the mother is left with a better physique than when she first got pregnant. There is always more milk than the baby needs. Without this energy present, she will experience difficulty with the milk. It may hurt to feed the baby. She does not enjoy it. When the energy is present, the mother experiences a feeling similar to sexual arousal as the baby sucks. She can have an orgasm and this is normal. It helps the milk.

This energy sets up in the female a disposition to give. She desires to give. And the act of giving is pleasing to her. In giving, and in seeing the target of her giving grow, the woman is made spiritually whole. The more this energy is cultivated in the woman's persona, the more generous is her attitude. The only thing that disturbs this cycle of regeneration is the issue of security. If the woman does not feel secure, her generous nature suffers.

This energy inspires in the woman a desire to form a family. It bonds her to the man in a family way. It takes her deeper into a yin profile and away from the outside world. Thus she gives over these external chores to a man to do, and he is charged to protect her and do the external things for her. Thus this energy causes a woman to seek out a man to regulate the 'external' stuff outside the door of the home.

The Seated Hawk

Icon: The icon of the Seated Hawk is a woman's body with the head of a hawk.
Image: The image for purposes of visualization is a wise and stern looking woman, holding a set of blueprints in her hand. She is seated on a chair of authority. Rays of power radiate out from the chair.

This energy represents the head, the plan, and the blueprint. When the master feminine faculty awakens this archetype, it brings on line the woman's intuitive function of the right brain. It is a woman's ability to intuit the solution or plan straight from the spirit world or DNA. It is without reason or logic.

This is the woman who is moving all things from behind the scenes. This is the queen bee who orchestrates the life of the colony of bees from a central place. She does not do anything herself. Everything is automatic, there is no thinking. This is the conductor who plays no instruments. She gives each musician a sheet with the notes on it, their own part, but only she has the big score, the blueprint. The woman is yin, and thus can not set the plans in motion herself. To do this, she needs a man, who sees the individual steps, and can follow in a linear step by step way. The male has vision, he looks ahead to see what is needed to do the plan, what obstructions must be removed first. But males typically do not comprehend the big picture. They are too caught up in the steps, and the separate pictures, to see that all is connected. The male has difficulty seeing that love is a circle; it connects the end back to the source. **It is in love that all beginnings and all outcomes have true purpose.** Men think you need to create a logical plan based on some purpose. The woman knows that the plan and the purpose are already there, you just need to sense it, to feel it. You can not always understand your way through life. You feel it first. Some men can see the big picture. But the masculine energy is left-brain in orientation. It is okay. They work well together.

When the woman has the full connection into her right brain hemisphere, men have the tendency to follow her. Why? Perhaps because she is nearly always right. The superior man will follow her and be happy. He knows following the right plan brings success. The inferior man may follow her, because he fears being wrong again. His ego has a problem giving her credit. He feels bad because he did not come up with the plan that worked. He does not know his role. As a man sometimes you follow, and sometimes you lead. Now when the woman combines the Seated Hawk attribute with the pleasure attribute of the Elegant Rose, men are compelled to follow her. They line up to do her bidding. But we must be careful here. A lot of women just naturally have their right brain thing going on. But most do not. They get a hunch here and there, but that is not what we are talking about. The right brain requires trance. You have to cultivate this faculty. To be pure the woman must not inject her left brain logic in there. So often the right brain intuition goes smack dead in the face of logic. Everything says go west, society says go west, your intuition says no, go east. You must have courage to follow. Understand that the womb is a direct connection to mother God. God is not seeking to make things difficult for us. He/She/It wants us to know the plan.

The Elegant Rose

Icon: The icon of the Elegant Rose is a splendid rose, on a pillow of silk.
Image: The image for purposes of visualization is a very voluptuous and seductive woman lounging on a couch. She wears a suggestive outfit, slit in the front to expose her smooth sleek thighs. She is enticing. She is effortlessly beautiful. On the couch with her are honey, flowers and frankincense.

The Elegant Rose imparts an essence and form into the woman that causes her to be experienced by the environment around her as being pleasing. She especially generates pleasure to men. More importantly, this essence of the Elegant Rose causes the woman to feel pleasure herself, from the act of giving pleasure and beauty to others. It is instinctively satisfying to her when she knows that others perceive her as being beautiful. She becomes wired so that it pleases her immensely to be touched, seen, smelled, tasted, and admired. She desires to place men into a trance, to intoxicate them. This is a power. When she combines her attractive energy with any of the other three archetypes it compels men to engage that function.

A woman generates this pleasure because she attains a harmony of form and function that is in harmonic resonance with key life vibrations. When fully expressed this energy or vibration even has a positive effect on plants and animals. The vibration of the elegant rose is resident in silk, a love ballad, sweet fragrance, the view from a balcony, and the curves of a voluptuous woman. And the woman who carries this vibration is in harmony with all other things that do. The rose has no practical purpose. It looks beautiful because it just does. The archetype of the elegant rose imparts a Feng Shui to all it touches that creates sensuality. It is like silk compared to burlap, a love ballad compared to plain speech, a balcony instead of a window, a flower instead of weeds, the smell of frankincense, and the taste of a mango.

It is self evident that the central theme of earthly experience is a sensual one. We have five senses to sense pleasure or pain. There is a component within feminine energy that supports and enhances our sensation of pleasure. The truest sensation of pleasure is natural to our being. In this sensation, nothing needs to be consumed; no one is hurt, nor is any quality diminished as this takes place. Natural pleasure occurs in the normal course of being what it is. In the female, the component of feminine energy that supports the experience of pleasure is the archetype of the **Elegant Rose**. Men and women are prototypes of the deity, serving as vessels through which the creator can come into the world and experience his/her/its creation. There are certainly many reasons why we were created, but a central theme of life is experience, in its many forms. Our destiny and evolution begins our journey into experience. Everything we must do to live and thrive on the earth is by nature designed to bring pleasure to us. Food by nature satisfies our appetite, bringing pleasure. Reproduction brings pleasure. Interaction with the natural environment brings pleasure. The earth has an abundance of stuff to see, eat, hear, feel, and smell. And when we live in natural alignment, most of this experience is designed to generate one pleasure after another. Of course if you abandon the natural way, if you live out of alignment with nature, you will probably experience more pain than pleasure. The sensation of pleasure is a central aspect of our creative and artistic faculties.

All females have the same hardware for detecting the vibrations of interpret these vibrations the same. The response is conditional. In other words our spirit determines how we perceive a sensation, rather we see it as being pleasing or not. This is an energy thing. One woman walks through the park and experiences breath taking <u>beauty</u>. Another woman walks through the same park and sees only trees and grass and scenery. One woman smells incense and it is to her a sweet aroma. Another woman smells the same incense and to her it stinks. Why the difference? It can be shown through hypnosis and other means that people can condition themselves to feel pleasure at sensations they otherwise had little reaction to. It is the change in her auric field, her energy which makes the difference. There is a similar component in the male human that has the same basic effect. When the master feminine faculty brings the archetype of the Elegant Rose on line in the female's persona, she gains the capacity to experience more and more sensations as pleasure. At the same time, this energy shapes that female into a being that generates pleasure to her entire environment. The key to her ability in this regard, is that the female <u>gets pleasure</u> from being pleasing, and giving pleasure.

When the master feminine faculty starts to awaken the feminine energy in a young teen girl she starts to act out a subconscious program that says she is joyous, beautiful, sensual, artistic, and carefree. She immediately wants to be seen, to groom herself different, and to explore her newfound sensuality. A young girl then looks to her parents and society for permission to experience this pleasure. If she continues to cultivate her feminine energy, and receives permission to enjoy pleasure, the extent to which the Elegant Rose can awaken is infinite. But there are many forces in our society that work to shut down her development. And few girls continue to cultivate this energy into their adult life. Unfortunately, in the typical modern female this is the most repressed and under developed portion of her feminine energy. Many of the false beliefs and fears that infest our society impact on our perception of pleasure. This is especially true of sexual pleasure. You would think that a society would encourage pleasure, as part of the experience of abundance. But in the scarcity model, pleasure is more associated with things you have to buy, and therefore permission to experience pleasure is associated with degrees of wealth. Sex is also closely tied to the ability to sell things in a commercial sense. The media uses sex to sell stuff, and therefore attractive women also associate their ability to give pleasure to men with a monetary value. Many women do develop the curves and physical features that make them attractive as a result of the early influence of this energy. But many more do not. And even many who do, start to reverse the effect in a few years.

When you walk on the beach and feel the sand and cool water it is naturally pleasant. The ocean is not hurt. You do not need to do something special to get the feeling. There is no consumption involved. When you look at a rose it is pleasant. If a man and a woman come together and kiss it can be just like this. If they are both attracted to one another, and both are willing then the kiss produced pleasure. This is then natural pleasure. In order for this to be so, the man must experience pleasure in the act of giving the woman pleasure. And the woman must experience pleasure in the act of giving the man pleasure. However if the woman has not cultivated her sexual energy, and the archetype of the elegant rose is not active in her persona, then she can give the man pleasure, but she will not experience pleasure from giving him pleasure. She kisses him because she likes him, but he gets a sexual thrill out of the kiss and is aroused. She just likes him, but gets no thrill from the kiss. Her elegant rose is not there.

When this archetype of the feminine energy is not developed, the female can not and will not experience any pleasure naturally or fully. Let me say that again. When the archetype of the elegant rose is not fully expressed in the woman, she will have a diminished capacity to experience sexual pleasure, or any pleasure. In such a state, her entire sensory array is thrown off balance. Her appetites attempt to compensate for this by over emphasizing the desire for other things, such as food. This is how many women start their teen years with dispositions for drugs, alcohol and cigarettes. The repercussions of this are wide ranging.

If the elegant rose archetype is substantially awake, the woman's sensory array is fully sensitive, and available for management. She is wired to experience a full array of pleasures. Her nervous system will interpret many common sensations and stimuli as being pleasurable. She may even find some things associated with pain, as having a pleasing component within. If this woman eats an ice cream cone, and a woman who does not have this faculty awake eats the same ice cream cone, it is not at all the same experience. The woman with her elegant rose awake will enjoy the cone, she will taste the flavors deeply, and probably be able to tell you what spices are in there. But she will have no compulsion to eat a cone next week, because this food is not in alignment with her biochemistry. It tastes good to her, but she can take it or leave It. Nor will she have a desire to eat this food when she is depressed or anxious. Now on the other hand, the woman without the elegant rose faculty will have a stronger reaction to the taste of the ice cream cone, even though she can not sense the flavors and textures of the components as well. The consumption of the ice cream treat is sexually satisfying for her on a low level. She is emotionally attached to this food, because it takes the place of something else she is not capable of fully experiencing. If she is depressed or anxious she will desire it. Even though some of the components of the ice cream are toxic to her, she will store these toxins in fat cells, to be able to process the negative memories that blocked her faculty, as well as the unnatural programming that gives ice cream an elevated status in her brain chemistry. The woman who has the elegant rose awake will be more optimistic, and have a more natural worldview. She will tend to desire to experience stuff more than normal, and be opposed to regulations and people who criticize her for enjoying life. There are no boundaries here, unless she is evolved in other ways. In other words she will tend to ignore moral, ethnic, legal or safety concerns if these seek to regulate or hinder her from her experiences of pleasure.

If the elegant rose archetype is substantially awake, the woman's sensory array is fully sensitive. Her hormones and dispositions are in harmony to this. She is wired to deliver a full array of pleasures to the opposite sex. The form of her body will be sexually attractive. In some cases her spirit body will be charismatic and magnetic. By magnetic, we mean that literally. Men who see her will be drawn to her by more than just her physical attraction. In the presence of her auric field a man who does not have full control of himself will be placed into a mild trance state. In this trance state, he can easily be influenced and programmed by her. She is built to give pleasure, and she enjoys giving this pleasure almost as much as she enjoys receiving it. She wants to keep the lights on during sex, because she loves looking at the face of her man as she sends him into outer space. Men will enjoy smelling her, and in extreme cases she will emit pheromones. Men will enjoy hearing her talk, regardless of the content. Just like mothers love to hear their babies make just about any kind of sound, so men are enchanted by the sounds she makes. If she can sing, entire crowds of people will enjoy it, and it will have the most profound effect on her mate. Her touch is very pleasing, and often has healing qualities as well. She will be capable of experiencing sexual pleasure through openings in her body not normally associated with sex. Her eyes, ears, mouth, and anus are erogenous zones. She can condition and train herself to experience pleasure with these openings in a number of ways. Such a woman is easy to arouse in bed. She might let a man tie her up or role play, but these things are not necessary for her, and may be a distraction. For her foreplay is more than preparation. She is getting more pleasure out of fore play than most women get out of sex. Her main challenge is to find a man who can satisfy her. Most men and women will judge her or seek to take advantage of her if they discover how deeply she can engross herself in an experience. Very few men are trained to be capable of bringing her adequate levels of satisfaction on a regular basis. Therefore they have two very serious potential issues. One of these is the danger of sexually transmitted diseases. Another is the very real probability of infidelity on their part.

As you will see, our creative faculty, our sexual experience and our sensation of pleasure of any kind are all tied together. The onset of the elegant rose faculty puts the woman into a state that is more right brain in orientation. Unless she intentionally cultivates a left brain presence through her job or other aspects of her being, she will appear to the untrained eye as being mentally slow, easily distracted, and somewhat illogical about routine things. A teenage girl in the midst of this dynamic can go from an 'A' student in math to a 'C' math student in a few months. She has not decreased in intelligence, but the equation between her right brain and left brain has changed. It will come back in a few years if she wants it to. It is what is called the butterfly effect. Butterflies rarely fly in a straight line, but they get were they are going. If a woman awakens her elegant rose faculty and the other archetypes of her feminine energy have not come on line fully yet, there will be a certain level of imbalance in her behavior. I have observed such women park their car, and leave the windows and sun roof open. At the time the clouds overhead clearly signaled that rain was about to come. They go inside their home, and it never registers that they should have put up the windows. In two hours they come back outside to go somewhere, and the car is soaked from the rain. There is no blame in this. She just needs to finish bringing her energy on line. Certainly this archetype can have its drawbacks at stages, but the benefits far outweigh any negatives.

Most women today do not manifest their elegant rose archetype to a great degree. These women tend to be more grounded in reality, more left brain in orientation, less attractive to men, and more focused on their careers. They may not see life through the rose colored glasses that the females with the elegant rose are inclined to. Therefore, there is the tendency for the underdeveloped women to judge the women who have awakened this faculty. Sometimes this judgment is harsh. This is counterproductive. For all women need to assist each other to full development of their feminine energy. No matter which of these four archetypes a female brings forward, she can assist other women by just being in their presence. Her energy will help them bring forth their energy.

The Treasure Chest

Icon: The icon of the Treasure Chest is a decorative chest, box or ting.
Image: For the purposes of visualization, imagine the chest or ting sitting on an altar surrounded by gold coins, precious gems, title deeds of property, ancient books, patent certificates, and treasure maps. Behind the altar stands the goddess with her wings outstretched. She grants a blessing to the things on the altar.

Inside the chest is the spirit of the goddess, the highest and best version of womankind. It implies abundance without corruption. It speaks to the gradual steering of mankind away from the inferior life to the superior life. It is the sacred use of material things, the alchemy of the mundane into the spiritual. It stores up treasure.

The Treasure Chest is talking about the internal drive of a woman to gather resources to support her domestic economy. Down through the ages men have been thought of as hunters and women as gatherers. So the Treasure Chest energy is the **nesting** and **gathering** aspect of the feminine energy. This is the source of the female urge to shop. There is a natural component of feminine energy that desires to experience the abundance and plenty of creation. But this is different from her maternal drive to reproduce and nurture. In fact in some ways it is the opposite of that drive. The attention of the mother is focused in toward her children. The focus of the female with the treasure chest energy is focused toward a collective, a group, a tribe. It is community. It is more selfish in that she wants to be a part of something bigger so that she can personally prosper and enjoy resources, society, wealth, and refinement. In the case of the moon energy she wants only to give to others. Here she wants to take, so that she can experience. In our society this urge presents her with many challenges and issues.
        In nature, the yin and feminine element is not aggressive against other life forms. The yang male is a hunter, but the yin female is a gatherer. Hunting is yang. Gathering is yin. Can you see that? Hunting

implies that you are going to kill and violate what you hunt. It is blood. This is not feminine. Hunting implies scarcity. Gathering is yin. Vegetables do not run away from you. There is abundance, plenty for everybody. You just calmly walk up and harvest it. You do not hunt rice, berries or mangos; you just pick or cut it. Hunting is about scarcity, gathering is about abundance. Now these same principles apply to harvesting men, money, property and intangible corporate assets. In the scarcity model, in the hunting motif, there is the implication that in order for us to have more, we need to deny somebody else. To carry this energy a woman has to purge this false belief from her psyche. The Treasure Chest energy represents the natural way we harvest the abundance all around us. The natural model is a model of abundance. But the average person may say, so what? Yes there are billions of dollars in the economy and tons of food on farms and tons of fish in the sea and all manner of stuff in stores and warehouses, but it is not mine. The individual person cries out, where is my abundance? How do I get mines? The golden chest represents this harvesting and collecting energy. How do we take the potential that exists "out there" and make that something we have personally. The goddess holds in her hand the key to this question. The key is unity. The image of the goddess conveys two themes:

- The way to best harvest abundance is through joint effort. Different tasks, but common purpose. It is a theme of unity.
- The way to best enjoy abundance after harvest is to share. Different contributions, but common sharing. It is a theme of unity

So the Treasure Chest energy is the gathering aspect of the feminine energy that seeks to bring about prosperity via a joint or group effort. It is one common unity. Therefore a woman with the treasure chest energy harvests what she needs, and does not "hunt" it. This applies to money, resources, mates, land and intangible assets. Some women today hunt men in an aggressive way, instead of gently gathering them in. Whenever a woman hunts something she pretty much is sure to damage it.

Femininity is an Energy

What is femininity? What is the definition of being "feminine?" The thing that makes a woman feminine is an energy It is important to note that while a woman is born with the tendency to be feminine, she can make the choice not to remain feminine. Being defined as a woman by gender, and being defined as being feminine by energy, are two separate things. The feminine energy causes a child to be born with female genes, and female reproductive organs. That is physical. Once the child is born and has these physical qualities of genes and reproductive organs, she is by gender a woman. But after that, she has a choice. If she decides to cultivate the male energy instead of the female energy natal to her, she can and will become more and more masculine, until it becomes hard to tell her apart from a man. She will start to look more like a man, and act more like a man. It is this energy that gives a human woman the qualities that make her female as opposed to male. It is not her physical womb or genes that make her female. In order to define this feminine energy, and the master feminine faculty, we need to introduce some concepts and terms that you may not be very familiar with. Try to bear with me. This abstract stuff is very necessary.

Humans are energy beings. This is the beginning of the deeper understanding of sex, gender, personality or emotions, etc. Our body, our mind, our life is what it is because of our energy. When we use the words spirit, auric field, energy body or life force, all these things are talking about energy. We can define feminine energy based on:
1. How it is different from masculine energy.
2. Based on the attributes it imparts to a living organism.

We start our lesson in quantum physics at the atomic level. Let's talk about yin and yang.   Yin and yang are opposites of each other. Think about electricity which has a plus charge and a minus charge. Yin and yang are like that. Yin and yang are elemental concepts. The yin defines the elemental nature of an energy. The proton of an atom has a yin energy, which draws things in toward it and creates the space or form or shape of the atom. The proton with its yin energy holds the electron or yang element in place, inside the field or form of the atom. The proton is passive outside of the atom. It does not react with other electrons outside of the atom. The masculine or yang equal to this is the electron, which is always seeking to escape the atom, moving about the perimeter and always in motion. The yang or electron is active outside of the atom, constantly seeking to act on or with other electrons. The yin is active and dominant inside the atom, controlling the yang electron. The electron or yang is dominant outside the atom, controlling interaction with other atoms.

Yin or Feminine	Yang or Masculine
Space	Light
Lowering of temperature	Raising of temperature
Increase in density	Decrease in density
Collection of energy	Dispersion of energy

Female energy is assigned to the yin polarity. Male energy is assigned to the yang polarity, the opposite energy. At the basic or elemental level feminine attributes are listed in the left column while the opposing masculine attributes are listed on the right. This is the classic yin versus yang definition that applies to non-organic as well as organic things. Yin draws inward toward itself, like a vacuum. Yang pushes out from itself, like an explosion. Yin traps energy. Yang employs energy or frees it. Yin creates space and boundaries. Yang creates reaction and expansion. Yin is more circular or triangular. Yang is more of a straight line, linear. These are general statements, they are not absolute.

Once you start talking about organic beings, the simple yin or yang definition is not complex enough. Feminine and masculine qualities at the organic level begin to incorporate aspects of mind, personality and behavior. At the next level we use general metaphors, describing the energy by saying what it has the general tendency to make a person do, think, or behave. These are the basic attributes of the energy. Thus we see similar dynamics to yin and yang in the organic cell. The cell membrane is the male or yang. The cell nucleus is the yin or female.

Feminine energy	Masculine energy
Attraction	Arousal
Receptiveness & flexibility	Assertiveness & rigidity
Capacity to give, without a sense of loss	An instinct to protect without concern for danger to self

Fertility	Potency

What is the difference between attraction and arousal? Why is one more female than male? For it is obvious that males can be attractive, and females can be aroused. Attraction implies drawing something toward you. The direction is important. Gravity pulls inward. Gravity is an attraction. Attraction is an action, not a reaction. Arousal on the other hand implies a reaction, not an action. It is male. Its direction is outward, away from the being. When you are aroused it implies that you wish to take action on something outside of yourself, the thing that aroused you. We see this direction of energy mirrored in the design of our reproductive organs. The female organs are directed inward. The male organ is directed outward. So there are two things we need to remember.

- First, when we say a person has "female" energy, or is "feminine", this implies a direction to the energy. This direction is inward, toward the person.
- Second, female energy tends to generate action, while male energy tends to generate reaction.

Thus the feminine energy is normally associated with first causes in life, such as nesting, fertility, etc. Thus we say one female attribute is the tendency to be submissive. Why? Because once a woman sets an action in motion, such as attracting something to her, the cycle is not complete until the thing she attracts comes back and acts on her. If she is not submissive or sitting still, the action she has generated can not be fulfilled. Thus the cycle is as follows: The female starts something by generating an action. Her "action" energy goes out and stirs up stuff, and causes a reaction. Her "action" energy goes out and bounces off all the male energy out there which wakes up, reacts, and comes back toward her to do the thing she has instructed to be done. She has to "sit still" or be submissive, and give the male energy a chance to construct or do the thing she has put into action. Can you see that? That is your lesson in quantum physics.

And many women live in daily violation of the nature of their feminine energy and do not even know it! Did you know that fibroid tumors result when a woman violates her feminine energy? A feminine woman is not attractive without being **receptive** and having a **cause** to be attractive. In other words sending out attractive energy without allowing it to come back and create something is unnatural and dysfunctional. That is how fibroid tumors come about. A woman's purpose or cause can be what she chooses. But her energy is not truly feminine unless she has one. Her purpose can be wealth. Let's say for purposes of illustration that her particular life cause at one given point in time is to generate wealth. This woman walks out of her door and allows herself to express her attraction. This is her action. Her cause is to attract wealth. Her action is to be attractive. **The final step is to receive the reaction.** A truly feminine woman will not resist this. Men will respond (react) to her attractive energy, and she welcomes and is receptive to this. Because the energy she sent out was associated with wealth, her energy will build up in the men who respond to her a desire to create more wealth and then bring it to her. The men do not know this, they do not need to. They simply respond, based on their ability to respond. The more attractive and mainly receptive she is, the more they will respond.

Arousal is more a male attribute than a female attribute. It is a reaction. It implies a projection of energy out from oneself. Sexual arousal results from the circulation of the hormone testosterone. Both men and women can secrete testosterone, but it is much more present in men. Males make and release testosterone directly. Females convert estrogen into testosterone and then release it. Males can be completely aroused by a female without setting up a field in advance. Just the vision of her doing something is enough to make them respond, because they are only reacting! This is not true of a female. Feminine energy is different. The female has to create the action first, before the reaction of the male has any impact on her. Feminine energy has to set up its cause and attractive field <u>first,</u> before it can be completely and thoroughly aroused by any male. The female controls this. It has nothing to do with the male. The female constructs a sexual program early in life. It starts with her father. It is influenced by what the women around her say and do. It is influenced by her religion. It is influenced by her early life experience. But every woman creates her own special program that says; this is how much I am going to let men arouse me, and this is the circumstance or conditions under which I will allow myself to be aroused." And this is her action, which determines how much the "reaction" of arousal will be. All male energy is filtered through this filter. This is the definition of the threshold of arousal for a woman.

Awakening The Master Feminine

The Decline of the Feminine Woman

Chapter 2 The Decline of the Feminine Woman

There is an African wise saying; "You are what you see. You are what you eat. You become what you think." Since World War II females in the west are becoming more yang. This results because what grows in us is what we feed our mind. If a woman feeds her yang or masculine energy, that is what will grow. If a woman sees society as being a place that rewards her for being yang, she will become more yang. Maybe in her mind that is what she needs to be a single parent. This may not result in the best life outcome for her. There are certainly many economic, social and political forces in this world pushing the modern woman in certain directions. I do not here advocate that every woman become a super yin, ultra feminine, passive, stay at home, diva. But I do believe the pendulum has swung too far in the yang direction, and we should begin to place a higher value on the feminine side of the woman.

Why are so many women becoming less feminine? Perhaps in the world as it currently is, women do not always perceive being feminine as being an asset. Keep in mind that we are talking about perception here. And if we think about the typical experience of a woman on her job, raising kids, dealing with money issues, maintaining a house, driving in traffic, etc., the case can be made that being strictly feminine will not always get her were she wants to go. Also, many women have experienced some form of sexual abuse or sexual bias, and I believe this is another factor impacting on how women perceive the value of being feminine. So often we find that modern women will sacrifice their feminine energy on the altar of modern progress, and social rights. We do not have to go back far into western history to see a time when women did not have the right to vote. Just two centuries ago the mistreatment and abuse of women were tolerated and in some cases institutionalized. Sub groups of women, such as Asian women and African American women, were not even considered human. Men treated their horses better than these women.

We can debate why women are becoming less feminine, but the fact is that they are. So it would appear that our society has embedded in it an internal conflict for a woman that is hard to avoid or resolve. Embrace your feminine energy and be taken for granted and considered weak. Suppress your feminine energy and discover that it becomes very hard for you to please men naturally, and your domestic life becomes a "chore". Everything from breastfeeding to cooking requires an "effort" and does not bring the joy it seems to for some women. Your ovaries dry up at thirty five and there is the tendency to gain weight. Without her feminine attributes functioning at their highest potentials, the woman experiences a loss in the quality of her life. Today massive sectors within the overall female population have experienced a substantial loss in the level of their feminine energy. So basically women today are becoming less feminine internally. On the outside they look more appealing and sexual than they ever did. Few women can live up to the expectations created by their outer appeal. They are loaded down instead with emotional issues and personality dysfunctions.

The older she gets the more her outside world demands that the modern woman be a yang, masculine production machine. Her job, her social clubs, civic organizations, and the credit and financial institutions all demand that she be like a man. But at the same time everyone in her intimate circle, including husband, boyfriends, children, grand-children, in-laws, and etc., desire to experience more and more of her feminine and/or nurturing side. And they become upset and act out when she will not deliver. Trying to do both in the absence of sufficient female energy is enough to drive the typical woman insane.

The Concept of Natural Sexuality

Natural feminine expression is what reflects the design in female DNA. We seek to reset the standard to the place where it always should have been. It should not be based on a social standard, but a natural standard, that always remains the same. Nor should a standard for feminine expression be crafted to create a race of woman ideally suited to serve the sexual interests of men. It is about balance. The natal traits of male and female, embedded in their genes, cause men and women to naturally come together in relationship and produce positive social outcomes. **You do not need to add anything to this mix**. It is by nature already perfect.

Each woman is born with the blueprint for being feminine already hardwired into her cells. For her to experience success in relationships, reproduction, community, and society, she only needs to cultivate what is already there. But in so many women today her natal feminine attributes lie dormant and unused. Instead she cultivates artificial traits and beliefs which are intended to equip her to cope with the machine world. She makes a fatal mistake when she relies on these artificial attributes of womanhood as her primary expression of her feminine nature, but fails to cultivate the natural feminine energy she was born with. It is important to note that a woman may have curves, and look sexy on the outside, but still have yang energy. To be feminine requires her energy to be feminine. The fact is a woman with natural feminine energy is no longer common these days. Most women today have what is called an Amazon persona.

We need to be clear now about what this <u>Natural Sexual</u> concept really means. It is saying that women already are pre-programmed to do the wife, mother, community, society thing from the DNA. If she changes the original programming, she will screw it up. And we are saying that the outside world, meaning her job, her parents, her peers, her organizations, her church, her banks, her merchants and etc., are demanding that she screw it up. They are demanding that she become yang, and adapt artificial behavior programs that run counter to her natural stuff. Thus if the woman refuses to become this yang, Amazon, consumer driven, production machine, society will punish her. But the more she conforms to the demands of a dysfunctional society, the more dysfunctional she becomes. The more she loses her feminine gifts. And at the same time everyone in her intimate circle, including her husband, boyfriends, children, grand-children, and in-laws, desire to experience her feminine side. This inner group wants all her nurturing, loving, pleasure giving, cooking, breast feeding, caring, and feminine stuff. And they become upset and act out when she will not deliver. They do not care about what she is doing in the world outside the house, because by nature they can not be normal without her feminine stuff. They must have it. It is the center of their world. The whole world, the family, the community the nation, the economy the schools and all of that rests on the foundation of the feminine mother and wife. When she withdraws her feminine stuff, the whole society starts to come unglued. We see it now. But how can she do both? How can she remain naturally feminine and still remain viable and productive in the machine world of modern technology?

So we are NOT saying that a natural sexual female should be a stay at home mom. We are certainly not saying that. Can she have an education? Does she need to have a job? You bet she does. And yes she does need to employ some of the yang energy and traits to be successful in her daily life. But she needs to cultivate the yang stuff as a secondary tier of attributes over her main feminine ones. She can not replace her natal feminine energy with the male energy and expect to achieve overall success. Each female is born with a Master Feminine faculty that allows her to reset herself. She has built in to her being the ability to restore herself to her natal default settings. This is the purpose of the master feminine faculty.

Awakening the Master Feminine

The Master Feminine Faculty

Chapter 3 The Master Feminine Faculty

The master feminine faculty is the part of her consciousness that determines which of her feminine attributes this particular woman will bring forward, and when to bring them forward. It is important to understand that this portion of the human subconscious is distinct from the main intelligence that governs our other development. The master feminine faculty becomes fully awake for the first time at about age 11 or 12 and starts the phase we call puberty. It begins to bring forward the feminine traits that become the woman's mind, body, reproductive system, personality, and emotional make up.

It should be self evident that each female human contains within herself a natal blueprint for becoming a woman. The faculty or mechanism for bringing her particular bank of feminine attributes into manifestation we call the master feminine. But the master feminine inside every woman encounters many obstructions as it tries to develop her into the highest and most natural version of a female that it can. Year after year it recedes further into the background as she replaces natural traits and natural lifestyles with artificial replacements. And eventually the master feminine faculty goes into remission and becomes merely a dormant element of her inner being, inert and inactive.

Science indicates that most female humans start their life with very similar genetic potentials as to their feminine nature. Of course women today present a wide range of body types, personalities, reproductive function, sexual postures and emotional states. But there is no evidence to suggest that the bulk of these are due to genetic factors. Science tells us that 98% of all humans alive today descended from one common bloodline in Africa just two hundred thousand years ago. From the standpoint of evolution, that is a very short time. Even five hundred thousand years would not be long enough for the human species to evolve into the variety of versions we see before us today. Therefore, we can assume that the wide variations in the expression of feminine traits has more to do with the development process of the female after she is conceived, than it is with the gene pool she started out with. So basically all women start off with an almost identical genetic template. If they developed into adult females that were a 100% reflection of that template, then women would be very similar in many respects, as are any other animal. The main differences would result from racial types, blood types and the geography of the bloodline. Human females, like other mammals are much more similar in genetic make up than they are different. In other words, humans are different more from their act of development, karma and environment than from any other reasons. The vast differences that we see in society result from a partial development of what is in their genetic pool, not as a result of major inherent genetic differences.

The flaws in the development process begin before conception, with the health of the parents. It continues in the womb, with the way different mothers carry the fetus to term. And these problems continue. There are deficiencies in nutrition, the level of Qi energy available, and etc. Ancient cultures tell us that the gestation period for a human embryo is one solar year, not nine months. In other words for the female child to come out of the womb with the maximum feminine potential then her mother would need to carry her for twelve months, not nine.

So why does one woman turn out tall and shapely with a provocative disposition, and the next woman comes out short and obese, with an aggressive and manly posture? Why does the master feminine faculty make the choices that it does? I do not know the full answer to this question. I doubt anyone does. But I do know that we can exercise more control over this development than we currently do. The master feminine faculty wants to do its job, but we hamper it in many ways. When the master feminine faculty awakens, it looks for input from us, but we seldom respond. In the absence of guidance from us, it goes to the default programs we are born with.

- Our forebears, going back seven generations.
- Our life mission.
- Our karma.

Thus in default our master feminine faculty uses the genetic makeup of our parents and the six generations before them. Each woman is born with a mission in life. So her master feminine faculty will seek to bring forth some traits which will help her with this mission. Each woman also has karma. She carries karma from her past life experience. And this karma reflects past traits she had in her past lives. And so her karma will also influence which attributes the master feminine faculty brings on line first. This is part of the default program. But we can and should try to influence the master feminine faculty if we are able to do so.

For the most part most women just never bring enough of their feminine attributes on line. They do not develop completely and fully. It is not that the master feminine faculty makes bad choices. The reality is that it is rare that a girl lets it finish its work. Most females shut this faculty down before they are 21 years old. The master feminine faculty is shut down, and usually before it completed even a portion of it work. In other words, most women enter adulthood without the traits and skills in place that her master feminine faculty intended for her to have. She enters the adult phase and tries to live life without all the tools she needs to do it naturally. Women have as much potential to be complete today as they did at any time. Her bank of feminine attributes can never diminish, decay or decrease. They are always available. But when the master feminine faculty is shut down prematurely, her main attributes remain dormant, and are not developed. Because of this partial development, her body will not be well defined, not a lot of curves, and her threshold to become sexually aroused may be high; and she may not find being a mother very joyful.

Why Does The Master Feminine Faculty Shut Down?

Everything the female is designed to do as an adult is suppressed and discouraged in her as a teen. Females are designed to get pregnant, be a mother, give sexual pleasure, gather wealth and resources, build a community and bring forth the plan for future society. If the parents, members of the opposite sex, and society in general is not actively working with a young girl to help her express all of the activities above, then in effect the attributes are being shut down. The master feminine faculty is the intelligence within a woman's subliminal programs that works with these four archetypes of her feminine nature. It takes a sleeping trait in her DNA and brings it on line. What happens is that the young girl enters her puberty stage and her master feminine faculty awakens and begins to bring her feminine attributes on line. In 80% to 90% of all teenage girls in our society the master feminine faculty awakens, and begins the process of bringing her four feminine archetypes on line, and then is forced to shut down and go back into remission.   But before the master feminine faculty within a girl shuts down, it does bring forth some of her feminine energy. Usually it develops one of the four attributes more than the other three. So most young women start their adult life with one of the four feminine archetypes active, and the other three archetypes still for the most part inactive and dormant.

Second Puberty   Moon Edition
The Reset Button

The master feminine faculty is a consciousness in the human spirit. It is not the feminine energy itself, but the mechanism or device that takes the feminine qualities and traits that reside dormant in the genes and aura, and then causes these to become active in her body, mind and personality.

The Master Feminine Faculty is not the aspects of a woman's nature that are specific to the female gender, but the controlling mechanism that activates her feminine traits out of a dormant, inert state and develops them as a real part of her physical, emotional and sexual make up.

The spirit of a woman is energy.   It is does not age, or diminish. The master feminine faculty can be awakened even after a woman has "retired" it.   There is a story of a woman in the bible; I think her name was Sarah.   I believe she was the wife of Abraham.   The story goes that at the age of ninety she conceived a child and gave birth.   If this story is true, it is an example of the power of the master feminine faculty.   If there is a physical requirement for the reactivation of a woman's master feminine faculty, it would be that she has good gland health.   She should be physically capable of the production of human growth hormone which requires a healthy pituitary gland.   And she should be able to produce estrogen, which requires that her ovaries be intact.   Even if she has gone through menopause it may not prevent the activation of the master feminine. Most females today do not cultivate and nourish their feminine energy.   Some do, but it is not typical.   Because of this the master feminine faculty often goes into remission while they are still in their early twenties. It should remain active their entire life.

The Awakening Circle

In the process of awakening the master feminine faculty forming an awakening circle is the first task. The awakening circle is a focus group of women and men. I suggest it include at least eighteen people or more. Many of the things that a woman can learn in this forum are best seen through the point of view of a male. Most men and women do not fully understand how the human energy field works and why it plays such a critical role in sexual behavior. It does not matter if the female is twenty or fifty; she needs to obtain an understanding of the pattern of her feminine development, and what her energy was broadcasting to males when she entered adulthood. There is the tendency for both men and women to blame the other sex for their relationship experience. And certainly males probably deserve some responsibility for her history. But each woman has a broadcast pattern, that is based on which of these four archetypes was dominant when she entered adulthood, and this will explain to her why she has attracted certain males to her, and why she has not been able to attract others. And it is fine to read this book and get the abstract meaning of this, but she will really only truly understand it by a thorough discussion of this within the circle.

Awakening Exercises

We divide the awakening process into four sets of awakening exercises.
- Restoring Reproductive Health. Reversal of Toxic Womb Syndrome.
- Restoring the Feminine Persona. The destruction of the counterfeit personality.
- Sexual Renaissance. Genital Reflexology.
- Building Your Culture of Abundance and Sustainability. Abandoning the scarcity model in your life.

The Awakening Regimen

Master Yao has designed several supervised programs for awakening the master feminine. The most common is a four month regimen with one month devoted to working with each of the four feminine archetypes, the moon, seated hawk, elegant rose and treasure chest. The actual process to awaken the master feminine faculty begins by the infusion of a catalyst into the woman's subconscious mind. There is a program already there. It is embedded. She is born with it. The infusion of this catalyst is like pressing the reset button on a machine. It sets the program back to its default settings, and starts the original program running again. It works sort of like hypnosis or auto-suggestion. And we could say this infusion is somewhat of an esoteric process. You can not do this without a coach or guide. But as you read on and see the female energy operating system you will discover that awakening the master feminine faculty is not as complex as it sounds. You can do it in a matter of weeks. Remember the last time you overloaded an electrical circuit in your house. You go to the breaker panel and switch the circuit breaker off and then back on. And the power comes back on again. Of course you first have to turn off the appliance that overloaded the circuit. Maybe you had both a hair dryer and an iron turned on. You turn the iron off, and unplug it, and then you turn the circuit breaker back on. Everything is okay. The master feminine faculty is like that circuit breaker. It disconnects the woman from the negative stuff, and sets her back to her original setting again. Of course you can not just pop the woman on the head and she resets. She is not a machine. It is more complex than that, and yet, it is still simple in each step. We are going to walk you through the whole process. We will devote a section in each chapter to this awakening process. We will introduce what we shall term **awakening exercises**. And we should mention right up front that women will find it easier to undergo these awakening exercises if they do so in groups. **Awakening Circles** are what we will call them. And all of this starts off with an **Awakening Regimen**. Our website is also a source of more information about the process.

- Awakening Exercises
- Awakening Circles
- Awakening Regimen

Thus a woman begins to awaken her master feminine faculty by hitting the "reset button." This is to undergo the awakening regimen. This lasts about three or four months. This puts her into a special second puberty stage where she can develop at an accelerated rate. Her sexual energy is way up high. During the regimen she is part of a focus group called an awakening circle, and this group has a very important function that we will describe later. The woman can stay in this secondary puberty state for months, even years, until she brings all the attributes on line she desires. After she completes the energy regimen, she can employ the awakening exercises any time she wants to. These are for achieving some specific sexual, relationship, energy, or reproductive goal. She does not have to do any of them, or she can choose to do all of them. This energy regimen employs a lot of exotic stuff. You do not have to understand all of it to do it. Everyone can do it. The regimen incorporates things like, Qi Gong, yoga, reflexology, diet, tantra work, table work, and special supplements as used in alternative medicine. It does not require a lot of time each day, no more than a half hour per day. It does not require major changes in your lifestyle. There are no radical diet changes or stuff. And the stuff you learn to do in the regimen can be transferred over into your bedroom experience, and into your mate relationship.

Vitale Structured Water

The special water used in the regimen is bio-available and clustered. This is H12 O6, rather than H2O. Drink one gallon of the special water each week. This is the most important physical aspect of this regimen. The restoration of the womb's water vessel is a key step in any healing. Most importantly, the modern female does not drink enough good water. In nature most fresh water used to be neutral PH, or slightly alkaline. Water running over the natural earth absorbs traces of minerals and develops entrains ions. But today most people live in urban areas that get their water from artificial sources. The water has been treated with chemicals. These may be very harmful to the female. Water has been changed, starting with rain. Industrial pollution has placed acid particles in the clouds. Even the rain falling from the clouds is not as it used to be. And the ground has changed. Much vegetation and natural foliage has been destroyed, replaced by concrete, roads, and lawns of grass, laced with chemicals. Lawns and farms and city streets are a major source of pollution. Water runs over these things and then into our drinking reservoirs. I have personally tested bottled water for several years. Almost all of it is acid PH, ranging from 6.0 PH to 6.8 PH. This is unnatural. It should be 6.8 PH to 7.8 PH. Some of the water you drink needs to be alkaline PH. The kidneys require this to neutralize acid wastes in the blood. Without a proper supply of correct water, a young girl can not stabilize the fluids in her body.

Diet

Many books have been written on the natural diet. If you buy it in a box, or the frozen food section, that food is basically worthless. The young girl needs all nutrients. But the absence of the amino acids, and the absence of vitamins 'A' and 'E' are especially harmful. Vitamin 'A' is critical for proper health of mucus linings. The omega oils help her to make hormones. There are some toxins that contribute to this issue more than others. Corn Syrup is a major problem. It is in almost everything. Free radicals are an even bigger problem. Her diet is full of them, especially in fried meats and fast food. Eating fast food, made with meat from chemically treated animals, then fried in putrid oil that is used over and over again, is a cocktail for reproductive death.

1. Buy a juice machine ($100-250). Make a serving of fresh juice twice a week. Use vegetables and fruits; especially root vegetables such as carrots, radishes, beets, etc.
2. Take 4,000 to 6,000 MG of vitamin C each day. Use Alacer brand.
3. Modify the diet to eat foods that contain omega oils. These are critical to make hormones, keep fluids the correct consistency, and for amino acid production. You will see a big difference in a week. Try not to take the supplements unless you have no choice. Get the oils from food if you can. Salmon, flax seed oil and cheddar cheese will help. (Cheese for the acid not oil.)
4. Check your iron levels. If you have heavy flows, probably need to supplement iron.
5. Avoid all salt and seafood in the diet for four days. Plot your cycle on a calendar. The three days before your flow, and the first day of the flow, do not take in any salt. It is the iodine in the salt, not the sodium that is bad. Seafood has iodine also. This iodine does something to the thyroid around this time. Naturally, the blood has the same ratio of salt to blood as salt to the sea. It is the thyroid which overcompensates.

The natal traits of male and female, embedded in their genes, cause men and women to naturally come together in relationship, and produce positive social outcomes. **You do not need to add anything to this mix**. It is by nature already perfect. Each woman is born with the blueprint for being feminine already hardwired into her cells. You don't have to add anything. For her to experience success in relationships, reproduction, as a mother, and as the center of her community, she only needs to cultivate what is already there. In each of the four awakening exercises above, we will talk about what has been added to our modern lifestyle that is artificial, and show how to remove it. Then we show what needs to be done to encourage the feminine faculties to come into greater prominence. And finally we show what benefit she will obtain.

Unnatural Sexual Habits in the Modern Era

There are natural life cycles and patterns that govern life. Indigenous cultures have followed the life cycles for centuries. In the West we have stopped following these cycles and in some cases we have forgotten that they exist. The Qi force is the raw energy field all around us which powers life. All life takes in Qi into the energy body and gives off an electromagnetic waste product. Qi levels rise and fall in a pattern that is in sync with the seasons. From a low point, Qi begins a slow rise in late winter until it reaches a working phase at the spring equinox. Life then renews itself. Qi rises quickly until it reaches a peak at the summer solstice. It then begins to drop and reaches the low point at the winter solstice. This is the cause of the seasons, spring, summer, fall and winter. Sexual energy, spirit energy and all organic energy starts with raw Qi. Therefore human sexual activity should begin in the spring, reach a peak in summer, and slowly taper off until the winter solstice. From the winter solstice until the spring equinox there should be only a minimum of sexual activity. To violate this pattern places stress on the reproductive system.

Humans are made to be active in the day, and resting at night. We are designed so that the hormones, mucus glands, organs and blood flow are primed for sex in the daytime. Sex at night places more stress on the system than sex in the daytime. Humans are 60 to 70% water. All activities involving the blood, the hormones, mucus, mucus linings and sperm are keyed to the ability of liquids to circulate. The lunar cycle clearly shows that sexual activity should peak near the full moon and reach a low point near the new moon. In indigenous cultures that have limited contact with western technology, women breastfeed their babies from one to two years. During this time they typically reduce sexual activity with their husbands. The same is true during pregnancy. In Europe, cow's milk was forced on young babies as a substitute for breast milk, to free the mother up to work or have the next baby. In Africa and Asia goat's milk was used. This leads to negative outcomes. It is one cause of reproductive issues in the female after she grows up. For some strange and troubling reason the growers of various farm animals decided to use growth hormones and hormone-like chemicals in raising their chickens, beef and pigs. Many of these hormones are almost identical to human hormones. The hormone given to chickens to make their breasts abnormally large is so close to human estrogen in chemical action that it disrupts the estrogen cycle in girls who eat that fried chicken. While many experts hint at these negative outcomes, no one really knows yet the full extent of the damage that this practice has for the current generation and for generations to come.   Artificial habits have a downside. It is clear that the shift in the ethos of the female gender from a yin and feminine woman to a more yang and masculine woman has had extraordinary repercussions.   In the last fifty years, there has been an explosion in the lesbian population.   Prior to 1958 the bi-sexual, or down low lifestyle was virtually unknown.   It is common today.   The divorce rate has ballooned over this period.   And health issues associated with the female reproductive system have escalated enormously.   Let's look at each issue individually.   How have unnatural practices and beliefs contributed to the poor state of female reproductive health?

Awakening the Master Feminine

Money, Power & Religion
The Herd Mentality

Chapter 4 Money, Power and Religion

Humans are born with the elemental natures of masculine and feminine. If these natal elemental potentials are cultivated into the actual adult personality of men and women, they will naturally come together in relationships that are guaranteed to produce positive outcomes. We are born with what we need. It is only necessary to cultivate what is already naturally there. Nothing else needs to be added to a recipe that is already perfect. When we add artificial attributes to the male or female personality that hinder or conflict with the natural ones, it destroys the harmony between the sexes. It upsets the energy equation. It is the dynamics surrounding money, power and religion that is behind the institutions which introduce the artificial attributes into the character of men and women. A "herd" mentality comes into being in which what is considered normal is not natural. Therefore the men and women who choose to conform to the herd mentality can not and do not properly cultivate their natural and natal attributes of feminine and masculine. The negative impact of this is most evident during the critical teenage years. As a result, during the formative years, when girls are developing into women, there is a tendency for her natural development to be stunted, and in the place of a natural feminine persona she develops a counterfeit persona instead.

The outcome of all this is the creation of masses of adult women who are under developed in such a way that they are not fully capable of conducting a marriage, a pregnancy, a cohesive family, a cohesive community, or a sustainable economy. Add to this the equally dysfunctional corresponding males, and we have what we have in our current social landscape.

Money

The influence of money is exerted through the commercial sector acting through corporate entities. Female sexual traits are redefined from natural male partnership to add value to commercial products. Sex is used to sell things. To sell the maximum amount, women and men are encouraged to be self centered. They are encouraged to buy and consume at rates that far exceed their needs, their means, or their ability to sustain such levels. In the face of this, society has become so driven by the needs of ever more income, and ever more growth, that now it is almost impossible to survive without conforming. You must live to pay tens of thousands of dollars each year in taxes. To have shelter you must pay each month, whether a 30 year mortgage or rent. To eat you pay each monthly cycle to purchase food from a distribution point. Food is no longer available from the environment anymore. It has intentionally been removed. And it is now against the law to acquire food naturally without a permit. Most people are required to drive a car to survive. To conform, one has to buy electricity. Even things such as cell phones are almost a necessity now, because so many people have them. You must have a "credit rating" to do many things that have nothing to do with credit, such as get a job. You must use a credit card to do many things. This dynamic of money acts to hinder natural female development.

Religion

Religious practice and religious beliefs are designed with good intentions. But 99% of the time the attempts by religious institutions to shape behavior to conform to a divine ideal have just the opposite effect. Most past spiritual masters follow the same motif. The holy man presents a system of evolution. It is through the process of attaining this evolution that man changes his style of life. The masters show the example of this evolution in the model of their own life. In following the system of evolution, the common man can duplicate in his or her life, the evolution that the master had attained. You rarely see these holy men judging people as being right or wrong. They are invested in getting people to evolve. The holy men promote a system, not a doctrine. Religions are based on doctrine. And this is the problem. They are founded based on a system of evolution, and then somehow transform into a doctrine. When they do this, they lose their effectiveness at influencing behavior.

It is the followers of these holy men who form and promote the doctrines. And thus religions are doomed to fail in this regard because by definition they are based on the premise that God is an external thing.

something outside and apart from us. You have to say this in order to promote a belief system based on a doctrine. If you agree with the original masters, and say that God is a part of us, and we are not separate from God, then you have a system of evolution. This is much harder to do, for you have to walk the walk as well as talk the talk. The clergy finds this difficult to do consistently. It is one thing to say you qualify to be a Christian because you follow the doctrine. It is quite another to say you are a Christian because you have duplicated the feats and evolution of Jesus in your own life. This would mean that modern Christians would have to equal the energy healing feats of the founder. It is one thing to say you are a follower of Islam because you follow the doctrine of the prophet. But it is quite another thing to be evolved to the point that you can go into a cave and commune with the angels at will. They talk the talk, but the proof comes in walking the walk.

It is impossible to separate God from the things that he/she/it created. And it is equally ridiculous to try to support any doctrine that separates mankind from God. But almost every secular religion attempts to do this, all with the same degree of failure. Thus they all follow the same pattern. The master leaves behind the system of evolution and the proof that it could be attained in the example of his life. In the immediate generations to follow, the disciples follow the system and evolve. Then in a few generations those followers who fail for whatever reason to achieve the desired result begin the process of converting the system into a static doctrine. Over the years the doctrine is modified to suit the times but the people following it stop the pattern of evolution. Inevitably the doctrine is reduced to a collection of false belief systems, which has the exact opposite result than what was intended. There are hundreds of forms of Buddhism, Christianity, Islam, Hinduism and etc. Each one operating under the arrogant and imperial assumption that somehow it is the one true authentic form. This is not to say that many individuals following a faith do not indeed lead a life of service and value. There can be no doubt of this truth. But the level of delusional thinking is incredible. That somehow a version of a religion created 1000 years after the fact could somehow be more authentic than the system set forth by the master himself who brought the original version to earth. To regulate thinking these institutions use fear, guilt, sin and an isolationist mentality. Such false beliefs obstruct and sabotage a female's natural feminine development and pervert her sexual worldview. They act mainly to divide a woman from her man, in the same way that religions divide the nations apart, and bring about divisions between parent and child, sister and brother.

The human spirit has three major divisions of evolution. These stages of evolution can be measured against very concrete standards.
1. Divine Man
2. Superior Man
3. Inferior Man

Until a human reaches the third and highest stage of evolution, the mind is not capable of even the conception of divinity. In the states of evolution inferior to this, consciousness, perception and reason is flawed, imperfect, and relative. Only after reaching the third tier is the understanding absolute and complete. It is a rare person who gets to this place. Perhaps only one person in every hundred million will reach this point. Thus the concept of an absolute, unconditional and fixed religious doctrine is an illusion. It is not possible to put such a thing in writing, for the people it would be intended for would by definition be incapable of comprehending it. Claims to the contrary are fraudulent. Religions have a place in culture. I am not against religion. There is much good there. But the negative influence a doctrine based belief system [faith based] has on the development of the modern woman must be considered.

Power
Every living thing needs and desires power. Without power, an organism stops being alive. The human desire for power is not only natural but essential to life. But power can corrupt. Then how does a superior man define the unnatural application of power? The lion hunts down the wild pig in the jungle and kills it. It is violence. The pig is killed. Is it improper? Is this a violation? No, it is natural. A hawk kills and eats a snake. This is natural. Nature is a delicate wheel, a delicate balance. There is an old African saying that "nothing lives, unless something dies." It speaks to the balance in nature. When power supports the balance in nature, the natural cycle, then it is proper. When power destroys this balance, creates misalignment, breaks the cycle, or prevents any living thing from living in the manner in which it was designed, this is a violation, a corruption. Much of the political power men and women crave today, is imperial in nature. It assumes the governing group has a better knowledge of how people should live than the group which is governed. And it assumes that the governing body has the RIGHT to enforce its dictates on others. Because this is often not true, we find one group imposing conditions on another that clearly interferes with natural personal development. The denial of women's right to vote is an example. Slavery is another example. But most of the time it is

something that seems innocent, but in fact is often very harmful. Such things as dress codes, building codes, styles, marriage laws, divorce laws, the regulation of education, interference by the state in domestic and family matters, welfare laws, and such things which hinder human spiritual development most. These laws and codes force a herd mentality. They prevent people from the pursuit of a natural and holistic lifestyle. They are not necessary for society to have order, nor do they contribute to any sustainable progress. For to be sustainable, people must do things of their own free will. Also the existence of so much regulation, law, and codes means that punishments need to be handed out for those who break the rules. So today millions are locked down in prisons. Millions are trapped in a welfare maze. The state requires a marriage license, and forces the divorce of the union if either party becomes irritated. Schools, offices and businesses require a dress code. If a family wants to Feng Shui their house, the county permit office will not allow it. The abuse of power, over-regulation, interference in the course of life, and imposition into individual sovereignty takes a massive toll on people today. They can not develop naturally under so massive a burden. To cope or compensate women tend to become more yang, more masculine, more rigid and more aggressive.

Finally we have the herd mentality. It is not unique to modern society. The herd people are most of us. They are the majority, the masses. They are the people who live their life as one constant reaction, to the actions set in motion by the creative people and the elite aristocracy. The elite aristocracies are the fence builders of life. They erect all these social boundaries that keep the herd people from really living. The creative people are always trying to set the herd people free. The elite aristocracy is the system, "the man", the conspiracy, the power behind the governments. They do not run the world. But they are constantly engaged in steering it in certain directions, and keeping men and women within certain boundaries. This is a major impediment to evolution. The elite aristocracies are parasites and the masses are their hosts. It is because the masses are so greedy for money, hungry for power, and satisfied with religion instead of evolution, that the parasites can control them. It is like parasites and viruses inside the human body, they focus their attack on the tissues that are weak.

Now when the young girl approaches the point in the cycle of life, her master feminine faculty awakens and starts to bring her feminine attributes on line. This is called puberty. There are four archetypes of this feminine energy.

5. The Moon   (maternal instinct)
6. The Seated Hawk   (right brain consciousness)
7. The Elegant Rose   (sensory pleasure)
8. The Treasure Chest   (harvesting, nesting and gathering)

As soon as she starts her development process to become a woman, the forces in society of money, political power, religious beliefs and the peer pressure to conform to the herd mentality, rushes in to shut her down. And for 90% of our girls these forces are too strong for her to resist. For her parents, the school system, her peers, her church and the government are the main agencies acting to shut her down. Even the daughters of the elite aristocracy are not immune. At first the young girls fight bravely to remain free, sovereign, and creative. They rebel against their parents, and society out of an instinct, but this does not prevail. In 90% of them the master feminine faculty eventually shuts down. Less than 10% of females keep the master feminine faculty awake into adulthood. In the rest it goes into remission and becomes dormant. But before the master feminine faculty is shut down, it does bring some aspect of the four archetypes of her feminine energy on line. In most, one archetype is dominant. And so most females enter adulthood with only a partial development of their womanly personality and attributes. They are in effect impaired. And they enter adulthood with a disposition to rely on one type of feminine energy instead of having the use of all four, as they should. Between the ages of 21 and 25 females enter a zone in which their worldview is dominated by one of four archetypes:

- Elegant Rose. They are driven by a worldview defined by pleasure and sensory experience. Life to them is like a game show. They want to have fun and be festive. They are concerned with such things as dress, appearance, hair, etc.
- Treasure Chest. They are driven by a worldview defined by money and status. Life to them is like a treasure hunt. They collect information, and seek higher education. The career is important. Social standing is important. They watch the news and want to know more than their peers.
- Moon. They are driven by a worldview defined by feelings and emotions. They are humanitarian. They care about people. They earnestly desire to become mothers. They are concerned and sometimes obsessed with security issues.
- Seated Hawk. They are driven by a worldview defined by control. Life to them is a contest or race. They seek competition. They view peers and even males as adversaries.

They seek some occupation or avenue which gives them an advantage over other women.   They desire to be the queen bee.

In all of these four profiles we see the central theme of dysfunction through which the main problems in their life will come, especially problems in their relationships.

Awakening Exercise 2

The relationship coach works with each member of the circle to discover which profile fits a particular woman.   There are other possible options, since some women have more than one archetype active.   When a woman has more than one archetype active, then the worldviews above need to be modified.   Each female member of the circle should have a basic understanding of their feminine energy. The men have a different workbook, but similar information. In the second exercise or session, the group will discuss the way men and women broadcast energy to each other. Each member of the group takes a turn, and describes their broadcast, and the typical broadcasts of the members of the opposite sex they have encountered recently.   Each woman is attracting a certain type of man to her based on her broadcast.   Each woman is attracting a certain type of relationship situation to her based on her broadcast.

In this exercise the men need to gain a better understanding of how women perceive their broadcast, and why it draws a certain type of situation to them. And the women need to gain a better understanding of how men perceive their broadcast, and why it draws a certain type of situation to them. The table on the next page shows the positive and negative broadcasts of each archetype of feminine energy. When during puberty a woman starts to bring the elegant rose archetype on line, she then begins to change her broadcast to males.   She broadcasts the positive version of this archetype which says:

"I Am Pleasing! Look at this good stuff! I am ripe fruit waiting to be picked! Pleasure me.   Be pleased by me."   But other women, who have not brought this archetype on line, will continue to broadcast the negative version of this energy.   So women who came into adulthood with one of the other three energies, the hawk, the moon or the treasure chest, then they began their adult lives with a negative pleasure broadcast.

The Moon	The Seated Hawk
Positive Broadcast I offer you my nurturing. I want to give what you need. I submit to you. Protect me. Be strong for me. Negative Broadcast I WILL NOT submit to you! I will not nurture you. I will attempt to undermine your power. I feel insecure.	Positive Broadcast I intuit the right plan. Set my plan into motion. Negative Broadcast I have no domestic plan for the community, only my own selfish agenda.
The Elegant Rose	The Treasure Chest
Positive Broadcast I Am Pleasing! Look at this good stuff! I am ripe fruit waiting to be picked! Pleasure me. Be pleased by me. Negative Broadcast I do not value men. I am hard to please. Yes, I attract and entice but I will not please you, unless you pay me!	Positive Broadcast I harvest the abundance through One Common Unity. Hunt, gather and build with me. Negative Broadcast I believe in scarcity. I manifest scarcity. I will not unite with others. I am not in harmony with you.

Now let us say a female came into adulthood with the moon energy dominant. She would then be broadcasting the positive version of this archetype which says:

> "I offer you my nurturing. I want to give what you need. I submit to you. Protect me. Be strong for me."

Note that all the women who enter adulthood with one of the other three archetypes dominant, will not be making this broadcast, but will be broadcasting the negative version instead. The positive moon broadcast is a very powerful thing, and men respond to it strongly. If a woman does not have a positive moon broadcast she will have problems with many men. This is the case even for attractive women. She may get his attention at first, but have trouble closing the deal. The failure of so many women to get men to commit to marriage is directly associated with this broadcast. So the majority of the women entering adulthood and seeking marriage are in fact broadcasting a negative moon energy that repels male commitment. It is an energy thing. It is subliminal.

I am confident that women who participate in an awakening circle will take part in one of the most awesome and profound series of discussions of their life. As some women get older they evolve and bring other elements of their feminine energy on line. We should encourage this as much as possible.

The Auric Field

In the language of energy, problems are described as "blocks", "choke points", and "brakes". These blocks, choke points and brakes can be seen in the human auric field. In regards to her sex life, these energy issues manifest as orgasmic issues, arousal issues, libido problems, toxic womb syndrome, poor reproductive health, and most of all relationship issues. As we have said, the negative social dynamics of power, money, religion and the herd mentality combine to infuse artificial traits into the female personality. The natural traits of masculine and feminine cause men and women to naturally come together in relationships that are guaranteed to produce positive outcomes. We are born with what we need. When we add artificial attributes to the male or female personality this destroys the harmony between the sexes. And so when the master feminine faculty shuts down prematurely after puberty the woman often enters adulthood with a counterfeit personality.

The Scarcity Model

The scarcity model is a political and economic model of internal social oppression. A division is intentionally created within a society in which one group is empowered, at the expense of a second group which is oppressed. It is the creation of economic classes. The difference in status and power between the groups is created as the first group has a parasitic relationship to the second group. The first group, the parasites, does not produce anything, but feeds off the work and production of the second group. The first group is usually a small group, who consider themselves to be an elite aristocracy. The second group, the masses, is usually larger, with less access to information, and held in submission by a central false belief. This false belief may be a religion, patriotic ideal, fear of the police, racial beliefs, etc. The scarcity model is the opposite life model to the natural model. Nature designed life on earth based on a model of abundance. There is an abundance of air, food, minerals, water, and resources to sustain life. There are enough people that everyone can have an attractive, healthy, loving mate. Scarcity must be created by man, it does not exist naturally. The scarcity model takes away the abundance of the masses, and concentrates this wealth in the hands of a small percentage. The elite have too much, more than they can possibly use. The masses do not have even enough to get by. The elite rich do not refuse to share with the masses because they need the wealth. No the elite deny the masses a fair share so as to keep them enslaved to the arrangement. Without ideas and the income, the masses never find the time or concentrate enough resources to break free.

There is also a psychological component to the scarcity model. For the elite parasites fix the situation such that the masses have so little power and control, that the masses must look to the aristocracy for the means of their very survival. Thus the members of the elite aristocracy set themselves up as demi-gods, more than human. They encourage the masses to worship them, and bow down to them. This is the basis for all aristocracies. After several generations, the belief of the masses in the superior nature of the elite keeps them in check and submission as much as any economic plan. The second group is the masses, the people who are being violated, and who allow this violation because of their false beliefs. Their abundance is taken away, even as soon as they grow, manufacture, make, or design it.

A nation or religion or trade house that operates based on the scarcity model has a definite advantage over a group that operates naturally. They can develop and deploy a military power quicker and easier. They can finance an economic project quicker and easier. So often in history a nation or group decides that abundance is not enough. They decide that the abundance around them is inadequate. Their appetite becomes artificially enlarged. They not only desire what is already available to them, but they also demand to have everyone else's share. They wish to oppress and control the resources and abundance set aside for others. Thus they become willing to cross the natural boundaries and violate others. In the scarcity model there is usually some military power in play associated with a false belief system that prevents rebellion and encourages the masses to conform. A government is set up to regulate the masses, but not the elite. You take all rights away from the people through laws. You ration food and goods, spread sickness, poverty, and force people into long hours of labor, to take away their most precious commodity, time. We find some system of taxation in all cases of the scarcity model.

All nations, religions, societies, and social movements start out as a rebellion against the scarcity model. But in a few generations, say fifty years or more, almost all nations, religions and social movements make a dramatic shift to incorporate the scarcity model. There are few exceptions. It seems this dynamic applies all over the world, and has existed down through all of time back to the beginning. The Founding Fathers started the United States on a platform of human rights and as a rebellion against tyranny, taxation and British injustice. And in the early 1800's the country begin to switch over to the scarcity model, and completed the transition in the late 1800's. We see that after the shift was complete, the country began to impose the personal income tax, something the founding fathers rebelled against. Females also apply this scarcity model in their relations with males. In the United States the shift to the scarcity model by the females is marked by the women's suffrage movement and the drive to secure the right to vote.

Females in every society from the beginning of time have also followed in a general way, the dynamic of the scarcity model. Once the society in general begins to shift from a natural model of society to the scarcity model, the women in that society begin a parallel shift as well. Their selection criterion for a male partner starts to develop. It takes on a financial component. Their worldview toward males gradually shifts. For women have something that men do not. They have a vagina. And they discover that while men need money or social status to transfer from the masses to the elite, a woman can sometimes accomplish an upgrade in her social station just through her sexual charms. It is called the art of acculturated prostitution, and women have mastered this art from all time. The same patterns and the same dynamic can be clearly and definitively charted for any society, nation, religion or ethnic group. Once the females in a society shift over to the scarcity model of relationships, a fundamental change in the family and community occurs. In our current situation is an empire of consumption. It is an advanced scarcity model. The industrial revolution and the technical revolution have created such vast hordes of abundance, that the elite are hard pressed to keep the masses from getting their hands on some of it. They do not want too many people crossing the boundary from the middle class to the rich. So consumption is ramped up to extremely unnatural levels. Prices are increased. Credit is encouraged so that people will consume to the maximum. And even this is not enough. So every ten years or so a war must be started, just to waste some of the abundance, and destroy some infrastructure, so that the masses do not make too much progress. People are taxed over 50% to keep them poor. The purpose of this taxation and government spending is not to support a government. For a government could be maintained with 2% of this amount. The true purpose is to keep the funds from the masses, so that they will not become the elite. Most of this tax money is wasted.

Females naturally apply the scarcity model to sexual pleasure. It is a natural progression that if all goods and services, all social prestige, in other words all things of value, by definition should also be things that are scare, that is, hard to come by, then so should her sexual favors. So women create an artificial scarcity of sexual pleasure, for the purpose of raising the commercial value of sex. The most attractive and feminine women reserve themselves only for those who are wealthy and part of the elite class. A few women may fall in love, but the vast majority of women who have the option, the most attractive women, use their sex as a bargaining chip, to gain what they want out of life. Her femininity is destroyed in the process of course. And this upsets the social eco-system and throws the male into discord. The master feminine faculty is shut down. Relationship harmony is secondary to political position.

The dichotomy is this, the scarcity model gives definite advantages in the short term, but eventually, it will lead to the decline and the demise of the group. They must decline after embracing the scarcity model, because it is unnatural. The elite aristocracy always undermines any real evolution because of the god-complex that they embrace. And the Amazon women who apply the scarcity model to sexual pleasure cause the exact opposite outcome to the one they intend. Yes it gives them some social leverage when they are young. But it blocks any real opportunity for them to achieve true sexual pleasure. Not only this, but as they age, they lose out to the younger women, who now look better, and have the same cut throat view toward them, as they used to have. And in each generation the whole social landscape declines and decays.

Commercial Sector
American values are now closely tied to the acquisition of material things. Thus a critical vehicle for affirming sexual worth and self esteem is income potential. Women often chose mates based on income potential over sexual compatibility or personality. Society programs women, and women program themselves, to obtain pleasure by seeking males who rank high according to social status. While a woman may be consciously aware that the connection between money, status and sexual pleasure is uncertain, that does not stop her from being governed by the subliminal programs. Of course her behavior has the direct impact of inhibiting her sexual pleasure and the pleasure of males.

- This breeds acculturated prostitution.
- This motif adds artificial components to the selection criteria women use to rank men. Thus the "select" and "non-select" categories of men have no natural sexual relevance.
- This motif allows the creation of a retail empire built around an artificial sense of self importance. This empire sells hair products, attire, facial creams, cars, skin products, wigs, shoes and hand bags that are thought to enhance a woman's self worth directly, and her sexual worth indirectly. But they do neither. It is an illusion.

In all cases this motif provides no value to the woman of any kind. Her assignment of value is purely artificial and is completely a self deception. In all cases the motif adds value only to the corporate and business entities that sell the products, period! But women have assigned value to these things. The business community did not create these concepts, women did. I am not saying that hair care products are bad. They have a place. What I am saying is that women have placed an abnormal sexual value on hair care products and such retail items and this assignment is not only inaccurate but destructive.

The Thought Police
It is through belief systems that people are enslaved. There is the truth, and then there are belief systems. The truth is always there, obvious and self evident. But it is hard to comprehend it, until the spirit evolves enough to ignore the exterior illusions, and turn inward onto the higher self. Until people reach such a state of wisdom, they are vulnerable to beliefs. There is no blame in this. Thus there is always a large segment of humanity seeking the right way, but looking to others to show them. Enter then, the thought police, the regulators of what we believe. Based

on rigid doctrines institutions create religious dogma, moral dictates education systems and political laws geared to enforce particular belief systems. These are used to regulate the actions of people to the benefit of special interests. Today we find that sexual activity and domestic life is highly regulated.

- The state requires a license for people to marry. And the same state will force a legal divorce if one party requests same. Like property, the state will grant custody of children.
- Religious institutions often regulate or influence dress codes.
- Religious institutions often prohibit members from marrying someone who is not part of the same faith.
- The state and religious institutions even believe that they have the right to regulate a woman's body. They believe they should regulate such things as abortion, adoption, the age of consent, the manner in which a woman has sex.
- In most patriarchal societies, including most cultures in Europe, Asia and America, the female gender is thought to be inferior to the male gender. It is a common belief in these cultures that the female role is to serve the males. Her rights to own property, travel freely, trade, and vote are inferior to that of males. Even in America, women were denied the right to vote until just a few decades ago.

In other words the state and religions operate on the belief system that only those in a position of power can know truth, and the woman can not find her own truth. The forces of the commercial sector, the thought police and the urban streets are always acting to inhibit the woman's expression of her natural sexuality and realization of pleasure. But she must consent for this to be so. She can not be forced to conform. We live in a society that is very much against any real and full experience of sexual pleasure. But we can choose to follow a different path. The machine culture is based on a model of scarcity that is anti-sexual. Each day each woman makes a choice to follow the machine culture or follow the natural path.

Abundance

There is no excuse for the modern woman to be complaining about a man. Mother Nature has given her plenty of men to have, hold and enjoy. And Mother Nature has endowed her with the power to make them into whatever she wishes. But most westernized women are in the business of giving good men away, in exchange for money, power and religion. And these women will not get good men back, until they realize who they really are, and what the source of their real power and pleasure is! Nature is a model of abundance. Scarcity is created by man. We chase after money, power and religion because society has convinced us that these things are superior to the abundance right in front of us. Women are constantly throwing perfectly good men away because society instills criteria in them which are artificial. These men are not smart enough, good looking enough, sexy enough, rich enough, cool enough or spiritual enough. These criteria come from the lure of money, power and religion. And yet women ignore the fact that they have an infinite power to reshape and recast males into anything women want them to be. Rather than make the investment, some women treat men like disposable toys.

Mankind is created in the image of God. Man is indeed a prototype of the creator, endowed with the power to shape and change the future reality. The law of manifestation is the outward statement of this manifest truth. Our individual future reality is constantly being influenced by the thoughts and visions that we energize today. We project what we believe into the elemental matrix, and it gradually becomes so. There is no aspect of human nature that more symbolizes mankind's creative divinity, than the female womb. The woman is the seat of creative power, the throne of the kingdom, with power to mold and influence the future nature of the men in her life in the most substantial way. She is a potential goddess. That is who she is. And until she realizes who she really is, and really takes responsibility for that, she will not get back any of the good men she has given away.

Awakening the Master Feminine

Toxic Womb Syndrome

Chapter 5 Toxic Womb Syndrome

Note
Nothing in this book should be used to diagnose or treat any individual aliment. Each individual is unique, and requires the attention of a qualified healthcare provider to make good decisions. The comments here are intended as general observations to be used to shape a new worldview of reproductive health.

To me, the female womb represents divinity more than any other part of the body, male or female. More than the brain or heart, the womb is divinity incarnate, for herein is the creation power. The female womb is not just a physical thing, but an energy thing as well. The womb is:

Physical reproductive system includes …
Ovaries, tubes, uterus, cervix, vagina, the G-spot, the tail bone or coccygeal spine, and the clitoris.

The energy womb or spiritual womb includes …
The sacral chakra, portions of the first layer of the auric field associated with above, the nerve ganglia and Qi meridians associated with the G-spot, and the cauldron.

There are seven layers to the human auric field. The first layer, the one closest to the physical body, is blue and fixed. It has the exact same shape as the body only it is expanded out about three inches more. Each cell in the physical body is anchored to a small bright blue dot in the auric field. This part of the auric field is the easiest to see with the naked eye. The physical G-spot in a woman is similar to the penis in a man. In the resting state it is withdraw up into the roof of the vagina. Normally, the G-spot is not 'in' the vagina. Only when a female enters the higher stages of arousal do the lips and folds of the vagina fill with blood and expand. The G-spot gets an erection, just like the penis does, and the head of it protrudes down into the vagina cavity pass the primary fold. The G-spot does not go into action until the energy womb tells it to. The cauldron is the core of the womb. It is located right in front of the base of the tailbone. If you drew a straight line from the bottom point in the 'V' of the vagina lips, to the tip of the tail bone in the rear, the cauldron would be located on this line right in front of the spine above the anus. This cauldron is the generator at the bottom of the power current at the core of the spirit body. This cauldron is what makes kundalini. The chakras take in Qi. This Qi is the raw energy that powers the energy body. The cauldron takes this raw Qi (yin Qi and yang Qi) and turns it into a higher more refined form of energy called kundalini. We will speak more of this later.

The physical reproductive system is controlled by the energy womb. The energy womb tells the vagina and uterus what to do. Humans are energy beings. By far, the energy womb is more important than the physical womb, for the physical reproductive system is but the hardware. The thing that makes the womb work is the software, the energy womb. This is critical to understand. To master your physical body and not understand your energy body is to remain in gross ignorance. A fine body and tight vagina are wasted on a female with no feminine energy. She might as well not have one. A male with a large penis and no masculine energy might as well be impotent. The masses cling to some serious false beliefs about sex that they need to abandon. It is time to come up out of the dark ages of sex. If you desire to master the operation of your thingy ting, let the old beliefs die.

Getting back to the physical womb, the first lesson for the female to learn is that the real womb is the water. The womb is the water! It is a water elemental spirit thing. Now reconsider what you know about such things as the blood, the eggs, the mucus, seminal fluid and the symbiotic fluids of the embryo sac. These things are nothing more than water vessels. The eggs in the female ovaries are little more than sacks of special water. The womb is a complex and wonderful series of water vessels. And the energy womb is the series of subliminal sexual programs that operate the water vessels. These water vessels of the womb are; the eggs, mucus, blood, seminal fluid, and sac fluid. Blood is just special water with red and white blood cells infused into it. Mucus is special water fixed into an emulsion. Whenever the womb wants to do something, it involves a movement and transition of one or more of these fluid vessels. It is the mucus which moves the egg each month during her cycle. If the mucus is bad, there is a problem or pain. The endometrium of the uterus can not hold an egg, or release it without a change in the function of mucus, a water vessel. A woman can not get aroused and have an orgasm unless the blood flows to fill the cavities. The right chemical balance must be present in the blood (a water vessel) for this to happen. It happens because the energy programs tell it to. There must be enough oxygen and the blood vessels have to expand to allow it. The energy programs are what do all this.

From the physical perspective the management of the physical portion of the reproductive system is the management of the movement, purity and make-up of her fluids. The master feminine faculty awakens in puberty, and brings some part of the moon archetype of the feminine energy on line. It is this moon energy that gives her the raw ability to be fertile, and provide for normal operation of the reproductive fluids that compose the womb.

The management of the energy or spiritual womb is the management of her subliminal sexual programs. When her sexual beliefs are not natural, her subliminal sexual programs are dysfunctional. Her master feminine faculty awakens in puberty and tries to 'download' all the good programs that make her reproductive system operate properly. But the young girl shuts the master feminine faculty down prematurely, before it can do the job. So about 75% of females enter adulthood without this sexual software in place. They are lacking the maternal energy, the moon archetype. Thus we have all these young girls running around with mature bodies, but immature operating programs. They are broadcasting the negative version of the moon archetype. We can envision the energy field of the young woman as a network of pipelines carrying energy. All over this network is a bunch of little valves in her energy pipe field. These little valves can shut the flow off, or turn the flow on. The moon energy gives her the capacity to open all these little valves to channel energy to all the things she desires. When a young girl holds negative attitudes toward males, or has had bad experiences with males, then these little valves are difficult to open.

The Womb Imprint

In the time frame from the age of ten to twenty years a young female shapes her womanhood. She can control this. If you ask school teachers, they will probably confirm that girls start to act different at about the fourth grade. In many girls, that is when her master feminine faculty starts to wake up. It is an important time. Now as soon as a young girl enters puberty, and her menstrual cycle starts, her master feminine faculty seeks a male energy model. In other words, the master feminine faculty seeks to not only make the highest and best woman it can, it also seeks to custom make her to suite a certain type of man. For at the beginning of the puberty stage, the girl's feminine genes wake up, and bring into her consciousness the very strong desire to be penetrated and confirmed. The desire is to be made love to by the <u>alpha male</u>. This is not ordinary lust. It is a strong primitive drive. This drive will pass away in time. Her image of an alpha male is a composite of her father, the positive male role models around her, and the local "champion". What defines a champion is different for each girl. She may exclude her father from the ranks of ideal men if her opinion of him is not high. When the girl is very young, she wants more than anything to have sex with this champion, this alpha male. It is a ritual. The master feminine faculty is behind this. Now the first two or three times she has sex a major event happens. The first two or three males to enter her womb act to imprint her womb with their masculine energy. She records their energy on her consciousness more than males after this. They **imprint** her womb! They provide the personality, body type, and attitude for her master feminine faculty to use to complete its model. She is designed sexually to fit that type of man. We mean she is designed to fit the composite of the first two or three men she has sex with. If he was indeed a mature alpha male this is a good thing. If he was an immature ordinary male then this is a very bad thing. For the male type which imprints her determines the type of man she will be aroused by in the future. She will broadcast her energy in such a way as to attract men like him to her. If this first male was a knucklehead, or if her first sexual experience was incest or rape, then her sexual behavior programming will be all screwed up.

　　　If you understand the significance of what we have said above you begin then to understand why many societies in the past arranged the marriage of young girls. If the first two or three sexual experiences of a young girl are bad ones, it sets her up for a life of misdirected sexual energy. In some indigenous societies the parents arrange the first sexual encounters of both male and female children to ensure they are positive experiences. In most situations today the energy of the male most young girls are having their first sex with is not a good energy at all. It does not leave a good imprint. Thus the master feminine faculty instills dysfunctional programs into her subconscious. We can go back and change this. And we should. That discussion is coming.

So now we can see three central issues with the womb. There are three main types of energy issues (blocks, choke points, and brakes) in the female auric field:

- As a young girl, between ages 2-7, there was a problem in the relationship with her father. Or perhaps the father was absent. Or the father was preoccupied with issues with the mother and pushed the young girl away.
- The master feminine faculty was shut down too soon after the start of puberty, and the young girl never cultivated her feminine energy in respect to the moon archetype.
- Negative original womb imprint from first sexual encounters. Her first man was a knucklehead, or the event was unpleasant.

Now we have simplified this stuff, and we have left a lot of the explanation out. But now you know the real basic stuff about the ting thingy. Okay so now we can start the discussion about the operation of the female reproductive system.

Reproductive System Issues

There are two sides to every problem with the reproductive system. There is the physical issue we suffer from, and the energy issue which caused it. In most cases the energy issue is the main problem. In indigenous culture both the physical and spiritual issues have the same name. It is toxic womb syndrome, or TWS. Some versions of toxic womb syndrome include:

- Fibroid tumors.
- Uterus Endometrium Disorder
- Premenstrual syndrome or PMS.
- Leucorrhea
- Infertility
- PCOS
- Cervical cancer
- Vaginal infections
- Various related conditions

Toxic Womb Syndrome is a psychosis of the human female and its most common cause is the premature shut down of the master feminine faculty in the teen girl before it can finish its job of bringing her feminine energy on line. Basically, toxic womb syndrome results when young females begin sexual activity before the female reproductive system has a chance to finish maturing. This is partly physical, but mainly energetic. Many of the women who have toxic womb syndrome do not show the symptoms of it. In other words they do not get sick or show any regular signs of being abnormal. In other words, even if a woman has the energy issues that are the root cause of the problem, she still can not get <u>physically</u> sick until certain specific things happen. First she has to introduce toxins into her reproductive tract. These toxins are in the form of parasites, bacteria or food chemicals. The type of physical condition she manifests often is directly related to the type of toxin circulating in her blood. For instance, fibroid tumors result from the introduction of free radicals, especially the burned oils of fried foods and the processing chemicals and hormones in some meats. Vaginal infections are either parasite or bacteria related. PMS is diet related, especially to food items the woman is allergic to but does not know it. The endometrial lining in the uterus is the source of many issues. When it swells and becomes inflamed each month it presses against the organs in the abdomen and produces cramps and other more serious events. But it really does not matter what form toxic womb syndrome takes. It is the same thing. The moon archetype is missing. And the woman has a negative imprint in her womb as a result of sexual activity with a male or males with negative energy. These conditions are all fluid related. There is something abnormal about the blood, mucus, seminal fluid, hormones or etc. The fluid is bad because her energy program is off.

Thus in the case of fibroid tumors there is hardened seminal fluid in the tumors or cysts. In uterus issues the mucus is often too thick or lacking. In vaginal issues the blood vessels are clogged with clots and plague from food toxins. We can treat the physical symptoms only, either through alternative medicine or via chemical drugs or surgery. But if the energy issue is left untreated, the condition will come back, and it will be worse than before. It is necessary to provide therapy to both the physical problem, and the energy problem. If you do not, **the energy womb will over time disconnect from the physical womb**, and this results in what you know as cancer. This takes a minimum of seven years to happen. In all cases, the physical treatment should be such that it restores the water vessel of the womb. To do this, the use of special water is a requirement. A woman can not restore the quality of her blood, mucus, seminal fluids, eggs and hormones without water that is "bio-available". For the main component of all these things is water.

PMS

PMS is basically the combination of two problems. It is inflammation in the reproductive tract. And it is abnormality in the mucus linings, the endometrium of the uterus. Both issues are directly related to the energy body and faulty programs. When you jam your ankle it swells up. It gets stiff. The fluids inside are changed. This is part of how the ankle heals. Now each month some females have the same condition in their reproductive tract. The jam to the ankle may have been the result of a sports injury. The trauma to the womb was internal. The reproductive organs are not operating right because her programs never got loaded right from the start. Her fluids are bad. Thus her mucus is too thick or too thin. Or part of her uterus lining is misplaced, and growing outside her uterus. Or the egg can not travel freely down the tubes. Or her blood is too thick. Whatever the issue, her sexual programs are not able to adapt and fix it. They should be able to deal with these minor issues normally. And then over the years she introduces toxins into the reproductive tract. Now her bad fluid issues are made into a more concrete problem. Each month her uterus becomes inflamed seeking to heal the trauma. At first her outward symptoms are mild. The swollen reproductive tract presses through the water membrane onto her organs. They call this "cramps." It is simply inflammation because the reproductive tract is in a semi-continuous state of mild trauma. She can receive some relief of symptoms by simply removing the toxins, whatever they are. She would gain even more relief if she can restore the water quality by drinking structured water and fresh juices. She will receive the most healing from energy work. But she can only obtain a cure by awakening the master feminine and letting it finish her development in 'second puberty'.

Her estrogen management system is already compromised due to lack of feminine energy. If the endometrium of the uterus is stressed and the fluids compromised, that is when menstruation becomes abnormal. Any damaged tissue in the uterus or abnormal mixtures of fluids must leave the body at the end of the cycle each lunar month. Some women retard the exit of these waste fluids by improperly wearing heavy pads and tampons. These devices are meant to regulate when and how the fluids exit the body. They are not meant to stop up the fluids completely and prevent their escape.

Fibroid Tumors

In the case of fibroid tumors, it is the logical outcome of the Amazon worldview of many modern females. Each feminine attribute has a natural objective. An attractive woman with the Elegant Rose energy is designed to please men. In pleasing men she completes herself. The Moon energy wants her to create and nurture. In creation she completes herself. The Seated Hawk wants her to have a purpose. And in having a purpose beyond herself she completes herself. The treasure chest designs her to be prosperous and to unite with other women. In common unity, she completes herself. But when the Amazon type woman negates these four purposes, she negates her own energy. Basically these tumors are the result of her sexual activity, which wants to do something but can not. There is no order. The energy has to do something. So it creates the closest thing to an embryo that it can. Amazon women are growing these false embryos all the time. Most get to be about the size of a quarter before she notices. When they get a little larger she usually goes to the doctor and has them removed. When they cut open one of these larger tumors they find that they contain all the components of a human being, teeth, nerve cells, skin, hair, bones, etc. But it is all mixed up and confused. There is no natural order to it, because there is no natural order to her feminine energy. These cells of a fibroid tumor are acting according to the commands of the auric field, but her auric field is in disarray because of her psychosis. When you see a really attractive Amazon woman, who really despises males, and she is all yanged up, you are looking at a fibroid factory! Fibroids may also contain the remnants of hardened mucous and fluids, that could not escape the body normally. But she does not need surgery to remove them unless they are very large and hard. Fibroid tumors are the leading cause of problems in childbirth, with endometrial issues close behind.

There are certain specific toxins that especially support the growth of fibroid tumors. Fried, low grade cooking oils, loaded with free radicals are the worse. Corn syrup and other artificial sweeteners are very bad. If she has an allergic reaction to cheese, nuts or other such foods and is unaware of her allergy, this is also a cause. Any foods which produce an excess of mucus in her intestines is a candidate.

Cancer

The cells in the flesh body do not have an individual will. They are bonded to the overlord. The cells **can not** do what they want to, they must do what they are told. That is why you are alive. Your spirit controls the body, one cell at a time. Each cell is ruled by a tiny intelligence in the auric field. The auric field is energy that is alive, it has a mind. It is your mind, the awake part, and the subconscious part. And there are billions of little minds in there, one for each cell. Each cell is anchored to one of these minds, a point in the blue layer of the auric field. And these micro minds tell the cells where to go, and what their mission is. The cell then looks into its DNA recipe to read the blueprint of how to actually do that. Now when the woman lacks feminine energy, and is overly yang, the "minds" in the auric field are giving the wrong mission to the cells. And toxins within the cells interfere with the reading of the DNA. These cells become cancer and malignant, when they are disconnected from the woman's auric field. Having no intelligence to guide them, they just do whatever. They aggressively attack surrounding cells.

The human being is an energy being first. With so much technology and emphasis on the body, we have lost sight of this in modern times. When we change elements of our personality, we change our energy. When our personal development does not match the natal blueprint in our DNA or spirit, we are out of balance, and this is reflected in the structure and function of our auric fields. The shift to the Amazon lifestyle is reflected in a distorted auric field. It presents as blockages and distortions. The table work, tantra exercises, Qi Gong, yoga, and sexual healing all help to heal the auric field of a woman.

If you do not use a part of your being that is given to you by nature, nature gradually takes it away. The recent spike in cancers of the breast, cervix, uterus and etc., are directly related to the sharp increase in the population of Amazon women. As we have been saying, humans are energy beings. You do not take your first breath as a baby until your "spirit" comes. When you die, your spirit body or auric field completely leaves your flesh body. Without your energy body, the flesh body can not live. The cells and organs do not know what to do. The intelligence which was operating the body is gone. In cancer, the same thing happens, but to only a small part of the body. A better understanding of cancer is coming. No cure for cancer can be found until the medical community recognizes the auric field and the role it plays. In severe cases of dysfunction, when the cells are so toxic, and the auric field is so blocked and decayed, the cells in the physical body become disconnected from their anchors in the auric field. This is the stage of necromancy. You call it cancer. Cancer is what we see in the flesh body, when that part of the body is detached from the overall auric field. Once cancer sets in those cells can not be saved. But if you remove the toxins from the surrounding cells, and repair the auric field, the cancer will go away, and that part of the body can be restored. I am not saying that this is easy to do. It is not. But it is possible.

Response from all 858 women whose uterus was removed with or without removal of their ovaries	
99.9%	Not informed of any or most of the adverse effects
78.2%	Change in personality
78.2%	Irritability
77.4%	Loss of energy
76.8%	Profound fatigue
75.2%	Diminished or absent sexual desire
68.9%	Loss of stamina
68.2%	Difficulty relating with and interacting with others
68.1%	Difficulty socializing
66.6%	Loss of pleasure in intercourse

I recommend you go to their website and review the documents. HERS Foundation, contact hersfdn@earthlink.net

Even if you disrupt the communication between the energy body and the flesh body there are serious repercussions. The glands are the messengers that help relay chemical messages from the auric field to the physical body. The ovaries are one of the major glands. Due to the reproductive issues that follow the Amazon lifestyle, many Amazon women opt to have a hysterectomy, in an attempt to stop some of the symptoms of toxic womb syndrome. In a hysterectomy the woman has parts of her reproductive system surgically removed. This usually includes the ovaries, but not always. Removal of the ovaries in effect breaks part of the communication link between the auric field and the cells, even though the direct link or anchor is still intact. To demonstrate what happens when this communication is broken, please refer to a chart below. One source that I reviewed while researching this topic, was the HERS Foundation, but it should not be implied that the Hers Foundation concurs with my findings. And the chart below is complied from a composite of information. In an ongoing study begun in 1991, the HERS Foundation received reports of harmful effects and adverse outcomes from 858 women who responded to HERS' questionnaire. These women were aged 15 to 65 and were hysterectomized from less than one year to 33 years earlier. These reports document the breadth and scope of the negative impact caused by hysterectomy to women, as well as to those who care about them and to the larger society.

The reader should especially note that women who had their ovaries removed reported a change in their personality, loss of energy, and difficulty relating to others, especially members of the opposite sex. This occurs, even though the women are taking hormone supplements to replace the estrogen. Our point is that the results are not limited to physical changes. Many of the changes are intangible, emotional, energy related.

Hormones
There are seven major glands in the human endocrine system. The seven glands in the female are pineal gland, pituitary gland, thyroid gland, thymus gland, pancreas, adrenal glands and ovaries. The endocrine glands are central to the function of the woman's reproductive system and the chemical function of her cells. Her ovaries produce estrogen one of the main yin hormones in the female. The pineal gland produces melatonin, the other key yin hormone in the human. These two hormones, melatonin and estrogen influence all other hormones in her body, and are the central chemical messengers through which the auric field conveys a feminine quality into her chemical and emotional being. Estrogen and melatonin are both yin in nature, together they represent a yin spectrum. But estrogen is at one end of this range, representing more the sexual aspect of yin, while melatonin is at the other end of the range, representing more the spiritual aspect of yin. Melatonin makes you sleep, passive, introspective and flexible.   Estrogen makes you incorporate water into the cells to make them heavy and fluid, it gives a woman curves, it makes flesh soft. It has a parallel affect to the emotions making her receptive and submissive to complimentary energies. The female also produces a small amount of testosterone. The action of testosterone is opposite to estrogen.

For estrogen to have any impact, it must be taken internally inside the cells of the brain and body. So it must leave the ovaries, go into the blood, and then into the cells. But for this to happen, a lot has to be in harmony. There is a 28 day reproductive cycle that governs this. Now in the Amazon woman this reproductive cycle is thrown off. The cycle is disrupted by the presence of excessive amounts of testosterone. The woman's system can only tolerate a small amount of testosterone and for only short bursts of time. In the excess yang woman the auric field generates an excess of testosterone production. The Amazon woman has an excess of testosterone in her ovaries and reproductive tract for too many days out of the 28 day lunar cycle. It displaces her estrogen, and her estrogen will not be motive enough. Progesterone can help.

Awakening the Master Feminine

Awakening The Moon

Chapter 6 Awakening the Moon

The Moon Archetype
Icon:
The icon of the Moon archetype is the moon, and inside the moon are a clutch of eggs.

Image:
The image for purposes of visualization is a young mother with her baby to her breasts.

This energy is an intuitive faculty of nurturing others. It is to supply the need implied by a growing thing. It is the capacity to give, and the desire to give, without a sense of loss. It generates an unending supply, based on the need to give unceasingly. We use the icon of the moon to denote the component or archetype of feminine energy that is associated with the abstract concept of an egg. It is the true essence of fertility. This is the yin energy that is designed to bring forth new life, or support existing life. To allow the generation of this energy the female must feel secure.

Broadcasts …
When this archetype of the feminine energy is active in a woman's auric field, she begins to broadcast. Her broadcast to the male energy is;

> I submit to you (the male energy). I give you the power you need to do. Protect me. Be strong for me, and make my dreams come true.

When the woman fails to develop the moon archetype, she feels a sense of loss when she gives. The act of nurturing others drains her. She is less fertile. In the absence of this energy in her auric field the female will broadcast the opposite message. Her broadcast to the male energy is;
> I do not submit to you (the male energy). I feel unprotected. I am afraid. I can not nurture you.

Examine the two broadcasts and understand. If you broadcast the positive moon energy men WILL desire to respond. The men, who have their masculine energy available, will respond in the positive. Men love to be the hero. They love to come to your rescue. But remember that the majority of them CAN NOT RESPOND. They do not have the energy developed yet. Do not get upset at these men. When you broadcast to them, and express your needs, it makes them feel impotent. They will act badly. It is because they feel incomplete. It is not your fault. Steer them in the direction so that they can become who they need to be. If you are broadcasting the negative moon message understand that men may find you attractive but will not commit to you. In their encounters with you they sense that something is lacking. They will come up with excuses as to why they will not do right. But your energy is what is giving them cause for pulling back.   The men will not change until you modify your broadcast.

The Moon archetype is one of the dominant feminine energies. But like all the archetypes, it is designed to work in unison with the other three archetypes.

Second Puberty   Moon Edition

To begin to awaken the moon component of her feminine energy a woman infuses a catalyst into her subconscious mind. This catalyst is like a key, and when the mind sees it the master feminine faculty awakens, and looks for the door it corresponds with to open it.   Now I guess this statement sounds a bit esoteric. How does one insert a 'catalyst' into the mind? Is it a drug or a cattle prod or do I stick my head under a pyramid? No, none of the above. This exercise is a series of things done together. It is done in a meditation format. During the meditations something is done to automatically cause the left brain to begin to shut down. And the right brain is opened up to be receptive in a special way. Special sounds are involved. Special breathing is involved.

There is a little trick to it that is private. These are instructions given out at the time of the regimen. Actually people who have done it find it very simple. It is organic. Each thing by itself is meaningless. But when done together, in the right sequence, these things form a catalyst. It may be hard to conceptualize this. But we are reprogramming our subconscious mind all the time. Every time we watch television, or sit in class at school, or go to a concert, or do anything with repetition. All ads on television are designed with certain colors, sounds, and themes that have some power to change your mind. We are programmed from birth to respond this way. And this exercise is perfectly normal. In fact everyone has already done it when they went through puberty the first time. They just did not know they were doing it. This time you are aware while you are doing it. The infusion of this catalyst requires a special CD. The meditation sessions last about 25 minutes. It is required to do the sessions three times each week. You will know that you have done something right away. And you will actually begin to experience results in about three weeks.

As soon as the woman begins the meditations, table work, and energy work her master feminine faculty begins to awaken. It then proceeds to go into her DNA storehouse and locates the set of attributes associated with the moon archetype. It starts to transfer them from a dormant state into an active state. They start growing into real aspects of her being, and stop being just potential traits. The extent to which she will achieve success, and the rate at which this transition can take place varies considerably.

While attempting to gain relief from the symptoms of toxic womb syndrome the woman should refrain from introducing the toxins into her system that trigger the problems.
1. No fried foods.
2. No corn syrup.
3. Reduce consumption of mucus producing foods.
4. During the three days prior to the flow part of the menses cycle, eliminate all salt and seafood from the diet.

Auric Field Detoxification
Healing the Reproductive Matrix
In the process of awakening the master feminine faculty energy work is a key step. This energy work is the detoxification of the spirit body or auric field. This type of energy work is done on a massage table, and a session is usually two hours long. Two such sessions are

suggested for this phase. This is a very special form of energy work. It is normally done by a healer familiar with the tantra. For females, only males can do this form of energy work. For males, only females can do this type of energy healing. The female client lies on the table and the healer introduces a special energy into her auric field that breaks up negative blocks and purges her field. The energy of the healer does not flow through the female client, but is the catalyst for a reaction within her auric field. In the case of energy table work for the purpose of awakening the master feminine faculty the male healing energy acts to neutralizes negative energy in the female's field. The presence of the special male polarity also stimulates the action of her master feminine faculty. Tantra energy work releases old memories. Females report that it provides healing to old relationship wounds.

The woman's age is some times a factor. It remains a factor only to the extent that an older woman has had a longer time to become rigid and inflexible in her belief systems and personality structure. Health is a factor. It is a factor to the extent that a woman has mistreated or abused her body so bad that restoration is impaired. In order for the feminine traits to become active, she must have the ability to secret human growth hormone from the pituitary gland. This is a requirement. The ovaries and estrogen also play a key role in the revival of the feminine nature. If a woman has undergone a hysterectomy, her chances of achieving success with this regimen are reduced, but not impossible. Prescription drug use or illegal drug use can damage the endocrine glands such as thyroid, pancreas, etc. This slows down the reaction. There are countermeasures to these things. But they make the process more complex. You must fully disclose any such history to your guide at the beginning of the program.

Energy healing or energy work is the second oldest form of medicine. Herbal medicine is thought to be the oldest. There are many forms of energy healing including Reiki, praunic healing, psychic surgery, hands-on-healing, table work, Shaktipat, Tumo, etc. are all forms of energy work/healing. Two of the most famous energy healers of ancient times were connected with spiritual orders. Imhotep was the high priest of the spiritual order in dynastic Egypt. Jesus the Christ is the name sake of the Christian religion. Both were advanced energy healers if the accounts cited have not been hyped up. From Russia, China, India, Africa, South America and especially the Native Americans of North America there have come credible accounts of what is termed "miracle" healing. In the past there was resistance to energy healing in America. This seems strange, since there is a large Christian population in the

United States, and energy healing was extremely popular with the early Christians.

Erasing Bad Memories
Detoxification of the Reproductive System

Our cells all hold memories. Memory is not just in the brain. Negative memories are stored in toxins held within the cell. Fat cells are must often used in this way. It is sometimes hard to get rid of these fat cells because of the toxic memories they store. We refuse to let go of the past, and so we can not let go of the fat. This reinforces the counterfeit behavior of the counterfeit persona. Women and men often cling to these memories and the fears and false beliefs that support them. This is not complex memory as in the brain, but a very primitive chemical message. This is not the same complex and blueprint-like memory that is held in the genetic material of the DNA. These negative cell memories are only triggered by specific situations or emotions, usually a fear or phobia.

Standing in the way of your new expression of feminine energy are old patterns of behavior and memories of how things turned out before. Until you break from this chemical attachment to the past, it is hard to embrace a positive future. Your mantra for this phase of the program is, "stop living in the past." Remember, what got you to here, will not take you to there (the place you want to be). Because when a woman brings the attributes of the Seated Hawk, Elegant Rose, Moon or Treasure Chest online, she wants to act like a feminine woman. To do this she has to trust men, feel secure, feel sexy, and feel special. The program is to develop curves, hype up the reproductive system, and change the energy profile. This proactive, positive, spiritual and upbeat energy is directly opposed to the negative, fear based, inhibitive energy that is locked into her cells.

You ultimately have control of your being. You have free will. We can not change overnight. But in a matter of weeks or months we can delete our attachment to the negative past. We can not delete the memories themselves that are held in the brain. But we can and we should use our will to free ourselves from the influence these memories have over us. Who is the boss of you? Is it your will or the memories? Are you the horse you are riding, or the rider of the horse? You are the rider, and you can get off the horse. Memories are powerful things to the extent that we continue to invest in them. Memories become impotent images of the past when we make our will dominant. Trauma and some negative experience may be hard to avoid. For instance let us say an adult woman remembers that her father abandoned her at the age of six. This was a trauma. Now the memories continue to haunt her and shape her present. The memories of being abandoned by her father got trapped in her cells when she was just six years old. She waited for dad to pick her up on the weekend and take her to his house. But this time he did not come. And then her mother told her that there had been an incident, and daddy was mad at mommy. Her father came to visit her less and less. Then comes the point of the final break from dad. The six year old girl is told that daddy has moved, and has another family. So she knows the whole situation has changed, and daddy may not be coming for a long time. She talks to dad on the phone and he tries to explain, but there is no acceptable closure in this situation for a six year old. This is when those bad memories get programmed into her cells. In goes in deep, because it hurt so badly. The break comes, and the crying, and the sense of loss. The memory is in her mind, and a copy of the memory is locked in the cells. The memories will stay with her, until she lets them go, or removes the toxins the memories are fastened to. As long as these toxins are in her cells, the negative memories will affect her behavior in an involuntary way. She believes she has no control over this reaction. And as long as she hates her father, and holds tight to the feelings of abandonment and anxiety, it will be hard to eliminate the fat. This is part of the role of the awakening circle. We talk about these things that bother us, and decide to let the past go. You can forgive, or choose not to forgive, it does not matter. The point is to disconnect and bring your will into play. It is better to forgive. But whatever you do, take control. The best way to start this cell detoxification is to talk about these episodes.

Cell detoxification is:

- Impose the will over negative memories.
- Use the language of victory. Talk about the past in the terms of how you want it to turn out.
- Use diet to support a purging.
- Exercise the thigh, hip and abdomen area. The exercise causes the blood to be pushed into the very small blood vessels and get into those cells in the corners and cracks.
- Act like you are clean and new when you start, to give your self the image of what you will be.

Your outer beauty and outer harmony starts with beauty and health in the cells. Of course, when we see a client in person, each regimen is tailored to their particular situation. Because if you have a serious issue like high blood pressure, diabetes, or liver disease, you may need to take extra measures to get the most out of it. We have already spoken about the diet aspect of the regimen. When you join a group and start the actual process more information is given to you.

Changing Your Broadcast

When your moon broadcast is positive it has a serious impact on men. In my opinion it is the strongest of the attractive forces. It says you will nurture them. It says you are receptive to them. What compels men about this broadcast is that the woman is saying "I need you." It is an acknowledgement of his worth. It says she accepts him, acknowledges him, and appreciates him for all he does. Males go into another space when they are in that "I am here to protect you and take care of you mode." If a woman is seeking marriage the positive moon broadcast will be her best tool.

A woman can tell when her moon broadcast is changing by her attitude to children and domestic things. Babies start to look irresistible cute to you. You gain a desire to cook and host parties out of nowhere. You find your kitchen no longer pleases you because it does not allow you to express your culinary side. You feel the urge to give to others. You are attracted to charities and doing good deeds to those less fortunate than yourself. Your moon is coming on line. Thus a change comes over her in that she has the ability to give, without feeling a sense of loss. She wants to give and nurture, and in fact is driven to do so. Some women tend to block this energy when it starts to emerge. Why you may ask? Because as young girls they looked at women who were giving and nurturing and saw that men were not doing their part. The young girls observe the last generation and often see that these moon women did not always have positive outcomes. Men did not protect them, did not care for them, men did not love them. In other words, young girls reject the moon energy because they observe an absence of older men who have brought forth their masculine energy. These men do not embody the house of the man. We will discuss the house of the man in another chapter. So there are all these issues of trust, security and caring. Once you begin this part of the regimen the energy will continue to develop until you stop it. You have to allow it. The past is the past. If you cling to it, your moon archetype development will be limited.

Awakening the Master Feminine

Awakening the Rose

Chapter 7 Awakening the Rose

Dedication

After many years of research, coaching and observation, I have come to the conclusion that the sexual life of most people in this culture is one of denial and quiet desperation. We live today in a sexual dark age. Few of us are satisfied. Few of us are whole. And most people have learned to settle for something less than the minimum. The issues and attitudes that have placed us in this situation are reversible. They are not inevitable. We could easily overcome them. It is ignorance that is our main obstruction. We are too filled with pride to even speak about the problem. And so in silence we suffer. Sexual issues which start off as minor things gradually grow into huge monsters of dysfunction. These horrible beasts of sexual dysfunction roam our bedrooms at will, scaring the begeebees out of man and woman alike. Some of us would rather go to our graves unfulfilled and alone than to face our false beliefs or seek viable solutions. But thank god, the tide is changing.

This chapter is dedicated to all the women and men out there who have summoned the courage to be honest about sex. They are standing up to the horrible monster, the sexual issues beast. I hope this chapter offers hope and provides vital information for the brave few who are struggling each day to come up out of the sexual dark ages.

Master Yao Nyamekye Morris

Awakening the Rose

The Icon of the Elegant Rose
Genital Reflexology
The Orgasmic Plateau
Her Lips & Mouth
Her Breasts
Tantric Mantra
Healing Through Table Work
Second Puberty
Female Beauty as Erotic Art
The Sexual Renaissance
Awakening Exercises
Case Study   Jennifer in the Rose Garden

The Archetype of the Elegant Rose
Icon:
The icon of the Elegant Rose is a splendid rose, on a pillow of silk.

Image:
The image for purposes of visualization is a very voluptuous and seductive woman lounging on a couch. She wears a beautiful gown, with a slit in the front. She is enticing. On the couch with her are honey, flowers and frankincense.

The Elegant Rose component of feminine energy imparts an essence and form into the woman that causes her to be sensed by others as pleasing, and for her to sense her environment as being pleasing. Imagine the image of you as that very voluptuous and seductive woman lounging on a couch. This is where the energy is trying to take you. The archetype of the elegant rose is the essence of sensuality. It is like silk compared to burlap, a love ballad compared to plain speech, a balcony instead of a window, a flower instead of weeds, the sweetness of a mango compared to oatmeal. This essence of the Elegant Rose causes the woman to feel pleasure herself, from the act of giving pleasure to others. She wants to ompronо hоrоolf iι οll ιφιιι ι li ιucli a way ιιιuι υιι αttracts males. This includes all five senses.   It makes her change to maximize the attractiveness of whatever attributes she has. It ignites a drive within the woman to achieve harmony with the male, even when there are fundamental differences between them. And the erotic energy generated from this arousal and pleasure is the engine driving our creativity.

To start the awakening of the elegant rose archetype requires the special meditations and tantra exercises again. This is the infusion of a catalyst into the subconscious mind that triggers the master feminine faculty to awaken again, and restore the sexual programs to their original default settings. This brings on the onset of second puberty. The puberty stage will progress and continue unless the woman refuses to abandon the false beliefs of the past, which shut down the master feminine faculty the first time. The process is the same as for the moon and hawk, but the keys and meditations are slightly different. This is the infusion of a catalyst into the subconscious mind of the female. This is done through a very special CD with music and instructions on it. If you are taking part in one of the regimens, follow the instructions of the guide. Also, a calendar is often referred to in this chapter. The calendar is given out in the first regimen session; it is not in this book. There is both a weekly calendar and a monthly schedule. These schedules give guidance on when to do the meditations and routines and tantra exercises.

The core of the concepts presented here are from the Natural Sexual Ideology, and not the tantra arts proper. Many aspects of the tantra art are incorporated into this chapter. But the natural sexual ideology is broader in scope and more general in application. While I have studied many disciplines and am given the title of master for certain past accomplishments, I am not a tantric master. This is a very specialized title for someone who has devoted a great amount of time exclusively to the tantra science.

About Tantra

The word tantra is actually the name of a volume of scriptures that go back to the Vedic tradition of the Dravidians (Blacks) of very ancient India. The tantra art is the infusion of spiritual and esoteric themes into a couple's sexual life. In modern times the word has come to be associated with special sexual arts. It is a controversial topic today, as it was in ancient times. In the Tantra Scriptures the subject of sex is dealt with openly and directly. The Vedic tradition celebrated sex, and saw it as a path to man's enlightenment. However, less evolved cultures have connected sex with sin, and the elevation of the carnal nature over the spiritual inner self. And of course any thing associated with the flesh, be it food, drink, dancing, money or sex, can enrich us or enslave us. It is always ignorance and bad intent which is the source of evil. Over the century's elements within the Hindu faith, Buddhism, Christianity and Islam have waged campaigns against the tantra arts. And today the art is often misunderstood and misrepresented. History shows that most of the objection to tantra did not originate from holy men, but instead from patriarchal cultures who view the female gender as being inferior to the male gender. Tantra celebrates the female as being equal to the male, a view most cultures and religions were not willing to tolerate.

About Natural Sexual Ideology

The natural sexual ideology is founded on the principle that the design of humankind is divinely inspired. Our design is not flawed. We are not born into sin. The blueprint contained in our DNA is perfect, if only we could fully realize it. Man and woman are born with everything they need to come together in relationship and produce positive outcomes. Natural Sexual Ideology seeks to comprehend how to bring forth into reality the potential perfection of our design. Problems arise when we stray from the original divine recipe. The creator did not make a mistake, nor is there a need for God to enter back into creation to correct something. He/she/it does not punish us or impede us. We punish and impede ourselves when we seek to change the original natural plan. Our mission on earth is to evolve into the beings we were intended to be and have the best possible experience on earth while we are trying to do that.

The elegant rose energy is about the experience of pleasure through sex and all other sensual experiences. There is a need to avoid confining sexual pleasure to the gratification of the animal nature only. This should be obvious; we should not even have to say it. When we engage in sex we should not restrict its benefits. Natural sexual interaction is intended to generate a range of benefits.

- It is a way to produce healthier more evolved children.
- It heals the reproductive system.
- It releases the energy into our creative minds.

This creative energy is required for us to evolve to become higher and better beings. A high Qi level is required for a female to carry a pregnancy to term. Naturally full sex raises this Qi level. Natural sex sends energy in wave patterns over the woman's body which has a significant healing effect. Typical sexual exchange is lacking this benefit. My critics point out that giving people the means to enjoy extremely intense sexual pleasure is an invitation to corruption. They are almost right. But as you see in the world around you, people do not need my help to find ways to corrupt them. They can handle that fine on their own. But if we deny people the choice to evolve out of the dark ages, we have done them an injustice. We should be less afraid of pleasure, and more afraid of ignorance.

Second Puberty
       The infusion of the catalyst, the table work and the tantra exercises will bring on the state of second puberty. The master feminine faculty has been awakened out of remission, and enters an active phase again. Changes and transitions are now possible that were not possible before. But with the elegant rose archetype, there are some dynamics present which do not apply to the moon, seated hawk or treasure chest. While there is some knowledge in this society about health, money, the brain and the personality, there is almost no real knowledge of the natural sciences with respect to sex. It is not just that the knowledge is lacking, but the false information and beliefs are so common and abundant as to present a real problem. Before we can discuss the second puberty of the rose and the regimen protocol, we must present an outline of some of the science. We will begin with the subject of Genital Reflexology. This subject was also presented in some detail in my first book, Amanmere, published in 1997. It is currently out of print, but used copies have been obtained on the auction web sites.

Genital Reflexology

       Reflexology is healing discipline of the nervous system. In reflexology one portion of the body affects another part of the body in a reflex manner. In the therapy, energy applied to one body area has a healing effect on the second part of the body. The genital area in the female is a reflex map. The entire vagina is a representative of the whole body. In other words, you can find a spot on the interior of the vagina which corresponds to all points on the main body. The Genital reflexology zone in the female includes the vagina, clitoris, and G-spot. A reflex map means that the surface of the vagina is divided into scores of mini-zones, each zone being a micro bundle of special nerve endings. Each special nerve bundle corresponds to one part of the body. So imagine that we took the vagina and spread it out flat like the map of a state. This vagina map is divided into little counties. Each county or micro bundle corresponds to a part of the body. One county is the lungs, another county the legs, another the head, etc. In other words each micro nerve zone in the vagina is connected to a specific part of the body. Just like an acupuncture point, when you apply energy to one of the micro points in the vagina, it causes something to happen to the corresponding part of the body.

Likewise, the entire penis is a representative of the whole body. The male genital reflex map includes the penis, scrotum, the perineum muscle, and prostate. Now the reflexology zone in the male is inverse to the reflexology zone in the woman. In other words they mate up. When the erect penis is fully inside an inflated vagina the two reflex maps are aligned. In other words, if a penis is fully inserted into a vagina the reflex points in one should line up point to point with the reflex points in the other. On a male, the spot on the penis which corresponds to the heart is near the tip of the penis, slightly north of top dead center. In the vagina, the spot which corresponds to the heart is near the very rear, adjacent to the cervix, north of top dead center. On the penis the liver spot is about 1 ½ inch from the base, at eight o'clock on the dial. This is about 5 ½ inches from the tip of a seven inch penis. In the vagina the liver spot is about 1 ½ inches in from the lip surface, at about eight o'clock on the dial. In other words, they are inverse matches. When the erect penis is making contact in the inflated vagina it is just like the contact that is made in an electric switch when two contacts mate. The connection is made and current passes on the wires. Energy is transmitted. Where ever the man's penis contacts a point on the woman's reflex map, it stimulates a current or energy transmission to the corresponding part of her body.

The illustration which follows is a two dimension image that suggests the location of the zones of a vagina reflex map. The vagina is three dimensional, but this Iridology chart shows the values if the vagina were flattened and the folds spread out.

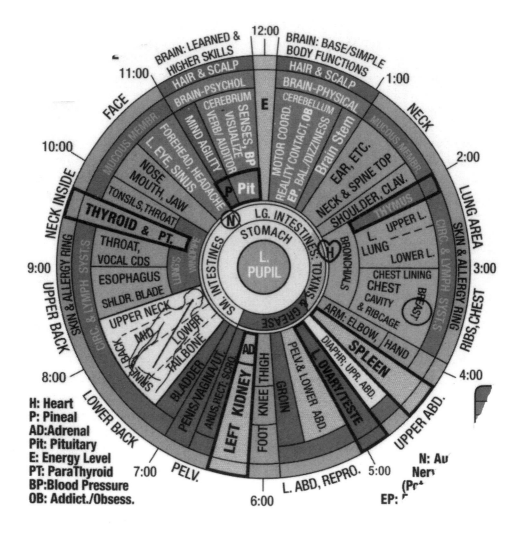

Now as most women know the interior of the vagina is not a smooth surface that is a cylinder, but an irregular surface with a series of folds. These folds are important. When she is fully aroused, blood fills up the cavities, and the folds stretch, and the mini-zones are presented to the penis at the optimal position for contact. The penis is designed with a rim or crown on the head, which during movement in or out, can make contact with the zones up in the folds. The more fully aroused a woman is, the more her "zones" are pushed out there for contact. There is significance to this. The vagina has the ability to grip or seize the penis. If the vagina loses its "grip" then for much of the range of movement of the penis within the vagina, the reflex zones on the penis surface are not being stimulated, and energy transfer is minimal. Not only does this reduce pleasure, but more importantly, it "chokes" energy flow. The muscles in the female vagina relax and lose tension with age. But we find that even in some young women their vagina has lost its grip. The main reason the vagina loses its grip is because the female pulls away emotionally from the opposite sex. We will speak more of this later, and show how the kegel machine plays a role.

For the most part, males and females who are compatible to each other tend to have matching genitals. And to some extent the fit of the male genitals to the female genital map is important. But the energy dynamic of the male or female is far more important. In fact when the male employs the natural sexual exercises and the tantra regimens, the physical shortcomings of either party can be overcome. If the male has a small penis this becomes less of a factor. If the female has lost her grip this becomes less of a factor. And as we progress through this discourse we will show how either party can use energy to overcome any physical short comings and heal the opposite sex party.

Now in respect to this reflexology map in the vagina, there are some other things we should mention. In the typical woman at age 21, more than 50% of her vagina surfaces are asleep and non-conductive. It was never brought on line. Why you say? Because her master feminine faculty was shut down before it could bring her entire reproductive software on line. More specifically the master feminine faculty did not get a chance to bring her elegant rose archetype on line. As she awakens her master feminine faculty, and brings the rose on line, so does the nerves in the vagina come awake. With males the same applies. Most young adult men only have a part of their penis reflex map active. Also health issues and lifestyles can deaden or make spots on her reflex map less sensitive. Smoking will make the lung spot less sensitive. Clogged intestines and colon make sections of the vaginal reflex map less sensitive. Diabetes, high blood pressure, obesity, and blood disorders also reduce the energy conductivity of the reflex maps of men and women.

Now the goal of the natural sexual protocol is to gain some control of the flow of energy during intercourse. This is the great secret to achieving maximum pleasure during sex, and receiving all the other benefits. Through energy management, the time of the sexual session can be extended. This will also increase fertility rates. By controlling this energy dynamic the healing power of sex can be realized. To achieve the goals of the natural sexual, the first step is to build up the internal energy in the body. And the second step is to achieve the ability to project this energy out of the body and into the nervous system or auric field of the partner.

In the case of the male, the first task is to delay ejaculation. In the male, the ejaculation reflex and the orgasm are two separate events. But most men ejaculate at the same time they have orgasm by habit. They never learned any different. Other men have an involuntary orgasm in sync with the female. The energy spike coming from the female triggers the male orgasm and ejaculation. This is unnatural. Males present this profile because they never fully developed their masculine energy or bonded to the female energy. They exhibit a general disconnect to the female energy. The act of having an orgasm without having simultaneous ejaculation is called "retaining the seed." It requires the prostate gland be strengthened. There are exercises to do. The mind must learn to impose itself on the nervous system. After this the male engages in a series of energy building routines that include Qi Gong, and tantra exercises. These build up the male energy. Then the man learns how this energy 'leaks' out of his body through diet, negative emotions and problems in the auric field. Then the male learns how to balance his Qi, and focus his energy in one place. Finally he develops techniques to project his energy out of his body through his organs, hands and penis. He is then ready to engage the woman.

In the case of the female, the first task is to unblock the circulation systems in her womb. The blood, Qi, lubricating fluids and acupuncture meridians must be cleared. The next step is to address issues in her auric field which prevent energy from building up. This blocks her from achieving higher levels of orgasm. Often, this involves addressing old emotional issues. Females develop sexual energy patterns from things like oral sex which must be broken if the vagina pattern can progress. Females with the Amazon persona will also need to shift to a more right

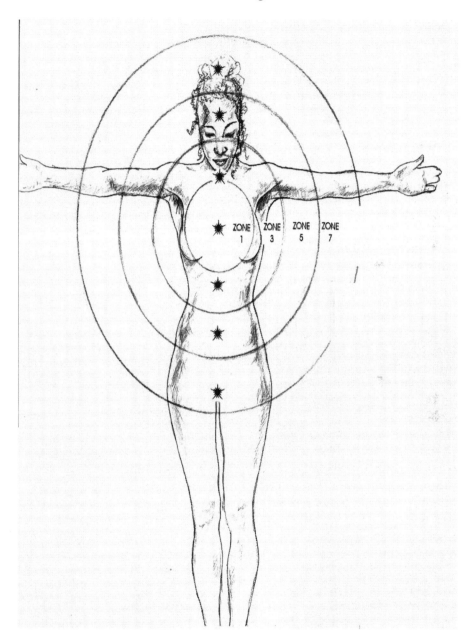

brain profile in order for the energy to really build up. After this the female engages in a series of energy building routines that include Qi Gong, and tantra exercises. These build up the female energy. Then the female learns how this energy 'leaks' out of her body through diet, negative emotions and problems in the auric field. The female learns how to balance her Qi, and focus her energy. Finally she develops techniques to project her energy out of her body through her organs, breasts and vagina. She is then ready to engage the man!

Let's continue with the reproductive science. The woman's body is divided into seven zones. The head is in zone seven and the feet are in zone one. Zone four is the heart, and is the center point. From the energy standpoint sexual activity should start in the heart, the center, and then move out to the other zones. These zones are connected to the micro zones in the vagina. The goal is to get the woman's energy moving. Then we want the energy to fill all her zones. See the illustration. The zones are not just divisions in the body, but in the auric field as well. To do this may be fairly simple or very difficult depending on the status of the woman. If the woman can fully engulf her body and aura in energy she can then achieve the full orgasm. We will talk about that shortly. She is then able to do all the things we talk about in the topic on second puberty. Now if the woman brings the elegant rose energy on line, and follows the regimen protocol, she should be able to correct the issues that may have stunted her sex life before. At the least she will see some improvement. It really depends on what she is working with from the beginning and how sincerely she follows through with the program. When we say her sex life will improve we do not mean she will just have a slightly better orgasm. We mean her sex life will look totally different, her entire sexual profile will move to a higher level. This will not all happen in the short time frame of the regimen. Improvement continues for many months after she first awakens her master feminine. We have mentioned some of the things that stand in her way. There are dead spots on her genital reflex map. There are blocks in her auric field. There are issues with blood circulation in the pelvic area and with Qi flow there as well. There are possible reproductive health issues such as fibroid tumors and PMS. But none of these things can stop the energy. In fact when the energy starts to flow again it will tend to clear up these issues. There are potential problems that can block her progress. We have already talked about many of them in the earlier chapters. And we are going to go into great detail about exactly what can undermine her energy flow in this chapter and the next. But the main issue is her lack of feminine energy, the Amazon persona. And Once she starts to reverse that through this process the main stopping point is gone. She is an energy being, and as her energy flows it moves the other issues out of the way. The main thing she has to do is just to allow it to happen.

We will return to this discussion of the movement of energy through the female reproductive matrix. But before we do we need to cover some points about the dynamics of orgasm and the purpose of the table energy work.

Achieving the Orgasmic Plateau

It is sad that so many men are against improving the sexual outcomes of women. It is surprising that so many women are against it as well. Now here are the stages and mechanics of orgasm. We can present only part of this discussion in a book. Some of it you learn by doing it. Full orgasm is not a climax. It is a plateau. There are four stages that she must pass through to get to this plateau. They are listed below. She does not have to experience them in the exact sequence as listed. Each stage represents a greater percent of her reflexology matrix being energized. In other words as more channels are opened so that more energy can flow, she feels more pleasure. When one system is filled to capacity, she expands to include more parts of her body. When the energy generated becomes trapped and can not escape, it builds up pressure, almost like air in a balloon or electricity in a house circuit. At some point the energy shock waves from the compression, and sends a spasm through her nervous system. The spasm may result in an orgasmic climax and the release of the energy. The climax is like a circuit breaking tripping from circuit overload. Or, the spasm triggers more reflexology meridians to open up, and the energy rushes into the next level. In this case sexual activity does not stop, by she bumps up to the next level and the pleasure becomes even more intense. She can still have an orgasm from the spasm, but it is not a climax. Most women have a climax when they reach this point, and sexual activity for them ends. This is however unnatural. The woman builds up to the plateau stage of orgasm through four pre-stages.

- Stage one involves the heart and blood and ends in a single spasm. This spasm can trigger an orgasm.
- Stage two involves the mouth, voice and breasts, and ends in a spasm which triggers multiple orgasms.
- Stage three involves the breath and auric field, and ends in more intense multiple orgasms. This sets up wave activity.

- Stage four involves the shut down of the left brain. The clitoris becomes erect. It ends in an intense ejaculation of a fluid similar to semen.

In the orgasmic pre-stages the energy zones are energized in the sequence of; four, three and five, two and six, one and seven, then in reverse order moving in concentric circles back to zone four. See Illustration. In other words the sexual energy of the woman flows in waves that cover an ever expanding circle that starts at the heart. This may not mean much to you now. By as you progress with the protocol it will.

The female orgasm is not a gradual rise to a peak, but a series of stages or tiers that she climbs up to a plateau of orgasmic bliss. When she completes one stage, the orgasm occurs as a result of her opening up to move a much greater volume of energy through her auric field and body.

Pre- Stage One of Orgasm
In the first few minutes of lovemaking, the majority of the female energy is focused in the body around the heart and lungs. The man and woman begin to breathe heavily. The heart of the man and woman begins to pump faster. After about seven minutes this zone (zone 4) and the fourth layer of the auric field is energized to the point of saturation. At least this is what should happen. In reality it rarely does. If the woman can saturate this zone with energy, then she boosts herself up to the next level. When this happens spasms of pleasure are triggered. In reaction to the spasms the female may have an orgasm. Some women never get this far, they are non- orgasmic. Others can not fully energize this zone, and have an orgasm and then stop. This of course is very pre-mature.

Pre- Stage Two of Orgasm
As the session continues more energy is put into motion, and more of the woman's body and aura are ignited. The circle that began at the heart is expanded to a larger circle. Eventually the circle includes the solar plexus and throat area. The throat is the same as the thyroid area, and the solar plexus is the same as the diaphragm area. So the circle from the throat to the diaphragm is ignited, and inside this circle the blood vessels expand, and the acupuncture meridians try to open up. Energy ties to flow. Blood sugar level drops. After about seven minutes this expanded zone becomes fully saturated with energy. The woman's energy is moving in a circuit. And once again the woman is boosted up to

the next higher level. As she is boosted up, the second set of spasms come, and possibly multiple orgasms in series.

Pre- Stage Three
In this stage the region of great activity expands again to include the brow area and the sacral area below the naval. If the couple can move to stage three of intercourse, the activity becomes intense. The woman's joints loosen and she feels the energy begin to penetrate deep within. She starts to lose awareness of her surroundings, and the time. The female should start to gradually lose consciousness in the left brain. After about seven minutes in stage three these zones should be fully energized. If the female can completely saturate these zones with energy, then the woman is boosted up to the next level. This bump up will trigger deep, throbbing spasms that may once again result in multiple orgasms.

Pre- Stage Four
At this point the circle seeks to expand to include the entire body, and the entire auric field. The skin tingles and the spine may become hot. As this stage progresses a strange thing occurs. The left side of the woman's brain continues to shut down. Her male side starts to come forward out of its dormant state, and her body is capable of acting like a male and a female at the same time. Her clitoris can start to act like a penis and become erect. Her uterus can act like a prostate. Her bladder is energized. If all her circuits are active and energy is running through her entire auric field then the female experiences an ejaculation similar to the male ejaculation. This ejaculation is different from her other spasms that lead to contraction type orgasm. It is a more intense experience. She actually ejects a fluid that is similar in viscosity to semen, but it is not semen. The left side of the brain is almost shut down. Only the right side of the brain is still awake.

        Understand that these orgasmic climaxes are preliminary. She is trying which each orgasm to complete a circuit, so that the orgasm can be held indefinitely. As the rose energy is brought on line, her circuits and acupuncture meridians gradually open up. This may take weeks or months. And if she allows the circuit to complete itself, her energy flows in a circular orbit and keeps the special junction of nerves and meridians at the base of her spine open, resulting in a continuous state of orgasm or bliss. This may last for ten to twenty minutes at a clip, depending on the woman. After one of these prolonged orgasms ends, another wave starts up in a short time. She may stay in this state for one hour or more. This is the orgasmic plateau.

It is at this point that the woman gains access to her power. Whatever she was born with, even occult abilities, she gains access to it. Only a very small percent of women have had this experience. But this is about to change. Of course a man does not have to train in a tantra regimen to have the ability to take his woman there. A rare few men just have such potent natural energy that they are rolling like that. I am not mad at them. But to reach the plateau she needs her man to remain erect and to project energy for 40 minutes to one hour. More importantly she needs to be open and receptive so that the energy can flow in her.

Her Lips and Mouth

Women and men have a power in their lips and voice. All animals make certain primal sounds before and during mating. Modern women have the tendency to stifle these sounds out of pride or humility. These sounds are important. In the center of a woman's top lip is a crest or peak. This V shape is the nexus point of one of the main yin meridians through which Qi flows. It marks the terminal where the yin meridian that begins at the base of the spine moves up the front of the body and ends. It is a major psychic point. During sex or table work the woman should part her lips slightly, so the top lip does not touch the bottom lip. Place the tongue on the gum line of either the top or bottom row of teeth. Allow the energy to build up, and then use the lips to make a sound. Project the sound out from the lips. Use any sound that comes naturally, or sound one of the mantras (next topic). When a woman screams out her sounds, waves of energy follow the sound. The more she projects the sound out, the more her energy courses over her body in waves. Sound is very powerful.

Kissing has such great power for this very reason. Many women will allow men to touch their breasts and vagina but resist contact on the lips, because it is a portal into the heart, just as the eyes are a portal into the soul. If a woman becomes advanced in the tantra, she will discover that through her lips and sounds she can project a power of love and healing. Before you can really feel a kiss, as a kiss was meant to be, you must purify your heart, and open it to the man you are kissing. In the Vedic tradition they say the lips and mouth are the second vagina. Loving words and sensual sounds from the sweet lips of a woman can arouse a passion in the man that rivals her womb.

Her Breasts

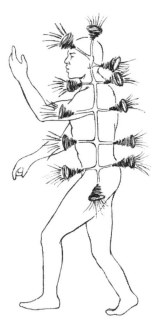

My mother nurtured me at her breasts when I was helpless and new in this world. Men feel connected to the earth and life through the breasts. When they are breast feed, the baby experiences his or her first sensual satisfaction in life from the breasts. More than this, a newborn receives comfort by being held to its mother's bosom. The breasts are very erotic. Both men and women have magnetism. And in the woman the center of this magnetism is the breasts. In females who are charismatic and magnetic there is a connection of the breasts to the heart chakra center. If you view the auric field of such a woman you will see bright emanations coming forth from the chest area both in the front and behind. In women who are dull and lack charisma there is a connection of the breasts to the head. These women live in their head. The auric emanations from the chest area are weak. They are not fully present in life. They hold back. Their ability to attract is weak. This is the woman who is excessively left brained. She thinks too much and feels too little. She is anxious and negative in outlook. Both men and women should take note of this energy dynamic with the breasts. There are seven chakras in the energy body. The crown chakra at the top and the root chakra at the bottom both have one cone. The other five chakras have a cone in front and a matching cone behind. One side deals with yin Qi, the other side with yang Qi. The heart chakra is at the mid point.

The auric field or energy body begins at the core next to the spine, and extends out about 3 feet from the physical skin. There are seven layers to it. The odd layers are fixed. The even layers have color. The fully feminine woman has an aura that is bright and full around the chest area. The energy is moving into heart chakra in a smooth helix flow. The

'petals' of the chakra are symmetrical. The breasts are connected to heart. In the Amazon woman the breasts are disconnected from heart, connected to head. The energy around the left breast and right breast does not match.

The breast on the right side is yang, the breast on the left side is yin. There is often a conflict within the heart of a woman rather to be a woman of virtue, or to be a woman of erotic desire. The elegant rose woman often slants toward the erotic side. The moon woman slants toward the side of virtue. But she is both. To choose either one side leads to problems. The woman should live from her heart. The breasts should have a strong heart connection. There should be balance between her two breasts. Adding to our past definition of the superior man we list the attributes below.

1. he can project energy out of his body.
2. he is able to retain his seed at orgasm.
3. he has some sense of her emotional state through their energy connection.

If the man is receptive and still inside, he should get a sense of her current state. He can feel if she is living too much in her head, or if she has that heart connection. He can then assist her by clearing and energizing her energy field associated with the breasts. When the man runs energy above and through the right breast it comforts the woman, and stills the thinking action of the left brain. The man should normally treat the right breast first. The modern woman works hard, and is often filled with stress. Giving pleasure to the right breast helps to release the woman from this stress. This is an important part of energetic arousal as well. He can use his hands to stroke the breast after the energy work. This is partly to give pleasure to the woman, and partly to get her blood flowing. This will also help women who have loss sensitivity in their breasts. When projecting energy, I often find it good to move my right hand above the right breast in a spiral motion, using elemental energy to release blocks in the breast. The motion starts about an inch above the breast, moving up gradually to the top layer of the aura, (about three feet out) and then back down again. The effect is subtle at first, it tickles, but the feeling will grow the more it is done.

Working with the left breast is more advanced and more difficult. The woman normally receives energy well in the right breast, but may resist in the left breast. This is especially true of the Amazon. The woman needs to be receptive to get the best energy flow through the left breast. The man may treat the left breast many times before the energy will penetrate. Do not get discouraged. She is blocking her yin side. Run energy into the field above the left breast in the same spiral motion as before, and sense what she needs. The more receptive the woman, and the more magnetic the man, the more this energy will penetrate in time. When the blocks here are finally released it leads to a deep intense erotic feeling within the woman. When the blocks are released here, and the left breast is connected to the heart it is like a dam bursting. The next time she is in bed with a man she will notice a major change.

This completes our discussion of genital reflexology. Of course we have only scratched the surface of the topic in this brief presentation. It is necessary that the reader gain some hands on insight before more advanced explorations into the topic can be undertaken. It is only when you begin to actually do this stuff that the words on the page begin to make sense. Now we move to other aspects of the natural science.

Tantric Mantra

MANTRA	PURPOSE	MUSIC NOTE
Ra (raaaa)	Increase blood and energy circulation. Increase Qi flow (yang)	A *above middle c*
Ma (maah)	Increase fertility. Shift more to Feminine (yin)	A *above middle c*
Yao (Yaw ooo)	Increase sexual energy and drive. (yin)	F+ *above middle c*
Khei (K EEE)	Heal reproductive system. (yin)	E *above middle c*

In the table above I have listed four mantra sounds, their general purpose and the musical note they should be sounded on. A simple and effective means to bring about positive change in your relationship and sexual life is through the use of mantra. The mantras are done alone and in private first. Seat yourself in a quiet place and chant the sound out loud. Repeat each sound in sets of nine. Do nine and then stop and be still for a bit. Do nine and then stop and be still. Do sets until about ten minutes elapse. You may do more than one sound per night. You can do these mantras in the presence of running water for better effect. The closer you are to the full moon the greater the effect. You need to do one mantra for about ten minutes each day for seven days before you begin to see the effects. If you are an advanced student, familiar with the tree of life, then you will recognize which sphere on the tree will support each mantra. You can then fashion other applications for each mantra.

Once you have performed a mantra for a few days you can take it to the next level. You can do this mantra with the full awakening circle. The larger the group the more powerful the effect is. Or take it to the highest level, and chant the mantra out loud in your lovers embrace. Chant the mantra in a slow steady cadence as you approach each pre-orgasm tier. This will really energize the goal. Place a vision in your head of what you want the outcome of the mantra to be.

Chanting the mantra during a love session sets up powerful wave patterns. It attaches a wave pattern or rhythm to your sexual energy. The regimen guide will give more details about this.   These four mantra change or redirect the currents of the elemental molecules in your body (Nitrogen, carbon, hydrogen and oxygen). The elementals are Fire, Air, Earth and Water. The molecules are h2o = water, c6 h12 glucose hydrocarbon = fire, o2 + iron (blood) = air, and nitrogen fixed plus various amino acids = earth. If this makes no sense to you do not bother about it. Some of the text here is intended for the advanced student. You do not have to comprehend all this stuff to get benefits. In the discussion of second puberty we keep it simple. In simple language, if I can exchange dirty water and put clean pure structured water into the woman's cells, I can change the way she experiences arousal and orgasm. If I can exchange the free radicals and damaged glucose in a women's bloodstream with pure, sound, structured glucose molecules, I can change the way she experiences arousal and orgasm. The mantra helps. If you observe some males or females right before they go into climax you see a point of hesitation, and then the body contorts and the climax comes. Some women vibrate while they climax like a shudder, twitch, or undulation.   Sometimes they twist up their toes or other body parts. These are signs that the body and energy are choking right at the point of climax. The real pleasure and the big climax are 'choked' off because she can not establish the wave pattern.

Here are some examples of the use of a mantra. She would chant the mantra **Khei** to break up fibroid tumors or reduce inflammation to heal PMS. If she has trouble getting aroused, chant Ra. If the blood is not getting into the small blood vessels chant Ra. If she has trouble with lubrication chant either Yao or Ma. For more staying power (male) or more intense sessions chant Yao near the full moon. More specific uses for each mantra are given during the regimen. The power of the mantra are cumulative. The more days you do a mantra, the more its power grows.

This concludes the outline of the technical concepts in the natural sexual ideology. We return now to the main discussion of the awakening of the elegant rose feminine energy.

Second Puberty   Rose Edition

The awakening of the rose archetype begins with the infusion of the catalyst. The next step is energy work. In the supervised regimen this takes the form of tantra table work, Qi Gong or one of the other styles we have talked about. Each week, there is a new routine of exercises. If you are a member of an awakening circle you also receive the benefit of those sessions, and the specific coaching provided for your individual situation. In about two weeks the typical woman should see changes in her feminine energy. She will start to feel different. These feelings are subtle at first. And then slowly but steadily the elegant rose starts to make herself know. If this is the first time a woman has felt the presence of the rose, it can be a pretty intoxicating thing. The elegant rose energy is not at all similar to the other three archetypes. It is a dominant forceful energy. It tends to undermine the cautious safe mindset. It is daring. It can feel strange and disconcerting to the nice girl type. When a woman brings one of the other three archetypes on line it is not such a traumatic event. But when she awakens the rose and sets that girl free, watch the hell out. While the elegant rose energy is very yin and feminine, it is not at all conservative, shy or passive! When a woman starts her adult life with any one of the other three archetypes, the treasure chest, seated hawk or moon, then the oncoming of the elegant rose will bring a level of dislocation and internal conflict.

As we mentioned in other chapters, the majority of females enter adulthood with a disposition to rely on one type of feminine energy instead of having the use of all four. Thus her worldview tends to be dominated by one of four dispositions. There are exceptions of course, but most women fit the rule.

Elegant Rose. They are driven by a worldview defined by pleasure and sensory experience. Life to them is like a game show. They want to have fun and be festive. They are concerned with such things as dress, appearance, hair, etc.

Treasure Chest. They are driven by a worldview defined by money and status. Life to them is like a treasure hunt. They collect information, and seek higher education. The career is important. Social standing is important. They watch the news and want to know more than their peers.

Moon.   They are driven by a worldview defined by feelings and emotions. They are humanitarian. They care about people. They earnestly desire to become mothers. They are concerned and sometimes obsessed with security issues.

Seated Hawk.   They are driven by a worldview defined by control. Life to them is a contest or race. They seek competition. They view peers and even males as adversaries.   They seek some occupation or avenue which gives them an advantage over other women.   They desire to be the queen bee.

We should take into account that a woman's personality is not static and rigid but changes as she grows older. Thus a woman over 35 may not align with the worldviews above as well as a woman of 21. Nevertheless it should be obvious that all three archetypes of the moon, seated hawk and treasure chest are going to have a problem with Ms Rose. That is human nature. Some women like to hate. And there is no type they like to hate on more than Ms Rose. So what happens when these women start bringing the rose attributes into their own personality? I think you can see where I am going with this.   Some of the young women with the rose energy are vane, self centered, lazy and deceitful. They have not balanced it with the other archetypes yet. From examining the worldview of the moon archetype, it should be clear that she would have a big problem with the elegant rose type. The moon types tend to be conservative, the rose type is not. The moon type women are some of the biggest critics of the rose type women. So what happens when a woman starts to become the very thing she used to disdain? Maybe she is going to be a little resistant, you think?   You are very right. The moon type wants to save the world, feed all the children, release all the prisoners and shut down all the hot night spots. The rose wants the whole world to admire her hot new look. In her mind children should be seen and not heard. She wants to date some of the prisoners and party at all the hot spots.   Are you getting a picture here? So what happens when you combine these two women who used to hate each other?   With the seated hawk and the treasure chest there are similar conflicts with the rose energy.

There are two markers or signals that the master feminine faculty has begun to bring the elegant rose into your feminine profile.

- You can tell that the Elegant Rose energy is trying to rise up when you find yourself hungrier for attention than usual. You will also notice that you become very much more sensitive to your surroundings. You desire to be surrounded by fine furniture, fine art, sweet music, soft beautiful fabrics, etc. If your bathroom and kitchen are not well appointed they will begin to disgust you greatly. You will strongly desire to upgrade them. You will feel an urge to wear outfits that are a bit erotic or risqué. Because women with the elegant rose thing going on like to be beautiful, like to be seen, and love to be admired.

- Your pleasure profile will change. At first it begins slowly. If you are single, you may not notice at first. The same stuff feels different to you now. Fabrics feel rough. People with uncouth voices, become intolerable. If you are in public, and men pay attention to you, it will give you a rush more than it did before. Your orgasm will come with a bang. If it was a bang before, it will be a much bigger bang this time. Your erogenous zones on your body come alive. It is like someone reached into your body and turned up the dial. The taste of food is more intense. Basically the sensitivity meter on your sensations detectors have been cranked up.

These changes can sneak up on a woman. There is a general opposition to people who are too intellectual and logical. There is the tendency to downplay mundane things and dismiss rules. She may become bored more easily and react with less patience to traffic jams, hospitals and people who can not live up to expectations. If the elegant rose was the first archetype to come forward out of first puberty a woman may not express herself well in a verbal way. She seems less intelligent. The rose woman is image driven, and creative in aspect. Go with this. Stop using your words. Use body language and riddles. It is part of the rose mystic. Know that this may drive your left-brain yang girlfriends crazy. So this brings up two challenges a woman will be faced with when this part of her awakens more fully.

1. Will she allow the expression of her beauty in a sensual context? In other words, will she allow herself to be projected in an erotic fashion?
2. Will she give pleasure without guilt and fear? Can she receive pleasure without guilt and fear?

In making any transition, a main sticking point is to continue to identify with what you used to be, while you are in the process of changing into something else. For females who did not start their adult life with the elegant rose thing going on, the erotic thing and the pleasure thing seem to be tough to express. They start to feel the energy, and immediately put the brakes on. If the woman is young and very attractive the transition is moderately difficult. Men would be surprised to know how many gorgeous women are uncomfortable with their looks. But if the woman is older, or if she believes her looks are only average, this transition can be a serious challenge. But the energy demands expression. And if you do not express it then you will find yourself in the same position as your first puberty, when you shut down your master feminine faculty prematurely! Each woman must build her own bridge to cross this gap. It is about your intention. It is about your definition of yourself. It is time for some new definitions.

The Definition of a Wife?
As a wife a female is a pleasure generator.

The Elegant Rose energy deals with the experience of pleasure. If we review chapter one some basic concepts about femininity were introduced. If the main business of life is experience, and the sexual relationship is an energy relationship, then what is the natural role of the female in the sexual partnership? The female is a pleasure generator. That is her main business. That is the main criteria by which men choose her.   That is the major challenge of her role as wife. If she fails to generate pleasure, the relationship fails. If she intends on elevating her energy level, it starts by accepting what you were meant to be, even if you have not become that thing yet. I do not believe most women see their role in a relationship this way. And that is partly why they fail.

Let us say for example that you own a fruit farm, and you think your business is farming. You invest in farm equipment. You plant the seeds. You pick the fruit and put it into baskets, but fail to advertise. No one knows you are in business. You sit there all day, and no one comes to buy any of your fruit. You are not in the farming business. You are in the fruit marketing business. That is your real business. When you understand that, you put ads in the paper, and set up a road stand, and then people start actually buying your fruit. And they like it.   And this is where so many Amazon women are today in their sexual attitudes. They think being a mate in a relationship is some sort of social position where the woman is the male's companion, friend and support partner. No, daffy Dorothy, it is all about pleasure, you are his catalyst for pleasure. And if you do that job right, all else tends to fall into place. Men cheat either because their wives do such a poor job of pleasure generation, or because the men themselves can not receive or give pleasure. Most of the women we have defined as the Amazon women do not seem to know this. But if a woman wants to maintain a high energy level she had better learn it.

A female sexual partner is a pleasure generator. That is the main aspect of this role. If a woman aspires to achieve a sustainable relationship with her soul mate, she must use her feminine energy to generate adequate levels of pleasure for herself, and then for him. The full awakening of her Elegant Rose faculty causes her to receive pleasure through the very act of giving pleasure. This is the key. Everything she does that gives her husband pleasure also gives her pleasure. This is so important to understand. Thus the women who have not yet brought the elegant rose archetype forward are in a catch 22 situation. Since they do not have the trait yet, giving pleasure does not yet bring them pleasure. But to awaken the trait she must live according to the truth of the energy. The rose archetype increases our capacity to experience pleasure. In the process, it changes the way we generate and move energy in our body and auric field. If you had not brought the elegant rose energy forward before, you may not be used to getting your share of pleasure. The man in your life may not be giving you all the pleasure you desire. But you must push through the transitional phase where it seems you are giving pleasure without getting your share back. Eventually you find that it matters less what your man is doing. Soon you will be getting what you desire, because the change coming through in you is bringing about a change in him. That is the secret to awakening the rose energy!

The sexual relationship is a spiritual energy thing more than a physical thing. What keeps people stuck in the inferior experience of sex is the focus on the physical. It is their focus on the mundane aspects of their life. How do I look? Am I cute enough? Is he cute enough? What will my friends think? The way you look is very important. But if you get the energy broadcast right, the looks will follow. When you start to generate pleasure in the act of giving pleasure, your subconscious will start to make your body get into shape. Let us look again at the rose broadcast.

Rose Attributes
Pleasure seeking; Joyous; Beautiful; Sensual; Artistic; Carefree,

Rose Broadcast

Positive	Negative
I Am Pleasing! Look at this good stuff! I am ripe fruit waiting to be picked! Pleasure me. Be pleased by me.	I do not value men. I am hard to please. Yes, I attract and entice but I will not please you, without attaching conditions to giving pleasure.

To maintain high energy levels requires that you feed the rose energy. To kill this energy in yourself you only have to feed the opposite of the attributes above. Whatever energy you feed through your thoughts and actions is the thing you will become. What you feed is the thing that will grow in you. The vessel of your spirit can not contain the sexual energy until you stop the leaks, and clear out the clogs in the auric field. No matter how much energy you or your man generates, it will not result in a true and lasting increase in your sexual pleasure and relationship success, until you stop depleting the energy by feeding the things which destroy it. I call such things brakes, blocks, and choke points. If a woman addresses these things, once her sexual energy is raised, it will stay up for a long time on its own. To become the rose you must live and act in accord with her attributes. You must reject the parts of you, which reject the rose. To become the rose you must begin to broadcast the attributes of the rose, and weave this state of mind into the fabric of your being.

The Non Orgasmic Female

According to published reports, very few women experience a full vaginal orgasm with a male partner with any degree of regularity. In fact many adult females experience orgasm only at an infrequent rate. I do not think anyone is surprised by this statement. If I am to believe what I read and hear, then there is a large segment of women out there who are for the most part non- orgasmic. And we just finished saying that women are pleasure generators. So let us say this one more time. Women are energy beings. For it is not the physical contact between vagina and penis which causes the main pleasing sensations. It is the stimulation of the reflex transmissions, or the energy which flows between the male and female that generates all the good sensations and wild orgasms. Physical contact between genitals where the spirit force is absent will generate about the same level of sexual pleasure as a good hug. Women suffer today because they have a basic problem with the concept of giving pleasure to a male. Men are the same way. Our society is the same way about money, property, political power and human rights. It is the old scarcity model thing. We fool ourselves into thinking that if we have power over something, we can deny others the right to enjoy it and increase its value. We look hot and we got the good stuff so if we play hard to get our stuff is more valuable. Wrong Daffy Dorothy! Math lesson number one, when you subtract from a whole quantity there is a net loss! When you have a whole society of people believing that the more they subtract from the whole the more there will be for them, sooner or later the laws of math will catch up to them. Well guess what ladies and gentlemen, it has. Your sex life is a causality. In chapter three we talked about money, power and religion. Now you know where all the orgasms went. Now you know why the pleasure generators are not putting out much pleasure. And there is nothing that says choosing the natural path is always the best choice. Maybe it is okay to give up our good juicy orgasms so 5% of the population can be rich. Maybe it is okay to give up one hour bliss sessions and the healing which comes with it so that the elite can control and govern us. Maybe the high divorce rate is something we just need to get used to. It is a small price to pay so that our patriarchal culture can instill fear in us through religious dogma. Women embrace fear so much, they can not bear even to talk about sex, much less feel free to enjoy it. But maybe this is okay? You Think!

The Violin

In a book I read long ago the author referred to the woman's vagina as a violin. And in a work from an ancient Asian culture the woman's womb was equated to the string instrument played with the hands. Are there similarities between the vagina and a fine musical instrument? It is said that the design of the violin was inspired by the curves of a woman. The sound made by a violin is thought by some to reflect the female emotions of humanity. And perhaps the man can be thought of as the bow used to play her violin. Romance has always been connected with the arts. We make love to music. We dance in the clubs.

Romance can not be separated from the arts. The elegant rose is about the sensory experience. Our sexual experience is affected by everything that our senses come into contact with. Everything that we see, hear, smell, taste or touch either increases or decreases our capacity to experience sexual pleasure. We can not separate our sexual appetite from the rest of our life. The more a woman or man refines and uplifts their worldview of sex, the more they will come to appreciate the metaphor of the vagina as a violin.

Female Beauty as Erotic Art

It is okay for a woman to look good.
It is okay for a woman to be beautiful.
It is okay for a woman to express herself sometimes as erotic and seductive. It is okay.
        When something is good, we should not treat it like it is bad. Beauty is good. Even if the female has an evil disposition, that does not make her beauty bad. Women must stop punishing other women for looking good. We must remove the stigma attached to the women in the 'sex' industry. Models, calendar pin up girls, playboy bunnies, video girls, even strippers, prostitutes and porn queens are isolated from the mainstream of women. The vast majority of these women came into adulthood with the elegant rose energy awake as their primary archetype of feminine energy. These females are born into a patriarchal society that does not value them. Men wish to abuse them, possess them and ignore their other virtues. In response, so many of them choose to make a living in the sex industry. It is important that these two groups of women be connected back together. Many of these women mature and desire to take other options later, but the door is often closed. And the mainstream group of women needs the elegant rose types to balance the female ecosystem. When the two groups are disconnected, neither group evolves. Can you see that? The reason the sex industry exists at all is because there is such a large group of Amazon women. It is because the master feminine faculty is shut down prematurely, that the sex industry has such a large customer base. The situation with males is the same. Women dress in one of two ways.
- They dress like a magnet, to attract energy to them.
- Or they dress like a shield, to repel energy away from them.

A fashion model, a clown in a circus, or a stripper in a strip club are examples of "magnet dressing." A judge, a doctor, or a woman in a business suit are examples of "shield dressing." Today most women in modern society dress to shield themselves. They are in the business of repelling male energy away from themselves. And there is no blame in this. With society in the state that it is in, women must be careful about how they present themselves. There are dress codes, the job requires a certain dress, there is the security issue and the sense of what is appropriate. Nevertheless, the rose energy is what it is. And the elegant rose energy is not in accord with shield dressing, the current popular choice. You must present the face that matches the type of energy you are trying to encourage to flow. For example if a woman was trying to manifest the treasure chest archetype she would dress for success. But the elegant rose archetype is a magnet dresser. She wants to attract attention to herself in an unmistakable way. Her broadcast is, "I am sweet ripe fruit, waiting to be picked. Please me, be pleased by me!" Her motif of dress has more to do with decoration, seduction, and art. She is not concerned about style, the way this culture thinks of style. The underlying theme of her dress code is erotic. In the rose motif cloth is not more beautiful than the bare flesh. Flesh is alive. Cloth is dead. In fact in the most pure expression of this energy, she probably would not wear very much at all. She might put some flowers in her hair, a lace brassiere, wrap a little printed cloth around her hips and head out to the mall. Well that is not going to do it for today's woman. So we have a dilemma. A woman sabotages her energy when she presents a face that is in conflict with the energy she is trying to carry. But keeping with the energy in this case may create some bigger problems. Every woman will have to deal with this issue in the best way that she can.

If you change your attire to reflect a more seductive and erotic woman you may feel silly or insecure. Maybe you feel like you need to lose ten pounds before you can dress a certain way. Stop sabotaging yourself. The beauty starts inside. It is the energy. Let your mind express what you want to be, and soon the body should follow. The Elegant Rose archetype of the feminine energy is not concerned about your pride, does not care about where you work, or what your children or girlfriends may think. It wants expression. It wants to generate pleasure and beauty. To raise the rose energy you must lose your fear of being the center of attention. The rose is pleased when men star at her cleavage. She wants men to stop and gawk when she walks into the room. It is not vanity, and it is not ego, it is an energy thing. A mango does not hide itself on the tree. It hangs there in clear view because it wants to be eaten. It wants to be picked. When it is ripe it advertises this fact by turning a bright color, so all can know that it is ripe and ready. A flower does not hide its petals. They are displayed. If you are not magnet dressing then you are sabotaging your rose aspect of the feminine energy. By dressing in a provocative way, the woman is forced to confront some of her issues about sex and pleasure. Once she finishes with this phase, she can go back to a more subdued style of dress.

The Beauty Thing
        If you are seeking to please a man it starts with how you look. Yes looks are very important. This is not a news flash to most of you. If you hear a woman say, "I do not want a man just to want me for my body!" you know right away that she has an issue with her rose. No woman wants to be short changed about any aspect of herself, but only women who have a problem giving men sexual pleasure will make a statement like that. Your mate can never want your body too much. When a normal man looks at an attractive woman, she puts him immediately into a mild state of trance. This is the first step to taking him out of his left brain space and into his right brain space. This is what he needs to tap into his energy thing. Stop requiring men to pretend to be civil and respectful in order to get you into bed. This is how men end up with erectile dysfunction, trying to accommodate all these women who get offended when a man looks at their ample cleavage. Let men be honest. The more they can be honest, the better their energy will flow.

Belly Dance
        When the rose energy comes on line and starts to invoke sexual attraction, it wants this to be reflected in the beauty of the physical body. It tries to take her body back to her natal template in the DNA. During the regimen period, I recommend all females engage in belly dance. If not belly dance then womb dance or pole dancing. If you need to lose weight, this is a good time to do it.

Surroundings
        The energy of the elegant rose is greatly affected by the surroundings. It is the true purpose of Feng Shui. If you live in poverty there may not be much you can do about your home, car and workplace but everything you can touch, see, hear, taste or smell affects your

expression of feminine energy. In the home, it is the bath room and kitchen that seem to pose a problem. The rose does not like dirt. The rose does not like colors which do not reflect harmony and beauty. In the home the rose functions best when there are clean lines of architecture, natural light, natural surfaces, plants, fresh air, and art. Organize your work station. Feng Shui the interior of your home. Place a small water fountain in the hall or something to keep the Qi moving. The toilet, garbage can, open meat locker, and damp packed closets are oppressive to the rose energy. The rose hates to live in a damp, dank basement with little light. Get your husband to clean these spaces once a week. Keep the garbage can hidden from view and smell. Use high quality incense twice a week to infuse smell. Place fresh cut flowers, or live plants (even better) in your space. Erect a small altar some where in your home. This is not a religious altar. Place only beautiful things on it. You would be surprised to know how much the mess, disorder and unpleasant smell of things in your home, car and workplace can pull down your sexual energy.

When I think of the elegant rose I remember the rose garden in the botanical gardens. The roses were everywhere, climbing, clinging, on trellis and stand. There were all colors. The aroma was heavenly and intoxicating. The beauty was so fierce, it pierced my heart.

Tantra Energy Healing

(Table Work)

Table work, or tantra energy healing, is the main form of energy work used to awaken the feminine energy. Only a male can do this for a female. It is normally done with the female on a massage table. The energy healer projects his field into the woman's auric field using his hands. The male uses his energy to break up blocks and choke points in the female's field. Have you seen the demonstration where a singer uses her voice to break up a crystal glass? The glass shatters as the singer attunes her pitch to the right frequency. When the superior male purifies his energy and builds up his spiritual strength his vibration gradually matches the original frequency of masculine energy. The abnormal energy in the female body and aura are like foreign structures and do not match the rest of the woman's vibration. And like the glass, they are broken up by the male energy. As the healer moves through her auric field removing these obstructions, her energy starts to flow better. It is like when a plumber snakes a clogged pipe. Then the healer places his hand on various points on the female body.   These points correspond to acupuncture meridian points. He again projects energy out of his body and into her meridian system.   His energy acts as a catalyst to move her energy along.   Depending on the health and age of the woman, there is an increase of energy released.   If he can get enough energy to move, then wave patterns begin to establish themselves above her body and in her body.   Women report that this feeling is similar to the arousal of foreplay.   These waves have a healing effect, opening up the reflexology points on her genital map, main acupuncture meridians, organs and brain stem. If the woman already has the elegant rose energy on line, it is even possible for the woman to have a mild orgasm during a session.

In my work, I find that older women often have flash backs in their mind to times they experienced sexual trauma or sexual joy.   In other words they flash back to an incident that stuck in their memory. It is either very bad or very good.   In the case of trauma, this indicants the memory is removed from their cell memory for disposal.   Younger women usually experience arousal more intensely, and are normally too busy seeking to suppress the arousal to receive the other impressions.   In either case the healing occurs.   After a two hour table session a healthy female will stay in an elevated state of higher libido and higher energy for two to three weeks. But if she fails to engage in a regimen to address the root issues, she will gradually go back to her previous energy pattern.   The best application of table work is at the beginning of a full blown regimen to awaken the master feminine.

Men can easily be trained to project energy out of their body.   In about four months a man can learn to project some level of energy out of his body.   But to do so often requires a radical shift in consciousness and abandonment of false beliefs about the female gender. More than anything it requires a belief in himself and consistent devotion to the training. The full discussion of table work is presented in the companion book to this, Awakening the Master Masculine.

Kegel
This series of small devices are named for Dr. Kegel. They exercise the pelvic floor. The original purpose of the kegel device is to help women who have bladder control issues from complications in childbirth. Master Yao has discovered another way to use them. Used as prescribed in the regimen the device changes the reflexology profile of the vagina. Use of the device tightens the muscles of the vagina that hug the penis during intercourse. This is discussed in the sessions. Used in conjunction with other exercises the Kegel also encourages the acupuncture meridians in

the reproductive tract to release and open. Small blood vessels in the vagina have very tiny deposits of plague built up over years in the typical woman. The Kegel may work to break some of this plague free. Most of all the Kegel exercise as prescribed alters Qi flow. Start with five minute sessions. Work your way up to twenty minute sessions by the end of the regimen. We mean you continue the exercise non-stop for twenty minutes. It sounds easy but may be harder than you think.

Qi Gong
Kidney Qi Gong is one of the main elements in the regimen. The kidney is a yin organ. These exercises build up the yin Qi in the female. More importantly, these exercises are designed to infuse greater Qi into the main yin meridian running through the main organs of the body. The benefits include better blood pressure control and invigoration of the important functions in the reproductive system. Other forms of Qi Gong are used to bring balance to the overall Qi system. When Qi Gong is used in conjunction with other aspects of the regimen, it has the effect of raising the kundalini slightly. And one of the main goals of the tantra art is the raising of the kundalini. The kundalini is the inner life force, the product of the combination of yang Qi with yin Qi. When the kundalini is raised, even a little, it has a very major impact to all life systems in the body. It has an impact on the master feminine faculty.

- The raising of the kundalini causes a marked increase in the secretion of human growth hormone from the pituitary gland. The secretion of this hormone is critical for the master feminine faculty to bring about many of the "feminine" attributes in the female that supercharge her physical appearance and libido.
- The raising of the kundalini brings on a state of euphoria. In this euphoric state the woman can face the challenge of changing her situation without the weight and inertia from past trauma, fears and anxieties crushing her spirit. It is like a tonic.

The Sexual Renaissance

Human beings are the prototypes of the creator. If the creator were an ocean, each human spirit would be a drop of water in that ocean. The spirit serves as a vessel of experience. In other words, through each human consciousness the creator is able to come into his/her/its creation and experience the creation. The creator experiences through our experience. We can have experience in a number of ways. But the intended way, the preferred way is through the experience of pleasure and joy. Our main purpose for being alive is to experience life as pleasure. We see this clearly in the young child. They find joy in the most simple and ordinary of things. This is why we are here.

Now of course having experience is not the only reason we are here, we are here to evolve also. The more we evolve the purer our ability to experience. And pleasure and joy is not the only type of experience. We can not know joy unless we have something to contrast it with, such as pain. Pain is there to show you the wrong path. And as you will see, the more evolved a being becomes, the wider the spectrum of things that can be experienced as pleasure. This is why some women experience unusual things as sexual pleasure. You can tie some women up, and do things that normally cause pain, but some females find these things to give pleasure anyway. What is happening? This is not abnormal, but a highly evolved rose faculty. It is the Elegant Rose energy. A woman can train herself to experience almost anything as a sexual pleasure, if the intent of the man is good.

The central theme of earthly experience is a sensual one. We have five senses to sense pleasure. Everything we must do to live and thrive on the earth is by natural design, designed to bring pleasure to us. Can it get any better than that? Food by nature satisfies our appetite, bringing pleasure. We automatically get hungry. Natural stuff is beautiful to look at. Look at a rose, a tree, a mountain, the ocean; they are all just beautiful without adding anything to it.

Awakening Exercise

Energy Foreplay

Important Note
The exercises, mantras, concepts and energy work described in this chapter are dynamic and intense. They should be done as part of a supervised regimen.   Major physical illness and problems in the reproductive system should be addressed or considered before attempting to undertake any of these procedures. The oral instructions given by the regimen guide should be followed. Any precautions given should be taken under serious advisement. If in doubt as to your fitness, seek professional advice.

The sexual experience is an energy experience. Orgasm is an energy event. It occurs in the auric field and nervous system first, and only then does the woman feel it in the reproductive system. A woman CAN NOT have an orgasm in her vagina until it first occurs in her auric field. If the man and woman do not know what they are doing, the penis and vagina get in the way of making love, more than they assist. In class when we are teaching the men, they are taught to make energy contact with their wife for 20 to 30 minutes before they actually undress and get into the bed. To do this, the man touches his wife in a special way. Or he holds his hand about four to ten inches from her body and projects energy out of his hand and into her auric field. Now this sounds like esoteric stuff from a comic book or something. I told one brother I was going to teach him how to project energy out of his hand and he said, "I did not know this was Star Wars class. Are you Obi I Kenobi or something?" And he laughed. But just so you know, he stopped laughing after he learned how to do it. His wife responded so well one time, he called me to thank me. And she made sure he continued to come to class. About 12 out of 100 men can project energy out of their body the first time they try. I do not know how easy women can do it yet. But everyone can be taught, because everyone has an auric field. You are always projecting energy. When you stop you die. It is just a matter of focus.

For this exercise the group will divide into men and women. The women will form an outer circle. And the men of the group should form a circle inside the females. Females should never attempt to do this with other females. It will produce harm. The females will turn their back to the men. Each man shall pick the woman in front of him, and stand right behind her.

Step One
The males locate the first thoracic vertebra on the spine of the woman. This vertebra is located near the base of the neck. It is usually the first vertebra to protrude out. It may be difficult to see on people with extra weight. The vertebra right above this is the seventh cervical vertebra. The spine is divided into seven sections that correspond to the seven chakras. The cervical spine ends at the brain stem. The thoracic spine is below it. The lumbar spine is below that. These are the main sections of the spine. Now the man locates the spinal protrusions of the first thoracic vertebra and the seventh cervical vertebra. Place the thumb of the right hand between these two protrusions, on the left side of the spine, about

½ inch from the bone. Press in, and then remove the thumb. This is the energy transfer spot.

Step Two
The woman should sit in a chair. She starts to take long deep breaths. The man will start his breathing pattern. The man will take a very deep breath and hold it, pushing his diaphragm out. Hold this breath in for 20 seconds then let the breath out. He will take his second deep breath and hold it, and place his right hand thumb on the spot again, pressing in slightly. He should not touch the spine until he starts the breathing pattern.

Step Three
The man continues to hold his thumb on her spine. He should take about three of these breaths for each minute. The out breath is quick. Hold the in breaths. Continue to transfer energy for about four to five minutes. The man then releases his hand.

Step Four
During the energy transfer the woman must keep her feet apart, and her hands apart. The hands should not touch each other. She should remain still and not talk during the transfer. The whole thing should take about five minutes. After the energy transfer the woman should feel a slight tingling in either her hands or feet. She may also feel the energy stir in her auric field.

It is possible, and even probable, that the woman may experience slight sexual arousal from this exercise.

For the next phase of this exercise the women should be seated. The men now rotate to the woman next in the circle. The men will each be seated directly behind the woman. The women will sit, with feet and hands apart. The men begin to breathe in very deeply, pushing their diaphragms out. Hold the breathe about 30 seconds and breathe out slowly, then in again quickly. Hold for 30 seconds. The right hand of the man is placed on the woman at her belly, right below her naval. His left hand is placed on the back of her neck, at the point on the thoracic spine he touched before. But he is using his flat hand now, not the thumb. The man will project energy out of his right hand, and attempt to direct his energy up her body, toward her head. The man projects his energy by seeing it in his mind. He must be confident and assertive in his projection. Hold this position for seven minutes.

Phase Three, Step One
    The men rotate again to the next woman in the circle. This is the third phase. They are still seated. The men start the breathing pattern again. Each man now places his right hand under her right breast. His left hand is placed on the back of the neck in the same spot as before. Then he cups the breast from underneath, lifting up very gently. The man projects his energy into her breast. He should take in about two long deep breaths each minute. Hold this posture for about seven minutes. Release the hand.
The exercise is over.

    Each man will have been with three females. Once the men finish, they switch places with the women. And the women do the same procedure to the men, all three phases. The group should take some time to discuss the results. After all three phases, the women should feel a slight tingling sensation on the skin, and running down the legs on the inside. Some women will also feel that their auric field is charged. The objective is that the women should begin to feel a sense of arousal, and a sort of euphoric feeling, or feeling of lightness. Women will feel aroused by the energy the more receptive they are to the male and to sexual energy in general. The more yin and feminine the woman is the more intense will the energy flow. A very yang and externalized woman will feel only a slight feeling in the beginning, which will grow to a more pronounced sensation the more times this exercise is done. Once the group goes home, they can teach this to their mates and continue to do the exercise at home. Practice this until the next meeting. Depending on the success of the group, the guide may give further instructions on how to enhance the exercise to get more intense results.
    This exercise is a form of foreplay. The more couples do it, the better the results. The women may not feel much at first. But give it time. Before women can get the full benefit of the energy flow, the men need to learn how to project their energy properly. It takes time. In time, a man can do this without touching the woman.
    Energy work brings men and women closer together emotionally. It changes the nature of the bond between man and woman. One man reported that after three weeks of this exercise he could smell his wife's perfume at work whenever he was stressed. He asked his wife about this, and she was surprised, she was unaware of what was happening to him, and was not trying to do anything that she was aware of. But she admitted that she had been refreshing her scent doing the day more than

normal, and after she thought about it, she noted that this was unusual. Some of these wives were taking the women's class and knew what their husbands were doing, but most had no exposure to the information, but responded just the same.

Case Example- Jennifer

Jennifer presented as self centered, judgmental, distrustful, and a little vane. Jennifer is a 26 year old woman of mixed race. Her mother was white and her father black. Jennifer was a very attractive young woman. She weighs about 135 pounds and is 5' 7" tall. Her cup size is 'D'. She dresses as a magnet to attract. Jennifer wears things which are form fitting. Her tops often show her ample cleavage. Men describe her walk as very sexy. Even when she is not trying, she sends off erotic vibes. She is broadcasting the positive elegant rose, and men pick up on this. But Jennifer does not have the use of the attributes of the hawk, moon and treasure chest. She does not nurture men, but judges harshly. Her right brain is out of sync, and thus she does not make good choices. She does not handle money well. Life to Jennifer is like an exciting game.

Jennifer likes her body, and enjoys male attention, but has trouble in one on one encounters with men. Jennifer is easily aroused, and once aroused she finds it hard to control herself. Her low threshold of arousal is something she is ashamed of. She once had an orgasm on the dance floor of a club after dancing constantly for an hour. Even though no one knew but her, she made excuses to her girlfriends and rushed home feeling very embarrassed. Jennifer has had relations at work, in the bathroom at parties and once at a museum behind a painting.

Jennifer took the metro to work every day. On warm clear days she always wore something a little sexy to work. On the way home, sometimes she got off the metro one stop early and walked the rest of the way to her car. She said she did this for the exercise. But the real reason was to engage in a form of voyeurism. Men from 16 to 60 would check her out as she strolled down the street. She made sure to bend over at the newsstand. She walked slowly by the construction site filled with many manly workers. Once in a while a man would follow her for two or three blocks, enjoying the view of her assets from behind. And this always turned Jennifer on, even though it was dangerous. But then she went into the secure private building where her car was parked. They could not follow her in there. On those occasions she often arrived at her car fully aroused and wet, her nipples erect. After this she hated herself for being so perverted. For that is how Jennifer saw herself, as having too great a libido. She wanted more control of her desire. Because while Jennifer could get aroused in public, she had trouble doing so in a long term relationship.

Jennifer's first complaint in counseling was that she could not seem to get into a serious relationship. She had not been in a relationship for three years, although she wanted to. Jennifer's second complaint was that she had lost her ability to have a vaginal orgasm in a normal relationship with a man. It had not always been so. But it seemed that she had developed a protective mechanism to keep her sexual drive from getting out of hand. If she was at the club with a stranger, or with some other woman's man, or in an unusual situation, she could easily be aroused. But she rejected men that she knew would be good for her, even if they were physically appealing. If he was too available she rejected him, on the ground that he could not turn her on. The funny thing was that Jennifer was blocking her natural attraction, and prevented herself from having certain experiences, even though the evidence was there. Her excuse was, "those men only seem to want one thing from me". It turned her off when men were too impressed by her body and sex appeal.

Jennifer responded to men who ignored her. She was intrigued by men who seemed unimpressed at first by her striking figure. Most of the men Jennifer dated were the roughneck types. She liked take charge men. They made her lose control of herself and give in. This was very intoxicating. Of course these men did not desire an emotional connection to her, just sex. And it was just a matter of time before her resistance would wear down, and she would give in to their demands. These men were able to arouse Jennifer, but she was not able to experience orgasm with them. What Jennifer did not realize was that she was blocking her orgasm because she was not emotionally connected. A part of her spirit rebelled against that. She would have hot sex for twenty minutes and the man would have his climax, but not Jennifer. She would fake it. Of course no relationship developed.

Most men of course were impressed by Jennifer. And among them were men who were compatible to her. Many of them she thought were cute, but she did not give them the time of day, even though they tried hard. If she remained in this cycle, she would not have much success in relationships. The "nice guy" behavior thing in men made Jennifer sick. But her counselor was able to make Jennifer see that her posture against nice guys was directly related to the guilt Jennifer felt about her sexual behavior and her lack of control. She was deeply self conscious about being so "easy". And in a deep part of her there was an insecurity that a nice guy might find fault with her where as a less virtuous men would not. Further coaching put Jennifer in touch with her feminine self, and removed the stigma. She finally decided to open up and consider dating men she had dismissed before. It did not take long for a man to approach her who would test her new resolve. They went out on a first date, and she liked him. He did stare at her cleavage too much, but she decided to overlook it this time. The more they went out the more she realized that she was getting attached to him, and it was a little frightening. After a while the moment of intimacy came. Jennifer had her first vaginal orgasm in many years, and the intensity of it shocked her. He was not a "roughneck" but she still responded to him. And then she realized that his excitement about being close to her was part of what aroused her. It was something inside her.

Jennifer was luckier than most women. Her Elegant Rose had developed a lot on its own. She was desperately trying to suppress it and was ashamed of it. Jennifer somehow had avoided any really negative sexual experiences. There were no rapes, nasty rejections, abortions or trauma in her past. Her father was there for her as a child. She did have a negative womb imprint from her first sexual experience, but it was not that bad. When Jennifer was fifteen, and fully developed, there was a policeman in her neighborhood who looked out for her. She saw his patrol car cruise by often as she walked home from school. He protected her and she was attracted to him. She seduced him, and lost her virginity in an alley. It did not end the way she thought it would, but it was not forced or bad. It did not shut down her master feminine faculty.

Awakening the Master Feminine

One Trillion Faked Orgasms

Chapter 8 One Trillion Faked Orgasms

The Sexual Dark Ages
   Here are the facts.

- Most adult females can not achieve an orgasm on a regular basis from vaginal penetration.
- A larger percentage of women are able to achieve orgasm with a man, through clitoral stimulation.
- Most women are able to achieve orgasm through self stimulation, especially with artificial devices.

And in the absence of fulfillment, billions of women fake orgasms. The billions of orgasms faked each year are the logical outcome of the lie we keep telling ourselves. We settle for the same old life. We focus the blame on the last partner we had or the flaws we see in our neighbors. But society itself has a cancer, and we need to face it. When it comes to sex our society is still deep in a very primitive dark age. Looking at television or the magazines or the Internet one would think that just the opposite was true. For images of sexual promise are everywhere. It is a façade that hides the fact that sexual anorexia is the reality most men and women are living everyday. The reality is that each year billions of women fake hundreds of billions of orgasms in the modern world. There is the mistaken notion that the current mass obsession with anything sexual is a result of moral decay. But the very opposite is true. Most people are suffering daily from a form of sexual anorexia, and in their desperation to correct the deficit; morals and decency have been abandoned. Basically, we have declined to the point that the sex most people are having amounts to little more than masturbation with a partner. It reflects the emptiness of our relationships. It reflects our disdain of the natural life. We invest so much time and money on fancy homes, cars, televisions, cell phones, and gadgets but not a dime on a book, a seminar or a self help program. We are in a serious crisis! The divorce rate, prison population and domestic violence are all off the chain. And we sit around as if we are on holiday. Well, you get what you pay for. Buy trash, get trash.

The picture we painted of a natural and full sexual life in the last chapter may seem unattainable to many. But it is not.   In the regimen the coaches can infuse the catalyst into your subconscious mind and you will enter the phase we call the second puberty where transformation is possible. This is the easy part. The hard part is to repair the conflict and bad blood between the sexes. It goes back generations. The hard part is not to let the negative inertia of the past drag you down into negative thinking, and self defeating actions. The only thing standing in the way of your sexual abundance is yourself, and the bitter, dysfunctional, underdeveloped males you must relate to. For the men out there are just as obstinate as the women are. The men are also their own worse enemy.

As stated previously, most females enter adulthood with only a partial development of their feminine energy, as their master feminine faculty shut down early. They enter adulthood with a disposition to rely on one type of feminine energy instead of having the use of all four, as they should. Between the ages of 21 and 25 females enter a zone in which their worldview is dominated by one of four archetypes:

- Elegant Rose. They are driven by a worldview defined by pleasure and sensory experience. Life to them is like a game show. They want to have fun and be festive. They are looking for Mr. Goodbar.
- Treasure Chest. They are driven by a worldview defined by money and status. Life to them is like a treasure hunt. The career is important. Social standing is important. They may take the option of acculturated prostitution.
- Moon. They are driven by a worldview defined by feelings and emotions. They are humanitarian. They care about people. They currently desire to become mothers. But often the husband takes a back seat to family issues.

- Seated Hawk.   They are driven by a worldview defined by control.   Life to them is a contest or race.   They seek competition.   They view peers and even males as adversaries. They seek some occupation or avenue which gives them an advantage over other women.   They desire to be the queen bee.

If the hawk then she tends to be controlling and right brain centered. Relationships are a contest to her, and she plays to win. If the moon she abandons the husband in favor of the kids, home and community causes. If the treasure chest she is the acculturated prostitute looking for money and rank in exchange for sex. If the rose she is looking for Mr. Goodbar. Relationships are a game, and she is trying to get as much satisfaction as she can. It is easy to see this dynamic in other women. And when we get to the discussion of men in a future chapter, you will recognize their archetypes with ease. But can you see this dynamic in yourself? That is what is important. This is where healing begins. Can you look at yourself honestly, and see your possible shortcomings?   But even with your shortcomings you desire to love and be loved do you not. Well men are the same. There are four archetypes of men. And their master masculine faculty shut down early too. And they have the same issues you have but in reverse. So don't they deserve an opportunity to grow out of it?

The regimens will work. But after the woman remakes herself and becomes this sexual powerhouse, she still needs a man to make it all worthwhile. Getting men to support you and go along with the program can be a beast. In the last chapter we get into that subject. We talk about the male energy and how men feel and react to stuff. So in this chapter we got to get you ready for the man thing. You got to shift from the fake your orgasm thing to swaying your man to bring it right thing. This chapter is a little on the heavy side. It can be a little depressing to talk about some of this stuff. Faking orgasms is no joke if it is you. I am not trying to depress you or make light of the pain that goes with that. Having coached many men and women with these type issues and worse, I can attest to the pain they feel every day. But hopefully the case studies and commentary in this chapter will bring you one step closer to your own solution.

Life Episode   Keysia

At the age of 13 Keysia already had the body of a grown woman. She had the curves and the look that men liked. Her master feminine faculty brought her elegant rose archetype on line early. Keysia went over to visit her aunt who was having a cookout. Marvin was there, a young man from next door that Keysia had known for years. Marvin was with a group of young men, sitting around a table playing cards. Keysia came over to the table filled with young men, and sat in Marvin's lap. She wanted to hear what the men were talking about. Since she was five years old she used to sit on his lap during card games and play his hand. But this was the first time she sat on his lap since her body had filled out so. The young men there took note of her appeal in a joking way. But Marvin did not seem to mind, and Keysia focused on the cards being dealt to her. At first Keysia was playful and teasing. But after a few minutes in his lap, she became aroused. Marvin's body was well developed, his six pack showing. Keysia was getting more and more aroused, but she kept up a poker face. She had very few opportunities to sit in a man's lap at home, and she was going to take full advantage of this one. But after fifteen minutes on his lap, Keysia had a quiet but intense orgasm, her first. She excused herself from the card game as discreetly as she could, and went up to her cousin's room to regroup. She was shocked, confused and ashamed. She did not understand what had happened. Her mother had told her nothing of sex or reproductive function.

Keysia's elegant rose archetype was developing fast. It was not just her body which was developing, but she was becoming more responsive to many sensations. Her pleasure faculty inside had become active. Immediately, Keysia started to learn as much about sex as she could. Keysia had her first sexual experience with a boy at 14, about a year after the incident at the card game. Her first sexual experience was very intense for Keysia, physically and emotionally. She remembers that before the act she was more concerned about pleasing the boy, than being satisfied herself. But the feelings were so intense that she got caught up and forgot everything else. Her climax was a series of intense throbbing spasms. Keysia's mother was strict, and during her early teens Keysia did not have many opportunities to be alone with males. But when Keysia was with a boy, it was always intense, wild and satisfying. She soon discovered that it did not seem to matter much what the boy did.

The Turning Point

At sixteen, Keysia had a fully developed body and her sexual programs were mature. Her elegant rose was on line in a significant way. Her master feminine faculty had activated early, but as with most girls it would not stay active long. It was very important to Keysia to be seen as being popular and attractive. At sixteen she was described by the boys as being "hot". But even so her self esteem was low. Keysia was subjected to a constant barrage of criticisms from her mother and older females. She was criticized for dressing too provocatively. She was warned not to get pregnant. The women advised Keysia to hold men in low regard, and they warned Keysia that males would only hurt her and disappoint her. The boys her age seemed very immature and rude. She desired an older man. Her opportunity came when she stole into a party attended by many older boys and young men. She had stashed a change of clothes with her girlfriend, and went to the party dressed in a very provocative outfit that her mother certainly would not have approved of. She was only at the party a short time when she was out on the dance floor, grinding on one of the young men to a reggae tune. After dancing awhile he lured Keysia upstairs to share a beverage. But upstairs he cornered her in a bedroom, and forced her. She did not resist much. She tried to yell out and he struck her. She finally just gave in to him in the hopes that it would all be over quick. Nor did she tell anyone about it. She was so ashamed and she blamed herself, based on the warnings her mother had given her. This was the turning point. Keysia's master feminine faculty went into a holding pattern. It took her two years to get over this and Keysia had no relations with a man for two years. But at 18 she fell in love and became sexually active again. At 19 she became pregnant and moved in with the young man. She hoped one day to marry him. But the pressure was too much for the man and he bailed out of the relationship, leaving her alone. She lost the baby in the fourth month. And by now her master feminine faculty was completely shut down. From 16 to 19 the social forces mounted many pressures to oppress her sexuality. By 19 her feminine development stopped. And from this point on Keysia started to go the other way, meaning she was becoming more yang and masculine. By the time she was 23 Keysia was confused and depressed. She did not trust men anymore and she was no longer interested in pleasing them. She hated the constant pressure from men to have sex. And to her dismay she discovered that it was no longer easy for her to have an orgasm. This was in sharp contrast to the throbbing, multiple orgasms she used to have in the early teen years.

Keysia started developing her Elegant Rose. But her development of that archetype ended at the age of 16. And at 19 she shut down her entire master feminine faculty. And though Keysia could not reverse her looks, she had suppressed almost all the other effects of the energy in her spirit.

Stop Sabotaging Yourself

With Anger or Fear

There are two postures or mindsets that prevent the average woman from reaching the upper levels of sexual intensity and orgasmic pleasure. In the presence of either of these dynamics, her master feminine faculty is hindered and may shut down.

1. She refuses to allow herself the full sensation of pleasure due to an internal fear. This fear is associated with either sin or a feeling of being unworthy. She is never pretty enough, righteous enough, or virtuous enough to deserve pleasure. Or sexual pleasure is something sinful, and she can not enjoy it directly.

2. In the second case the woman harbors a deep resentment and anger toward men in general, and she refuses to allow the energy to flow because of this great anger.

Most women today are very much against either giving sexual pleasure or receiving sexual pleasure. It does not matter whether they are married, single, cute or plain, old or young, the resistance is there. It is deeply subliminal and internal. They are not completely conscious of this posture. In their mind they want sexual pleasure and joy. But under the surface, in her subconscious, she has erected these blocks to her energy. She can not stop it, until she recognizes that she is doing it. The typical woman will undermine her pleasure more than support it. When I have been successful at getting a woman to release just one of these "brakes" or "blocks" while she is in the second puberty phase, she immediately experiences an elevation in her sexual energy level that is noticeable. The very next time she is intimate she feels the fire a little hotter. Let us return to the discussion of the three main events in a female's life which shape and determine her energy body.

- Event one is the childhood relationship with her father. (age 2-7)
- Event two is her womb imprint. She receives the energy signature of the first two or three men she has sex with.
- Event three is the first puberty, specifically the time period during puberty when her master feminine faculty shut down pre-maturely.

Fear

If the woman's counterfeit sexual posture is fear based, then the brakes, blocks and choke points were erected by her during these events above, either because of a fear of sin or a feeling of low self worth. The first type is a fear issue and/or a self esteem issue. The fear is rooted in the religious doctrines of original sin. Common religious beliefs are based on doctrines created by man, which fully ignore natural law. It is fear based on the false belief that all things sexual are sinful by nature. This strange notion that God's main role is to punish us is unnatural and perverted. They have it backwards. We are not born in sin. We are made from God and therefore are born divine. We must choose a path of sin, we are not born damned. It is true that some people are born with obstructions from karma. But this is something they did, not God. Why do we wish to slander God like that? God is good. God creates us to be happy and to be vessels through which he/she/it can have experience. The concept that God can or would punish anybody or anything is flawed and ill conceived. Creation is perfect. There is no need for God to come back in after the fact and correct something. This is foolishness, the thought of a mind that has not evolved. If your child was young and immature and disobeyed one of your rules would you punish them for the rest of their life? Then turn around and punish your grand children for what the mother did?

The low self esteem issue is rooted in the patriarchal nature of western society. Men often still feel superior to women in many respects. A stay at home mother is less valuable than a working woman. A sexually expressive woman is a slut or bimbo. Right brain centered females who do not test well or exhibit left brain skills are considered dumb. These views are often expressed to the young girl right in her face by father, brothers or uncles. If her family was poor because the father was not around, she may feel second class. If the boys who had her first did not respect and treasure her afterwards, she may feel unwanted and confused. During puberty there are any number of events that can crush a young girl's spirit. Most women do not have to look hard to see how events that occurred in the three reference periods above can cause the program of fear to be implanted in her subconscious.

Anger

The second issue is internal anger. When we look deeper we see that it is also a self entitlement, ego thing. The woman feels entitled to be angry at all men because of an ego issue she has. In the second case the woman is angry at men, arising from a great subliminal rage fermenting just beneath her surface. This anger is not visible on the surface; she hides it beneath the smile she wears.   Her anger results from some incident in the past, maybe the absence of her father, or some man touched her in a bad way, or rejection by boys in school, when she was young, or some such thing. She refuses to allow the energy to flow because she has disdain and anger for men, and she does not wish to give them any pleasure. Her reaction in this way is driven by the little girl reflex, and reflects immaturity.   Her anger is expressed in a frigid temperament, and resistance to being aroused or controlled by a man.

Now we profile two types of women.   One type restricts her pleasure because she feels fear and low esteem. Now the second type of woman is angry, and has negative intent. This is a bigger problem. In the case of a woman whose energy is blocked and choked by anger, the first step toward release is to address any issues with her father. She will need to go back and come to grips with any issues of abandonment, incest, rejection, prison, child support, drug use or divorce. She does not have to forgive her father. But she needs to do all she can to make peace with his past actions toward her. It is important that she do whatever is proper to have some level of a relationship with him, if she can do this without danger of abuse to herself. Maybe just a once a week conversation may be all it takes to bring closure. Her goal is to connect to the male gender in general, by closing out any ill feelings she is still clinging to about him. As with the other type, she should bring up this subject in the awakening circle sessions.

Young Female Indoctrination Into Negative Pleasure Culture
Fear & Anger

From the age of about 5 years young girls are intentionally indoctrinated to prohibit them from giving sexual pleasure to men. In their youth most young girls are indoctrinated into a negative pleasure culture by parents, church, teachers and older women.   The more physically attractive a young girl is, the more pressure she is subjected to. She is taught to view sex through a prism of fear and sin and entitlement. Young women need a lot of coaching from the mother in order to perfect a good sex life. It is not just a matter of dating. It is not enough for her just to take her panties off and do it. There is much more to it. Young females often think that if they are with a good looking, sexy man then that is enough. It is not. And by the time they are thirty most women know better. But by then the damage is done. Of course young girls require a level of regulation in conduct. I am not advising when they should start sexual activity or under what circumstances, marriage or such. But there is a positive way to do this, and a negative and destructive way to do this. It is important that a young girl feel that parents and guardians are working to assist her in cultivating the attributes that will ensure her to have a quality sex life when the time comes. There is this perception that a young girl can generate pleasure without assistance. But they need help. And if this defines what your puberty was like, then you probably have some anger or fear left over from puberty.

A man told a sad story at a workshop. He talked about losing the custody battle for his daughter. He wanted joint custody of his daughter. The mother won sole custody. The father was restricted to partial weekend visits by his daughter once or twice a month. The mother sometimes reduced the daughter's visit to one overnight per month. The father could do nothing against the power of the court. Over the years he watched his daughter grow further apart from him emotionally. And her attitude grew more and more disdainful of men. The subtle influence of the bitter mother took its toll eventually, and by the age of nine his daughter had negative opinions about men, and disdain for them. She grew even disrespectful of him. The father reported that by 11 (her current age) his daughter and her immediate girlfriends had become male bashing, diva want-to-be's scheming as to how to run games on boys. The mother did not see the danger in this, and encouraged it. The father expressed his sincere sadness at the way his daughter had turned out, and predicted the outcome of her early relationships with boys could be nothing but a disaster. He declared, he would not wish to be one of the young men seeking to engage a young woman like his daughter in a relationship. He saw no hope for the next generation. If a young girl is already fully cynical, distrustful and scheming at age 11, before she has even had a relationship, what hope could there be?

In Search of Goodpussy

(Living Without Love)
Jennifer and Erica
Case Study

In Search of Goodpussy was the title of a popular book by Don Spears in the 1970's. The book talks about how men search for sexual gratification to replace the love they are denied. In our story David and Kenneth are both "searching for goodpussy". They are two men in their early thirties who claim to be just out looking for sex. But what each of them really wants is to be in a real relationship. Each of them has been hurt in the relationship game before. Kenneth had a nasty divorce. David had finally hooked up with a woman he thought he could get used to when she got a chance to land a part in a movie. A week later she landed the small role in a big movie. And a week after that she moved away. At first David tried to hang in there with her. But her new career opportunities made her push David way down on the priority list. The distance between them and his loss of status was too much for him to bear and he reluctantly ended the relationship he had such high hopes for.   David and Kenneth were friends, and being manly men they felt obligated to always put up a masculine façade. To the world they were just two secure single guys out enjoying the dating scene. But they could see through each others façade. But true to the code, they never spoke this truth.

The book In Search of Goodpussy describes the social status of so many men today of all races. They are seeking gratification on a surface level to replace a deeper more spiritual fulfillment that they have come to believe is out of their reach. They must keep up appearances. It would not do for other men or women to know how much they felt unfulfilled. David and Kenneth had jobs, drove decent cars and had their own places. They were not "losers'. Kenneth was tall, about 180 pounds, trim and fit. On a scale of 1 to 10 he rates about 6 to 7. He is considered "select" because of his job, and he owned his own house. He is classed by women as a 'masked man'. David is tall, about 190 pounds of solid muscle. He played sports in college. On a scale of 1 to 10 he rates about 8. He makes less money than Kenneth, but he is also considered select because women think he is very cute. He is classified in the category of Mr. Goodbar. Both men were relatively popular. They had opportunities to date available women. But both men felt that getting women to love them was a high risk low reward venture. They knew their issues all to well. And why did they have to go through that type of ordeal anyway? (Be reminded of their issues) It was so much easier just to settle for sex. They considered themselves victims of the system. Women were to blame. Because the women they encountered had too many issues to love them. At least that was their side of it. Either the woman had too much baggage and it turned the men off, or the men had too much baggage to commit, and the women cut it short. And once in awhile they ran into their greatest fear, the female player. "A woman with no heart", was their label. Basically a woman with the same dating philosophy as them. The worse blow to their pride came from women who just used them, and then lost interest for no reason. It was okay to be players and for failure to commit, or not calling enough. But it was tragic and unseemly just to get dismissed for no reason.

What Kenneth and David failed to consider was that the men of their father's generation were responsible for shaping the attitudes of their female peers into what it had become. And David and Kenneth needed to take care, or they would turn out just like their fathers. So many males from that generation got divorced, and spent the better part of their life, "looking for goodpussy". They prematurely gave up on their quest for love. And in the process ruined any chance they had of ever really finding it. Not just for them, but for their sons and daughters as well. By reducing the female to only a sexual object, they insured that the next generation of men, their sons, would face a group of angry and fearful women.

In each episode the women are slightly different. But they maintain the same archetype profile all through the book. David met Jennifer. And Kenneth had an encounter with Erica. That is where are little story begins. Jennifer and Erica do not know each other. Erica is governed by internal anger. Erica embodies the energy of the seated hawk. Erica is definitely looking for a husband. She is the queen bee, looking for a good worker ant. Erica is governed by internal anger, directed at men. Erica embodies the energy of the seated hawk. Erica is 32 and has no children, she has never been married. Erica is 5' 8" tall and weighs 142 pounds. She is cute, but she has not developed the curves and sexual presence to match Jennifer. Plus she dresses as a shield, to block not attract. Her elegant rose is not developed much at all. She almost never wears high heels while Jennifer has 24 pair. Her hair is plain, and she thinks showing too much cleavage is not classy. She prefers style and class, and does not seek to project an erotic flare. Her broadcast is the positive aspect of the hawk, and men listen to her. Men follow her plan at work, in the neighborhood and in her family. She is a leader, and other women look up to her. She has more male friends than female, and she bosses them around. It comes natural to her. Erica is bossy and sometimes even controlling. She has no trouble getting men to be friends with her. But finding a romantic partner is more difficult for her. Into her life has come a man to woo her. He is "searching for goodpussy". Kenneth is dating Erica, unsure of where the encounter will lead.

Kenneth and Erica

Kenneth is very dissatisfied with his relationship history. For the most part he has failed at relationships. And he tells himself that a serious relationship is not for him. His standard procedure is to just tell women what he thinks they desire to hear. He is not seriously invested in the outcome, having little hope that it can be positive. But deep inside he hopes the next woman may somehow be different. He is doing everything to discourage a real relationship. But deep inside he hopes in this he will fail. He and Erica have been dating for three weeks. It is still new. Erica leads a very externalized lifestyle.   Her main focus is her job. The cultivation of her feminine energy is not a priority. Pleasing a man is not a priority.   Really she is mainly looking for a man to please her, while she continues to pursue her career and life value objectives.   With Kenneth, she decides to perform the old bait and switch routine. In the first weeks she has been putting on a good acting job. She pretends during this time to broadcast the positive version of the Elegant Rose. She has been wearing more attractive attire, tight fitting outfits, low cut tops, etc. She almost put on high heels one evening. She pays attention to what perfume she has on. But Erica can not hide her energy. She is not receptive. And acting feminine takes a great effort on her part, because she is in part faking.

After dating Erica for only three weeks Kenneth starts to see signs of her issues behind the façade. Kenneth is always looking to detect a woman's issues. At the slightest hint of dysfunction, he puts her actions under a microscope, and goes over and over the scenario with his buddy David to figure it out. Kenneth was very impressed with Erica at first. Erica had so many good things going on. She had a good job, no children, and she seemed to know where she was going in life. She showed maturity, and in many ways demonstrated that she could compliment a man in many ways. On his second outing with Erica he became concerned that Erica was just a little too serious. Just when they started to have fun, and things were headed in the romantic direction, Erica would change the mood, and start to ask Kenneth a lot of questions about some serious topic. On the third date Kenneth noticed that Erica got very upset at their waitress over a small matter. The waitress was cute, and Kenneth made it a point not to even look at her, but Erica still seemed overly annoyed at the girl for no reason. A red flag went up in Kenneth's brain. He and David talked about the waitress thing for half an hour.

It did not take long before Kenneth saw glimpses of the regular Erica. Behind her smile Erica is angry. Kenneth also noticed that Erica was a bit controlling. In the fourth week Erica got a call from her half sister It was about her father, and the call really upset Erica. When Kenneth asked Erica about her father she released a torrent of angry criticism of her dad. Apparently he had not been there for her growing up, and now she resented him tremendously. Her dad had left her mom when Erica was three, and he went to stay with another woman, the mother of Erica's half sister. But he did not stay with the second woman long before they too split up. The half sister was trying to patch things up between Erica and their common father. But Erica was not having it. Kenneth discovered that Erica had a lot of anger directed at a lot of people. She was angry at her boss, her dad, her ex-boyfriends and her landlord. He and David had a second long conversation about Erica. Most men know that women with father issues usually give men a harder time.   David advised Kenneth to cut his losses now, and get out. But Kenneth decided to continue seeing Erica, but placed her on probation.

The reaction of women to men in the bedroom does not hinge entirely on the male performance alone. Kenneth thought that he was fair to good in bed. He was good for 10 to 20 minutes most nights. When in bed with him women were normally vocal and responsive. He was never sure who was faking it and who was not. Kenneth tried not to think about that. The woman brings something to the table that determines what the limits of her reaction are going to be. We can for example sake create a measure of the sexual reaction of women to sex using a scale of 1 to 100. The highest rate of response is 100 points. The lowest rate of response being 1. Using this scale Erica would grade only 18 points maximum. Erica did not have the rose energy active. Erica was in the group of women who are non-orgasmic. No matter what Kenneth does,   Erica only has the capacity to respond so much. If Erica met the most attractive man alive she would become very highly aroused but sex still would not result in an orgasm. It was very frustrating.

Erica was attracted to Kenneth. It was not that he had a cute face, but more his body, and his manly ways. Kenneth had a deep voice and a manly posture. But she pretended that he did not move her at all. Erica did not dress seductively, and she was visibly uncomfortable in the romantic settings that Kenneth created. Kissing was awkward for her. Erica decided to sleep with Kenneth because she knew it was expected of her. She did not want to lose him to another woman. The night of their first sexual encounter came, and Erica was very nervous and anxious. She did not seduce Kenneth; she did not burn candles or put silk sheets on the bed. In her mind she was doing Kenneth a big favor. She thought her role was just to take her cloths off and let him have her. There was not much reaction on her part. She enjoyed the sexual episode, but she did not have an orgasm, or even lubricate much. Really she did not become that aroused, but this was normal for Erica. Erica did not feel much in the sexual department until the man made some emotional investment in her. Of course after all that waiting, the event was a big let down for Kenneth. Kenneth thought he was good in bed. At least the reaction of other woman to him was a lot more intense. Erica barely made any noise. Kenneth was very disappointed, to put it mildly. He debated with himself for two days if he could continue the relationship. He decided to continue, hoping she would warm up in time. Erica was on pins and needles for two days waiting for him to call after that first night. Finally on the third day Kenneth called her, but his tone was different.

Of course Erica's girlfriends told her to heat things up a little. So she invited Kenneth to go dancing and Erica put on a dress. And she allowed Kenneth to have sex again and threw herself into it a little more this time. Erica even faked an orgasm this time, like her girlfriends told her to do. Now that Erica was intimate with Kenneth the clock was now ticking. Since she had given him some, it was time for his behavior to change. In her mind Erica had a list of stuff that Kenneth was supposed to do now. But she never made Kenneth aware of any of it. There were definite rules. But men do not always know when these rules apply. And it is now, at this point that the relationship began to unravel. It is now at this point that the error of communication took place. It is now at this point that intervention and bridge building was necessary, but Erica was stuck in the Dark Age programming.

The Crossroads Point

This is the crossroads point. Erica and Kenneth reached it. At this point the relationship still had a chance to be saved. If the correct actions were taken now, they could both end up with what they wanted. The first time a couple is intimate is sometimes the crossroads point. Or maybe it is the first time you meet his family. The crossroads point is when the dynamics of a new relationship start to shift. **It is when one party in the union changes course**. It is that critical point in the relationship when your issues surface, and either the man reacts, or you react.

Status:
After the first time, Kenneth was disappointed with the sex. Erica was already on probation. But Erica still had many good qualities that mattered. Kenneth still wanted the relationship. He had hopes that the sex thing might improve.
Up to this point Erica is feeling Kenneth. But she does not have the elegant rose, and her negative pleasure broadcast is killing her standing.

But she is not really hosting any real communication with Kenneth. It is all a façade. She is so focused on what her girls say, that she is missing all the negative signals from Kenneth. Erica is ready to move forward. Kenneth is starting to pull back.

Erica felt that since she was now sleeping with Kenneth, the clock was now ticking. In her playbook, Kenneth now had three months to get serious with her. And from that point, she felt she had the right to intrude on his privacy. She checked out his credit report. She gradually exerted herself into other aspects of his life. And more and more Kenneth saw Erica display her anger, jealousy and tension to the people around her. But in her distraction, she neglected to address the basic stuff. Erica never put her cards on the table with Kenneth about her issues with men. If she gave him the real history about why she was so angry maybe he could understand. Then tell him that she would never direct her anger at him. Ask him to help her heal this place in her heart. This would have pulled the male into the issue with a positive spin. And Erica needed to get real with Kenneth about the sex. She needs to know where she stands. Her negative performance was not the issue. It was that she did not even see it as a problem. If she just made it clear his satisfaction was a priority, she would have been okay. On the other side, Kenneth had not fully brought his masculine energy on line. Therefore, he would not stand up straight. He is not about to expose his emotions. But if Erica were to meet him halfway, he would do the right thing by Erica. But Kenneth has lost faith and pulled back in general from women. He felt it was just a matter of time before he would be in her crosshairs. But he still wanted a relationship with her. The clock was ticking for Erica. Three months after they became intimate she demanded that Kenneth make a decision about where their relationship was going. Kenneth was waiting to see changes in Erica that never came. When Kenneth failed to give the right answer, Erica fired him, ending the relationship. She spoke to him one last time in which she dismissed his objections, and expressed her gross disappointment that he failed to take life and her more seriously.
End of Erica and Kenneth

Jennifer and David

Jennifer is governed by sexual fear. She embodies the energy of the elegant rose. But she does not yet have the other three archetypes to balance it out. Jennifer does not know exactly what she wants. But she means to have fun while finding it out. And she is not too concerned about who gets hurt in the process. In this episode Jennifer is 30 years old. She has a very seductive shape. She weighs about 135 pounds and is 5' 7" tall. Jennifer wears things which are form fitting. She dresses as a magnet to attract. Even when she is not trying, she sends off erotic vibes. She is broadcasting the positive elegant rose, and men pick up on this. She knows they all want her, to have sex with her, but beyond that she does not understand what motivates men. Life to her is like a game or show. She wants to enjoy this show. But a man has come into Jennifer's life who wants more than just games. On the surface, David is "looking for goodpussy". But what David really desires in his heart is to be loved and healed. Jennifer is too filled with fear to do either.

Jennifer refused to go out with David at first. But after a while she consented to go out with him. She told David not to get his expectations up. But the way she came across she did not sound serious. It sounded like a standard line of hers. David was used to being around attractive women. And he had seen all the games. In his mind, he had no idea of what Jennifer's bottom line really was. He did not know if Jennifer was playing hard to get or if she was really aloft like that. This was the part of the game that Jennifer liked; being chased, admired, flattered and pampered. David's first goal was just to get in those panties. Jennifer had it going on. Without trying, the subtle little things she did turned him on. He kept up the chase. Jennifer decided in the first five minutes of their meeting how things were going to go. There might be some sex after awhile, but nothing more. And David would have to "put in his time" before he was getting any of that. And David played her game, and soon he got his reward.

One night during the week Jennifer called him and announced she was coming over in a few minutes. She wanted to catch him off guard. When she arrived Jennifer had on a long coat but it was not that cold outside. Underneath her coat she had nothing on but her panties bra and high heels. David's eyes were that big. His heart was pounding fast. David went to work the next day with a big smile plastered on his face. He felt that he had rocked Jennifer's world last night. He thought that now that he had rocked her world she would stop playing hard to get. But he was wrong. His ego was fooling him. In fact she did not rate his performance in bed with the top ten. Jennifer was just being Jennifer. Jennifer reacted wild and intensely with every man in bed. Women have a built in arousal program that determines their limit of response to men in general. Jennifer was just generally more responsive in bed. On the 1 to 100 scale Jennifer would grade as 33 points. This is versus the 18 rating for Erica. Jennifer had not one but several orgasms with David.

After her arrival, the two only made it as far as the kitchen before David had her pinned against the countertop. Before it was over, they had employed whipped cream and fruit from the fridge, and Jennifer ended up on the kitchen floor. Neither of them remembered how they got there.

Of course David did not keep his smile for long. They too had approached the relationship crossroads. After the wild episode in David's kitchen Jennifer did not return his calls for a few days. It was her way to cool him off. She did not want him to get too invested. But when they did speak next, she was invasive in her responses. Jennifer liked David, but she had set boundaries on the relationship from the beginning. The strange thing was that David was starting to feel a thing for Jennifer that went beyond just a casual thing. He was starting to feel chemistry between them. They reached the crossroads. And it was from this point on, that the arrangement between David and Jennifer began to unravel. It is here that communication failed. Right here Jennifer had the power to ensure that the outcome of their encounter would be good. But Jennifer was stuck in the Dark Age programming.

Crossroads Point

At this point the relationship still had a chance to be saved. David and Jennifer were compatible with each other. But Jennifer would not be ready for a serious long term relationship for two more years. She had some serious maturing to do. But in two years when she finally realized that she wanted to get married, David was not going to be available anymore. And she would look at the other men and realize that he was the best candidate. The crossroads point is when the dynamics of a new relationship start to shift. **It is when one party in the union changes course**.

Status:
Jennifer was ready to pull back. She had set boundaries on the relationship. It was not part of her game plan now.
David was starting to see something in Jennifer that he had not seen in awhile. He was feeling a chemistry that he thought indicated some long term potential between him and her. He thought Jennifer was in the same place, but she was not.

The best outcome for both David and Jennifer was to remain in the relationship. It was time for David to get over his old hurt. It was time for Jennifer to get over her fears of intimacy and commitment. If she missed this opportunity with David she was headed for an exciting encounter with a foreign diplomat and the sexually transmitted disease he was carrying. But Jennifer refused to be honest with David. When she saw him, she told him that she needed time to get used to her feelings. Jennifer did not know how to tell David that she did not consider him "serious" relationship material. Jennifer did not see a real future in it. Jennifer just wanted David to "hit it" once in a while. Had she been honest with him, he would have been okay with that. But by her not being truthful, she allowed David's feeling to grow. The relationship was getting more serious, and he wanted to take their relationship to a serious level. At first Jennifer went along to avoid a confrontation. But the confrontation came anyway, when Jennifer backed out of going with David to a formal Black Tie affair. And then Jennifer broke the affair off. She stopped returning his many calls. David did not understand. He and Kenneth debated what had happened until late into the night. David finally got the message and moved on. Jennifer thought that she had done the right thing. But Jennifer's girlfriends reminded her that this was a pattern for her, and pointed out that David was just the latest installment in an old cycle. They felt that there was nothing wrong with David, and Jennifer was just afraid of serious emotional involvement with any man. One year from that date Jennifer received the call from the clinic. She had an STD. She had rolled the dice one time two many.

End of Jennifer and David

Both Kenneth and David had been dumped by their girlfriends in the same month. They sat in the café on a Saturday morning trying to make sense of it. This was getting old. The conversation went something like this.

"With these women it is always something! If there is a way to mess it up, they will find it."

"I just still wonder what her real program was. All this time I thought she was moving in that direction, and now I realize I never really know what her thing was." I still don't know man!"

"History repeats itself, did you really think things had changed?"

"No... But actually I was starting to get a little different vibe this time. It doesn't matter anyway, it may be all for the best. If they going to sweat you and put you through changes like that, it's better to get it out in the open in the beginning. The things a man got to go through to get a little bit."

"Well it is no sense in looking back. What is on the docket for tonight? More of the same I guess."

End of Episode

So what have we learned from Erica, Jennifer, Kenneth and David? The message is learn to recognize when you reach a crossroads situation in a relationship or potential relationship. That is when one party starts to change course. At this junction you should consider the following.

- Get outside your box. Think outside the box. Do not do the same old thing and expect a different outcome.
- Talk to a member of the opposite sex before you make a decision. Don't just depend on your girls for feedback.
- Get expect help. Read a book, go to a workshop, hire a coach, or call an elder.
- Consider a change of course yourself, to stay aligned to your mate.

Think about the four worldviews. Life is a game show, a treasure hunt, a charity event or a contest. Which one are you? What mistake are you likely to make? Which one is the man? What does it take to keep him in the game for a few more months? What would it take for him to develop more of his masculine energy during that time? Remember, you choose him. What was his intent toward you? Does his mistake indicate bad intent? Or is he just suffering from ignorance? Ignorance can be forgiven. Bad intent is a deal breaker. Most men start their adult life with only partial development. When they are in this phase, a man will not stand up straight in their relationships. **Standing Up Straight** is the mark of a fully masculine man. He is going to try to do right even when it hurts. Do not expect this level of honorable behavior from males who are not mature. If you are still acting like a little girl, do not expect the man who stands up straight to put up with you for long. The majority of young men are working through their own issues just like the young women are. It is not always that they intend harm, but often the woman is hurt as a casualty of their circumstances. For when a man encounters the deep seated anger we spoke of, often he just turns away inside. When a man confronts her deep seated fears, often he just turns away. Men can easily become bitter, cynical and full of apathy. When they come to the crossroads the weak man may just turn away. Only a fully masculine man will seek to work through the issue with you. Most are going to take the easiest way out.

Men and women are born to compliment each other. The natural way is perfect; nothing else needs to be added to it. We need only to cultivate what is there. But each man and woman must choose to reject their history, and be sexually reborn again. We must choose to leave the sexual Dark Age behind us. No where is this more difficult to do than in our sexual life. But in his rush to obtain power, money and social superiority, western man has been eager to sacrifice the natural path. And this has plunged the modern world into the sexual Dark Age. The masses have chosen to abandon the natural path and the ancient and timeless wisdoms. And they have paid a steep price for doing so.

Awakening the Master Feminine

The Amazon Woman

Chapter 9 The Amazon Woman

The tales of the Amazon woman are more than just myths. The myths are based on real life bands of warrior females. On the radar of history the Amazons pop up briefly and then are quickly gone. There is some archeological and historical data about Amazon cults, but there is not enough. When she did appear in history she did not remain around for long. Perhaps they came into existence because the male population was wiped out by war or disease. We do not know. They did fight as warriors, sometimes by themselves, and other times alongside their men. The tale of the Amazon comes to us via the ancient Greeks, Russians, and Africans. There is a brief mention of her in the history of Brazil. The latest mention of Amazon cults are in Russia, about 1,000 years ago. She lived among the horse cultures on the step plains to the south, and east of the Baltic Sea. And even further back in history we find mention of them in Northern Africa again among the horse cultures along the desert rim.

While the Greeks glorified her, it would seem her real life was less glamorous than the myth. For the most part it seems these cults of yang women were outcasts, misfits who were exiled from the main body. They were not welcome among the villages and settlements of the mainstream population. Most indigenous cultures that were in existence at the same time were intolerant of overly masculine females. I expect in reality a band of warrior women, unnaturally masculine, were about as popular and esteemed as a colony of lepers. Now as fate would have it, she has popped up again in the world, in modern western culture.

Officially the modern Amazon woman is the child of the femininist movement in the sixties. But more astute observers know that she had her true origin in World War II. The Great War changed the established order of society. So many men went away to fight. And the women left behind were asked to leave the homes, and go into the factories and industries to build weapons, and ships, and goods of war.   Few understood the spiritual and energetic affect this would have on these women. More importantly, she passed this masculine war energy into her children.   These children were the first of the baby boomers. Twenty years after the war the energy rose up in protest in her female children, now grown to adults. The feminist movement burst forth with great anger and retribution. The women burned their bras and gave men the finger. But still the scholarly men of the time were ignorant of the energy. The protest was really about World War II and its evils. And the women and the Blacks turned and looked at the next war, the war in Vietnam, and in anger they shut it down. But still nothing was done to heal the energy in these women. Nothing was done. And so in the third generation of baby boomers after the war, in the 1980's, the Amazon women appeared.

Definition of an Amazon Woman

- Her female energy is significantly suppressed. Her master feminine faculty started the process of bringing some of her feminine archetypes on line, but she blocked this development before it could be completed.
- Her male energy is overdeveloped. She embraced a yang lifestyle.

Identifying Amazon Woman Behavior

What does the male see when he encounters the Amazon woman? What is the male point of view?

- It is very difficult to satisfy the Amazon woman, and she is not easily impressed.
- The Amazon woman only seems to become passionate about negative things.
- The Amazon woman can not accept criticism or testimony from a male, without prejudice. She strongly resents male authority figures.
- The Amazon woman is to some degree an acculturated prostitute. Acculturated prostitute means that she engages in forms of prostitution which are socially acceptable, and which involves virtual sexual acts, as much as actual sexual favors. This is something like the "gold-digger". The Amazon woman is not able to get the same benefits from sex that the feminine woman does. And her attitude is that men do not deserve pleasure.

The Amazon woman is a female spirit with an abundance of masculine energy and male like attributes in her personality. In some cases, her energy is so masculine, that when she is intimate with a male her energy repels his energy to some extent. This happens under the surface. In other words, he may be very attracted to her body, and she may be very attracted to him, but their energy clashes. She finds that there seems to be a hidden "force field" that seems to push them apart.   Being an Amazon woman does not mean you look masculine. She can look very soft and attractive on the surface. It is in the personality that the Amazon nature is seen. And even more so, it is in the bedroom that it shows up. He may like what he sees at first. And often, he wants to look forward to spending some quality time with her in just her panties and maybe a wine glass. But too often she is busy, this is not her priority. She comes home and degrades him about something, and barks out commands.   The mood is spoiled and she does not care. Pretty soon, the less attractive, and more yin waitress at the coffee shop starts to look real good to him. The Amazon woman at home depresses the sexual performance of most males. The more masculine his energy, the more negative the effect of the Amazon on him.   Lesbian and bi-sexual women do fall into the category of Amazon women.   But by far most of the women in this category are heterosexual and date men. Since the arrival of the Amazon woman, the divorce rate has gone wild.

Every human being has an energy field, or auric field or aura. This field is always broadcasting. It is daily attracting some things to you, and repelling other things from you.   What this field attracts to you depends on what you are broadcasting. This is the really short explanation of the Law of Attraction, a sister principle to the Law of Manifestation.   In respect to the opposite sex, our field is always broadcasting based on our energy and personality. This generates a sexual response in all members of the opposite sex that we encounter which are still sexually viable.

The fully feminine woman is broadcasting four positive signals to men. These are the four archetypes of energy we spoke of; the hawk, the elegant rose, the moon and the treasure chest. This has the effect of attracting positive and productive events in her relationship experience that lead to positive outcomes for her. The Amazon woman is not.   The Amazon woman only has brought forward one of the archetypes, and in some cases she is sending out four negative broadcasts.

What grows in our personality is what we feed it. The Amazon woman is only feeding her yang or masculine energy, and that is all that is growing. If we look deeper at how this manifests in her daily life we will easily see how males perceive her. This leads to conflict between the sexes. It is unnecessary conflict. In the awakening circle, discuss how this shows up. There is no blame. It is an energy thing. This conflict is the result of men and women attempting to relate, who have not properly developed their masculine or feminine energies. Fully develop your energy and the conflict will go away! Too many men are struggling every day in a relationship with a woman who is trying to fulfill the roles of both male and female. In other words she wants to "wear the pants" in the household. She wants to make all the decisions in the home. The Amazon becomes threatened, anxious, and combative if he asserts himself on even a small issue. Too many women are struggling every day in relationships with men who will not stand up straight. He is apathetic. He refuses to commit. He does not assert himself where it is needed.

The Cup is Half Empty

The Amazon woman only seems to become passionate about negative things. She complains, but does not really listen to the male's response. For his response does not seem to make any difference. The Amazon woman is not experiencing life in the same way the fully feminine woman is. The same events and climates do not hold as much joy and satisfaction for her. She argues with him over nothing, and refuses to compromise, because she desperately wants to experience passion about something, even if it has to be something negative!! So her spirit indulges in a counterfeit substitute. The Amazon woman is going to experience more pain and misery because that is what she is attracting.

So what happens when the male in a relationship encounters his Amazon woman and her negative broadcasts? What does she do to a man when she projects her negative broadcasts? What the male experiences is that she is invalidating him. Validation is expressed as acknowledgement, acceptance, approval, affection, appreciation and admiration? But what the male receives instead is the negative side of that; rejection, disapproval and disdain. This gradually kills his spirit. The typical male response is to withdraw. He stops being present. Depending on the situation, he may stay in the relationship. But he will not be fully present with the Amazon woman emotionally. It is at this point that he may look for another woman. He looks for another source of validation.

With the Amazon woman he is just going through the motions of a relationship. At the same time most men are struggling with their own issues.

The non- select males experiences rejection, disregard, and disrespect from the entire peer group of females, consistently.   Pop singers make fun of these men. And groups of young women enjoy the pastime of bashing them. Often this is done in an arrogant and dismissive manner, so that the men end up with low self esteem. There is a red flag here. This has devastating consequences. These non-select men are destroyed spiritually. And it may seem to the woman that the incident is over after the male slinks away with his tail between his legs. But usually these men will only turn and plague other women they encounter. Our social system is a closed system. These men are not going anywhere. There will always be some female for them to abuse or oppress.

Don't Tell Me What To Do!

The Amazon woman can not accept criticism or testimony from a male, without prejudice. She resents male authority figures. She automatically invalidates male opinions that are critical of her, even from experts in the field, due to the fact that they are male. She seeks to undermine the authority of her boss, her school principle, local politicians, and any male figure of authority in her vicinity if he presents as too masculine. It does not matter what his platform, stance or views are, she is unconcerned about what he stands for. What angers the hell out of her is that he had the gall to stand up to her, that he is assertive, that he defends his ground. She sees this as a challenge. It is like one male lion becoming furious when another male lion enters his hunting territory. The first lion just does not want to occupy the space with any other male lion. She will however tolerate and welcome the opinions and contributions of homosexual men who are yin in nature, passive men, and men who are creative and artistic in a feminine way. She looks up to these men.

The Amazon woman is hard to impress. She resents male authority. She is difficult to satisfy. It is just hard for her to be emotionally impressed or satisfied. The man buys her flowers. They are beautiful. But she only feels a little joy. In a few minutes it wears off. He does not get any real credit for his act. To be impressed by any man, regardless of his accomplishments, a woman must be "fully present" in life. Things must <u>matter</u> to her. A woman is impressed by men to the point that she is invested in them. To connect with men, she would need to have feminine energy. And so the reaction to the Amazon woman is that men stop TRYING to impress her. And the men in her "select" category, go out of their way to let her know just how much they are not trying to impress her. And they ridicule any man who tries to, because only the "non- select" men do that.

The Counterfeit Personality

Human beings are born with certain traits and dispositions already fixed in their natal personality. This is called the natal character map. If these natal attributes are naturally cultivated in a woman as part of her upbringing, then she will develop an adult personality true to her inner nature. She will tend to naturally live in sexual harmony with the opposite sex. Her master feminine faculty will not diminish and go into remission. This adult will naturally seek to relate to the opposite sex in a productive manner, and will offer only minimal resistance to living by a natural code. But because Western Society is out of alignment with nature, it does not support such natural spiritual development. When a woman accepts false ideas and illusions about reality in the place of the reality itself, then she must become something counterfeit. She will develop what is called a counterfeit personality. Men will just say that "that woman got issues man."

1. Because the dominant culture is saturated with unnatural themes, toxic false belief systems have become the accepted norm by the majority.
2. The acceptance of these false belief systems sets up a series of subconscious programs that block the psychological development of self. The acceptance of an illusion of reality in the place of the reality itself, has the effect of creating a counterfeit version of self, in the place of our true natal self.
3. The vacuum created by the premature halt in natural development calls forth into being abnormal development. To compensate for what should be there naturally, but is not, we form something artificial in its place.

To support the work of the master feminine faculty, the adult woman will need to undergo a partial detoxification of her personality. False beliefs shape life experience and personal development into an unnatural mutation of what they were designed to be. The counterfeit persona is the definition of what is socially dysfunctional about us. We have issues, negative emotional issues, and this stuff gets in the way of any transformation back into a normal state. People believe very firmly that this shell is us!! And getting a person to recognize that their counterfeit persona is indeed not their true self, is a major challenge, to state it mildly. We all know that most people have different "faces" for the different sides of their life. They show one face on their job, another face to their family, and a different face to the opposite sex when first dating. It may be shocking to know that these vastly different faces -- all belong to the same person! We often evaluate a future love mate based on the wrong face. These "faces" are matrixes of personality that we gradually construct during our lives. They comprise our coping mechanisms. They're your scars, badges and the lessons you've learned. But these faces don't reflect the inner you, the real you, the core of the "you", that nature designed you to be. A woman tends to grow out of her counterfeit persona. As she does she may also grow out of the relationship that she is currently in.

It becomes important now to define or label the counterfeit personality. This makes it easier to recognize it. And this makes it easy to talk about how to fix it. Women need to recognize what it looks like in the males they encounter. And women need to recognize what it looks like in other women. There are five versions of the counterfeit personality. See the table.

1. THE SCHIZOID PERSONALITY
2. THE ORAL PERSONALITY
3. THE PSYCHOPATHIC PERSONALITY
4. THE MASOCHISTIC PERSONALITY
5. THE ANAL or RIGID PERSONALITY

One of the issues with the Amazon personality is the disconnect between the right brain and the left brain. The hawk energy restores the equilibrium between her right brain and her left brain.
By definition, females tend to be more right-brain in judgment and worldview. Men tend to arrive at conclusions, solutions and plan through a thought process that is either deductive or inductive. These are logical and linear thought streams. Normal women tend to arrive at conclusions, solutions and plan through a thought process that is synergistic or intuitive. It does not follow a lineal pattern. It is not logical. Amazon Women are somewhere in between. In the modern workplace this may help her. But it usually hurts her in relationships. Men look ahead with vision and then go step by step to get to a place in the future. Women look at the whole thing in the now, and see only the final desired objective. They do not like to dwell on the steps in between. Often they have a feeling, and intuition about it. They do not know why or how, but it

feels right.   In the last fifty years women have been forced, or have chosen, to be more and more left-brain in thinking. And this bleeds over into her personality.

Schizoid Personality
She believes that males are naturally born with defects of character and the behavior that results is to blame for her negative experiences. Her reaction is anger and hostility. Personality is fragmented. One week she is fully engaged, the next week her hostility restricts her to a partial expression of life.
Oral Personality
The woman with an oral personality structure fears that her mate will abandon her emotionally. Her reaction is an Entitlement posture. (selfishness) "I am entitled to certain benefits from life, regardless of whether I make a contribution or not. If my mate does not gratify my entitlement needs in the relationship, it is a sign that they intend to abandon me.
Psychopathic Personality
She believes that she must be in control in a relationship in order to receive the benefits from mating that she desires. Obsessed with Control Manipulates mate and others.
Masochistic Personality
The masochistic female believes that males are incapable of treating her fairly. Passive/ aggressive as a form of Rebellion. The "Victim" who undermines the agenda of mate because of her belief that cooperation equals submission. She picks partners who tend to be abusive, and when she rebels without reason they tend to mistreat or abuse her.
Anal Personality
She believes she can achieve love in a relationship without risking the exposure of her true feelings. She believes that companionship, sharing money, space, sex and material things equals a relationship. Trust Issues. Fear of risk. Insecurity. Fear of rejection. Remains on the surface.

Awakening the Master Feminine

Awakening the Hawk

Chapter 10 Awakening the Hawk
Restoring Intuitive Thinking

The Seated Hawk

Icon:
The icon of the Seated Hawk is a woman's body with the head of a hawk.

Image:
The image for purposes of visualization is a wise and stern looking woman, holding a set of blueprints in her hand. She is seated on a chair of authority. Rays of power radiate out from the chair.

This aspect of the feminine energy is the intuitive function of the right brain. It is a woman's ability to intuit the solution or plan straight from her DNA or spirit. It is to think from the intuition first, and to rely on reason and logic second. It is synergistic, inclusive, and holistic. This is not to function from hunches or "feelings", but to have the ability to access real information from an internal source.

There is a real difference in the way females and males process information. This is not a learned skill, but something which is built in to the DNA. When a woman restricts her model of thinking to a non-feminine carrier, this also restricts her energy. It in effect changes her personality. Part of the reason why the master feminine faculty shuts down prematurely is the education system in the west. And part of the reason why females fail in relationships is because males have been conditioned not to comprehend their communications. Further, men do not place value on the natural thinking process of the female. This is very significant. John Gray began to address this issue in the book, <u>Men Are From Mars, Women Are From Venus</u>. But the issue has relevance far beyond just a communications issue.

Most women can identify with the elegant rose energy or the moon energy. We easily associate being female with the maternal thing or the sexy pleasure thing. However, women seem less familiar with the natural thinking patterns of the female. Our society does not generally discuss the various polar dynamics of the genders, such as the left brain versus the right brain, or anabolic versus catabolic, sympathetic versus para-sympathetic, acid versus alkaline, etc. But if a woman wants to diet, dance, be creative, have intense orgasms, work, exercise, or sleep, and she wants to get the maximum out of these activities, she definitely wants to know about her right-brain ability and its connection to her feminine energy. So bear with us as we take a short detour and discuss the operation of the brain, and the western education system.

Human intelligence is expressed through the human brain in one of four ways. The brain arrives at conclusions and makes a judgment based on one of four processes. These are:

1. integration or intuitive revelation
2. synthesis or synergistic observation
3. deductive reasoning or logic
4. inductive analysis or analysis

Deductive reasoning (logic) is linear, left brained, and microcosmic. It is a process of being informed. It separates the subject into small parts, and analyses each one in turn based on the problem. It is to learn by definitions. The conclusion is then deducted from the information gained from the parts. (Sciences such as chemistry)

Inductive analysis (analysis) is abstract, left brained and microcosmic. It separates the subject into its components based on the like functioning of the components. It then employs abstract analogies to work backwards from the desired conclusion to determine what steps must have been involved to get to that conclusion. We understand one thing, by comparing it to another thing. (Math, investigative reporting, criminal investigation)

Synthesis is holistic, right brained and macrocosmic. In synthesis you start by an examination of the big picture, in respect to how the parts of the whole fit because of the system that connects them together. You are not so concerned with knowing the parts, but an understanding of the synergy that allows the system to work. (Common sense, ecosystems, biology, carpentry, apprenticeship, naturopathic medicine)

Integration is intuitive, right-brained and macrocosmic. This method requires the person to be in a trance state such as watching television, dreaming, day-dreaming, meditation, yoga, prayer or just absent minded. A vision or image of the thing is placed in the mind. Remove any pre-conceived notions about the thing. The right brain then opens to the subconscious mind, and automatically indexes to the sources of information about the thing. It will even penetrate down into DNA, or past life memory. When trained, the subject can even open to the elemental realm, or plant, animal or insect kingdom to retrieve information. Wisdom or information is then transferred from these sources into the awake mind for processing. Once these inputs are received and transferred by the right brain, the left brain must then figure out how to integrate these insights into a conclusion that makes sense. Often the person will arrive at a conclusion and not really understand how they did so.

Women are born with a predisposition to process information through the brain using either the synthesis or intuitive models. It is based on a 'big picture' format. Men are born with a predisposition to process information through the brain using either the logic or analysis models. It is a 'step by step' format. Of course we all have some capacity for all four models. Specific women have excelled in all four models as have specific men. But in general we find that each sex is geared to a yin or yang model. There is nothing wrong with females using the logic or analysis models. But if she only thinks in the left- brain way it will change her energy. Men brought up in a western style society look down on women who employ synthesis or intuition in their normal thinking regimen. Thinking in this way is seen as being inferior to the more scientific and logical method. The truth is that intuitive right brain thinking is the most complex and by far offers the most value of the four. Synthesis and analysis are both critical models in today's climate. Logic is the least complex, and offers value in respect to technology, but has almost no applications in respect to life and living well. To consistently apply logic to relationship situations is to guarantee oneself a steady stream of failure. This is the definition of being a nerd. Before we return to the main discussion, and the greater relevance of all this, we need to devote a paragraph or two to the education system, and the racial profiles.

There are four main racial types. There are four basic types of education systems in the world. The table which follows shows the correlation.

Gender, Race, Education Models

RACE, GENDER,	EDUCATION MODEL
White race, male Left brain, Analysis	Military academy, boarding school Regimented. Students learn by problem solving and following strictly an example. Compliments the army and economy.
Yellow race, male Left brain, Logic, science	The current public school system. Students learn by being informed by the teacher. Mainly memory work. The curriculum is a series of subjects each seen as a separate life unit, and each taught as a science. Students 'copy' knowledge from books but do not need to understand it.
Red race, female Right brain Synthesis, ecosystems	Outdoor School/ apprenticeship Students learn by observation. The surroundings are the classroom. The student spends time mastering a system or environment. Then use synthesis to comprehend the part or action by how it works within the system. To understand the big picture first, and base all future information on this central understanding.
Black race, female Right brain	Initiation System Students learn by intuition. The sixth sense is trained through some rite of transformation. The student gains the ability to channel information seemingly, from out of nowhere. All occult, psychic, intuitive and mediums are related to this system.

The public school system is based on the logic (science) and analysis (problem solving) models. They are both left brain centric, and geared to the male learning pattern. This system has its origin in ancient Asia more than Europe. Academic and religious institutions in the west belittle the other two models, which were very common in Europe and Asian in the past, and are still common in indigenous societies. As western society moves toward a green consciousness and sustainable forms of living, the right-brain models are gaining in popularity. We need all four models of course. To restrict the population to only the left brain side is to cripple the development of men and women.

We all know women who have that sixth sense. Mothers sometimes can just sense things about their children. Wives just know certain things about their mates. The best books, songs, music, and plays are written via inspiration. They just come to the creator seemingly just "out of the blue." In science, business, and the arts the greatest discoveries are not via research and analysis, but from pure inspiration and intuition. In the past women operated from their sixth sense much more often, and the faculty was trained to a much greater refinement and power.

When the woman gains the ability to really tap into her right brain hemisphere potential, such that she can genuinely make judgments and give insight from a higher source, she becomes a resource that men respect. Males are then compelled to follow her. This is the woman who is moving all things from behind the scenes. This is the queen bee who orchestrates the life of the colony of bees from a central place. The evolved woman knows that the plan and the purpose for everything in life are already there, you just need to be able to sense it.

In the Ausarian religion of ancient Egypt, the Tao of China, the Vedic Scripts of India, the Sacred Path Texts of the Native American high cultures, and the Kabala of the Sumerian and the Hebrew, all share a similar concept called the Tree of Life. At the top of this tree is a trinity of three entities said to play a major role in the life and evolution of mankind. One of these entities is always a female, usually depicted as a woman's body with the head of an animal. The woman is always seated. In her hand are symbols of power. The ancient Kemitic (ancient Egypt) version is Sekert, she is pictured as a seated hawk. Scholars in the west have for centuries misunderstood the imagery and metaphoric language of these early cultures. Only now is the true meaning of the woman with the head of the hawk being understood. The early Egyptians were not worshipping a hawk-headed god. That is silly; they were way more spiritually sophisticated than that. The image of the woman with the head of the hawk meant that she represented a "hawkish" quality within an otherwise yin and feminine profile. That the hawk headed woman was seated was very significant.   It implied that her power was such, that it was unnecessary for her to leave her seat or take any external action in order to achieve her needs. She was a feminine "hawk" that did not need to "hunt' to obtain its prey.

The metaphors and icons of each archetype give us clues about the way feminine yin energy works. Implied in all of them is the concept of indirect action. It is the passive/ aggressive dynamic. The yin dynamic looks passive until you get up close. The male yang motif is like an eagle, swooping down on its prey. He is a hunter. It takes direct action. He has to think a certain way to be like this. The female yin motif is more like a spider, which spins a web and waits. Also we could think of a fisherwoman, who baits her hook and waits. Can you see that? To be this way you have to think a certain way. The seated female hawk is just as hawkish as the standing male hawk. But they are hawkish and obtain their objectives in opposite ways. The male is openly aggressive. The female constructs a trap or employs some agent to work on her behalf. And the thinking model for male and female is based on this dynamic. The male must research, explore or analyze to obtain information. The female gains access to the wisdom that is already inside or in the environment at hand. It is difficult for her personality to develop fully or her sexual energy to mature fully, if she does not connect the two halves of her brain, the left to the right.

We are simply talking about what is. This is the way feminine energy naturally works. The feminine woman sets up a cause, she defines a purpose, but she does not take the actual action to obtain her goal.   That is the job of the male. Females achieve their objectives without ever leaving the nest. It is in the very act of bringing forth the plan from within that she sets up the matrix that determines what the final outcome will be. She brings forth her plan from within. The plan is set. It is not based on what she observes 'out there', but from what already is in the DNA. Her plan is in alignment with natural law, the cycles, DNA, the ecosystem. She does not need to do anything more, except get out of the way and let it happen.

At this point the female stops, and hands this plan off to the male. She hands over her goal to the male and becomes submissive. She is submissive in order not to interfere in the actual completion of the task. It is an energy thing. If her energy continues to be dominant while the male is doing his thing, it will hinder the male. Also in the act of turning her energy around, and being submissive, she throws a boomerang; she draws back to her like a vacuum what she has sent out into the matrix to be done. The male looks around to see what is required to do this thing handed to him by the female. He has to be left brained and practical so that this dream of the female, this ideal vision can be made into a real thing. This is not easy. There may not be enough money, time or plans to complete it. He may say no. Or he may say yes, but with these changes. He is in charge, but in charge of accomplishing her agenda. He completes his task, and brings the finished product back to the female. She becomes hawkish again; she is back in charge now. It is his turn to become passive. She is in charge of how to use or distribute these goods once he has produced them. Can you comprehend how the sexes compliment each other? Neither sex is in charge absolutely. The male is the executive of the family, responsible to carry out the plan. The female is the board of directors, responsible for coming up with the plan, purpose. But life is in charge. Life is telling both of them what to do. This question of who is in charge is silly. We all are trying to learn our lessons as fast as we can, so our butt whipping of life will not be so severe.

To be a seated hawk, a woman has to be hawkish about the future of her family, her community, her country. It is unselfish. To sit on the throne carries great power, but also great responsibility. Without an understanding of the seated hawk archetype they are handicapped. Women are too quick to let society, men, or commercial interests set the prime agenda, the first cause. She has to produce a vision of where her family and society needs to go. It must be naturally aligned. It should be sustainable. The Amazon woman only works from her plan. Men resist cooperating. The seated hawk woman intuits a natural plan that is inclusive. Men are compelled to follow. She can rein her man in, and change the course he was on without upsetting the balance in her relationship with him. She does not have to bash him, or break him, or rebuke him to get him to see things differently. A truly feminine woman has tremendous power of influence over a man. Women may seem passive on the surface, but they are by far the more powerful of the sexes. She does not need to go toe to toe with a yang male to achieve her ends.

The women who are serious about achieving Goddess status must get out of their egos, and get over themselves. I am talking about the whole issue of submission. It has become a dirty word to most women. But women need to come to grips with some stuff. Men want to fight for you, do for you, put your needs first, and be there for you. The reason some of them stopped doing those things for women is because females blocked it. They blocked it by trying to be men. It is the same issue as patriotism. The common man is looking for something to believe in, he wants to put his country first, but the politicians keep making him lose faith. In domestic situations it is the same. Men want to be good fathers and sons and husbands, but often make the wrong decisions at the crossroads. Keep in mind that these men are not fully developed. They are operating with 25% of the masculine deck. So the boy is stumbling through life in the first place. His father never told him what his role was, because his father did not know. In most domestic situations the male is responding to something the female did. This does not excuse his poor behavior. I am just telling you like it is. If the female works her role, and stays the hell out of his, he will very likely come around. And his role sometimes means being in authority. When one person is in authority, the other person is being submissive. And maybe at first he will not know how to handle being in charge. But he will never get it if you jump out of character every time he asserts himself. It is an energy thing.

Being submissive is not about being passive. You never let people abuse you. Not man or woman. But men are meant to regulate women. Just as women are meant to regulate men. It is about staying in your role. It is by definition a check and balance relationship. In any relationship only one person can be in charge at a time. When a client walks into the doctor's office the client is in charge. The doctor is working for the client. The doctor is submissive. But once the client tells the doctor what is wrong, the client becomes a patient, and submits to the doctor. Now the doctor is in charge. You do what the doctor says. Once the doctor finishes your treatment you are back in charge now. It is time to pay him. You now decide if you liked the treatment or not. Then you pay him. Being submissive is about knowing what in creation your role is. When you are doing your thing everyone else needs to sit down and shut up. But when it is your man's turn at the plate, you need to learn to sit still and shut up. It is time to follow. It is just that simple. But when the woman can not do this, it will almost certainly follow that the man will act out in a negative way. Now a lot of men do not respect the opinion and role of the woman. But when she gets that right brain mojo going, he gets a fresh respect for her. It is the queen bee thing. He learns to give you your proper respect.

The Counterfeit Personality Trap

The right brain yin thing is so very powerful. We see examples of women seeking perfection every day. They invest time, effort and money into this. And then these women striving for perfection enter into a relationship and fail. Why? It is the absence of the seated hawk. From time to time we see individual women who rise up to demonstrate perfection in some sport, art, music, work, or creation. And when we see what some women are capable of, it reminds us that each of us has this potential greatness within. The highest calling in life is to strive to become the highest and best version of something possible. But the woman lacking the seated hawk archetype often neglects to perfect her personality. Her mantra is... "Accept me as I am", no matter how dysfunctional that may be. Strange, her job, arts, talents, appearance, car and home are worthy of investment, but apparently not her personality. Your body and face may get you into a relationship, but your personality will make it work. You have to live with the situations you create. Why live in the dark, damp basement when you could live in a mansion? A sustainable, holistic and natural woman has a naturally feminine personality. In our discussion of the personality we will often use the term **counterfeit personality**. If your current version of personality is not a reflection of your natal spirit, it is not genuine, and is therefore counterfeit. If your current version of personality reflects a bunch of masculine traits and attributes, and very few feminine attributes, and you have a vagina, then your personality is counterfeit, and does not reflect your natal gender. To qualify as your natal, feminine personality, it must reflect your natal core self, and a distinctly feminine signature. The shift from an Amazon, masculine and counterfeit personality is a dynamic shift from left brain lineal behavior to right brain intuitive behavior. Your core self is internal, it is not external. It is not artificial faces, facades and masks that we wear. Thus the shift from the counterfeit personality is a dynamic shift from external faces and facades to a heart connection. The archetype of feminine energy which awakens the right brain and repairs the head to heart disconnect is the Seated Hawk. Therefore in this chapter we will present an awakening exercise, and a case study which attempts to assist a woman to do this.

Second Puberty Hawk Edition

A woman begins this phase of the awakening program by infusing the catalyst for the seated hawk energy into her subconscious mind. This is begun by a series of meditations based around certain sounds, rhythms and notes of music. It is organic. Each thing by itself is meaningless. But together it is a sequence that unlocks a key. You must be supervised by a guide to do this. You can not do this by yourself. We dare not give too much detail on the actual process because some person would try to fill in the blanks or take short cuts. The master feminine faculty goes into her DNA storehouse and locates the set of attributes associated with the seated hawk archetype, or the intuitive right brain program, and starts to transfer them from a dormant state into an active state. They start growing into real aspects of her being, and stop being just potential traits. With in a matter of weeks, and maybe even days, the woman's persona begins the shift from a left brain and masculine paradigm to a right brain and feminine persona. Once the catalyst is inserted into the woman's subconscious mind, her master feminine faculty will activate the programs almost immediately. It will begin to happen in a few weeks, even days. And most likely, the onset of this will throw the typical woman into conflict!

A battle is about to be waged between your masculine, left-brain, counterfeit personality, and the feminine personality trying to displace it. Which one will win? The one that you feed the most will always win!! If you successfully awaken your right brain and learn to intuit knowledge, it will be the coolest thing! Your teen daughter goes out and has a drink. In your dreams you see her clearly drinking alcohol, and you see the name of the bar, and the time. You confront her. She can not understand how you knew. You meet a new man and he seems to be okay. But a thought pops into your head from out of no where saying "check his driving record." You check his record and discover he has three DUI convictions. So you know better than to give him drinks and then let him drive. He may kill someone. When you bring the Seated Hawk on line the reaction of men to you will change. It is like you are the sun and men just orbit around you. They may not be sleeping with you, but they feel a connection. When you call them they will come. You stop competing with men. You no longer feel any need to argue, convince, or confront men or woman. You intuitively know the secret law of manifestation. You visualize what you want done, and they will do it for you. Of course you had a plan, which was more than just your own selfish agenda. Let us be clear. Men are compelled to follow your suggestions because you are in alignment with the energy of the times. You are intuitive. They are following you because of the energy, not because you just want them to.

Awakening Exercises:
1. Visualizations to encourage right brain development.
2. Identify your counterfeit personality.
3. Identify your external faces, facades and masks. Get a preview into the faces, facades and masks of males.
4. Align your personality to its natal position using the table of validation.

These exercises require group participation to be done properly. At this stage, you should have assembled your awakening circle of women and men. These are the women going through the awakening program with you. The awakening circle should be an honest forum, open, safe, and private.

Identify Your Counterfeit Personality

Awakening Exercise

The hardest part of any personal transformation that involves the personality is the recognition on the part of the person that they need to do it. Our society does not encourage critical self examination. Politically correct speech today avoids even using words that directly refer to any negative or uncomplimentary trait. People do not normally acknowledge that anything is less than perfect with them. People always ask you how you are doing, but they definitely do not want you to tell them. You are expected to say "I am okay" no matter what the truth is. People do not wish to speak about something being wrong. And even after a problem is first pointed out, many people began to force this thought out of their mind as soon as they wake up on the next day. In my experience with people, I have found that only a very small percent of humanity are able to embrace being confronted by knowledge of their counterfeit personality. These are perhaps the most evolved among us. People enjoy pointing out the issues with other people. But they can stubbornly cling to a state of denial about their own issues even in the face of overwhelming evidence.

In this exercise, each woman shall attempt to list two "issues" or negative traits that she has been labeled with. Sit in a circle with paper. On one column on the paper each woman is to write down two issues that a male in the past has accused her of. On the other side of the paper she is to write down two issues her family labeled her with. Only allow seven minutes for this. Then each woman will read her list, and the group will pick two of the four issues. The group will choose issues that correlate to one of the five versions of the counterfeit personality. People who can not write something down in seven minutes are your best candidates for denial. Now each person has two issues.

Next buy a white board and erect it in the front of the room. Now each man and woman in turn will write their two issues on a clean board. She then stands in front of the group and explains why these are not her issues. The group then tries to determine which of the five personality structures from the table most closely describes her current counterfeit personality. Remember your counterfeit personality is supposed to be negative. The group now picks one personality type for you. Write this down. It is your assignment for the next session. You may disagree with the choice. But the fact that they see it this way is important to note. Do not worry. You will get a chance to amend it. Each of these five personality structures is caused by one of five central false belief systems.

1. THE SCHIZOID PERSONALITY
2. THE ORAL PERSONALITY
3. THE PSYCHOPATHIC PERSONALITY
4. THE MASOCHISTIC PERSONALITY
5. THE ANAL or RIGID PERSONALITY

After the Awakening Circle has assigned each man and woman a counterfeit personality, give the group a few days to think about it. Then at the next session each person can change and pick their own choice. But they must give a reason why. Until you stop feeding your counterfeit personality it will not fade. Now comes the hard part. You have to examine all the evidence and determine if there is a need to change anything. Few people, male or female, have full control of how their life starts.   But each of us comes to a point in life when the past circumstances no longer control our future destiny.

The awakening circle is the best way to uncover the counterfeit personality. For one thing, if a woman has not brought forth her seated hawk archetype of female energy, she may have trouble visualizing what that looks like for her specifically. It helps if she can see it reflected in another woman. It helps a lot if they can speak to another woman who has had the same experience they have had. Of course the men have different archetypes. If this is done correctly, it may be one of the most moving, emotional, eye-opening, and intense experiences of your life!! Every woman needs to be heard.   If the meetings are going to be successful there must be honesty.
This is the end of the exercise.

Our Faces
When a woman accepts false ideas and illusions about reality in the place of the reality itself, then she must become something counterfeit. Our friends respond to our façade. We get so used to

operating under the façade that we believe in time that this façade is us!! And getting a person to recognize that their counterfeit persona is indeed not their true self is a major challenge, to state it mildly. We are very young when we start doing this. Some examples:

- We use clothes, garments and attire to present a "face" of who we are. If our attire is classy and elegant, then we believe we become classy and elegant. But you can put on any attire which you can afford. You do not have to change inside to present a look through attire. You can look sexy, but not feel sexy. In short there can be a disconnect between your presentation and what you really are.
- We use our friends to project an image of ourselves. Rather we mean to or not, people judge us by the people we hang out with, and where we go with them. Are we a gangster want-to-be who hangs out in the inner city and goes home at night to the suburbs? In short, there can be a disconnect between your peer group and what you are really about.
- Our automobile amounts to another layer of our persona. Like in a Batman movie, our car is like our exo-skeleton. It is this complex machine which we control. Our automobile has an emblem which denotes we are something special. Our persona merges into it. We can afford this car. It indicates our social standing. We present an image of ourselves based on the image of the car. In short, there can be a disconnect between your image or façade, and what you really are.
- And we can add many layers. Our job title. Our blackberry. Our badges and trophies. We identify with them. It is all exterior stuff. And the people in your vicinity believe that your façade is you, and you are really your façade, the public face, peers, events, car, house, and achievements.

There are so many facets and layers of the modern counterfeit personality. It starts with the "mask", the face we put on for the public. But these faces don't reflect the inner you, the core of you. Our true feminine self is buried under there somewhere. We are no longer in touch with it. We are no longer present in life. It is our counterfeit persona which makes the decisions for us now. We have lived the life that society said we should have lived. We dress the way that is socially proper. We express our sexual appetite within the set boundaries. We no longer even remember what it feels like to be fully present with a man, to risk all, trust all, give all, accept all, and be all. And this is where the typical woman disconnects from men. For she is born with a longing, an aching desire, a destiny, an inner burning to be something, to do something. And she disconnects from her longing in life when she stops being fully present in a feminine way. She disconnects from men.

Awakening Exercise
The Table of Validation Exercise
        For this exercise make a copy of the table below and blow it up to 36 inches by 24 inches or larger. You can also put this image in a power point slide and project it from your notebook computer to the front of the room. Go to our web site to find assistance www.masteryao.com

        When a woman expresses the Amazon persona in the presence of males it broadcasts to the males the messages of disregard, disrespect, rejection, and etc. In this exercise, the group should discuss how this dynamic plays out in everyday life. Refer to personal situations when this is possible. Talk about the male reaction when he is placed on the bottom part of this chart. Talk about the male reaction when he is placed on the top portion of this chart. Also discuss how women feel when males place them on the bottom portion of the table. When do males acknowledge, accept, approve, etc., of women in the group? Why. Being physically attractive is one example. What are the others? In the conclusion of the session, discuss what changes in personality are necessary to keep relationships on the top portion of the table of validation all the time.
End of Exercise.

The Table of Validation

	Hormone Boost	Blood PH	Feminine
ADORATION	Melatonin Melanin	9.6	Feminine
ADMIRATION	Human growth hormone & L-dopamine	9.2	Feminine
APPRECIATION	Thyroxine	8.8	Feminine
AFFECTION	Endomorphs	8.4	Feminine
APPROVAL	Insulin	8.0	Feminine
ACCEPTANCE	Androgens	7.6	Feminine
ACKNOWLEDGEMENT	Steroids	7.2	Feminine
		PH 7.0	Neutral
DISREGARD	Acidic toxins	6.8	Amazon
REJECTION	Toxic neuro-chems	6.4	Amazon
DISREPECT	Toxic neuro-chems	6.0	Amazon
DISAPPROVAL	Toxic neuro-chems	5.6	Amazon
HATRED	carcinogens	5.2	Amazon
MALIGN	carcinogens	5.0	Amazon
REVULSION	carcinogens	4.8	Amazon

Kim   Life Episode

Remember Kim?   Kim is in her late thirties. She is the single parent of one daughter Michelle. Kim lives in a very fashionable section of the city, makes a six figure salary, and drives a fine car. Kim has never been married.   Kim is the third generation of what was becoming a single parent tradition in her family. In fact, in the last ten years Kim has not had a relationship which has lasted for more than six months. Kim grew up in a climate of male hatred.   In the absence of a father at home, Kim never fully connected to men in general.   It was typical for Kim to put in long hours at work, and spend time supporting her favorite two pastimes, her sorority and her alumni chapter. The men Kim dated came fourth on this list of priority for her time.

Kim wanted very much to connect with a man. She felt that she had a lot to offer, and genuinely wished to finally make that soul connection with a man.   But her history with the opposite sex was filled with a lot of painful memories that she found hard to shake. She did not have a lot of confidence in herself with men. She was unwilling to make a full effort in the beginning of her encounters, because frankly most of her past efforts did not pay off. Kim did not understand the signals given off by men. And since the age of thirty Kim's weight fluctuated between 165 and 180 pounds. Being overweight did not help.

Kim is an Amazon woman. If you remember the House of the Woman, there were four archetypes of the feminine energy, Seated Hawk, Treasure Chest, Elegant Rose and Moon.   Kim especially had problems with her Rose and Moon. She was not much of a nurturer. Nor was Kim very comfortable at giving men pleasure, or even with receiving pleasure from men. She was awkward in intimate situations. Kim dressed conservatively. She rated 8's and 9's on style, but did not come across to men as particularly seductive or sensual.   She thought of herself as classy.   She felt that dressing to seduce a man was not something a woman of her caliber needed to do. For Kim, getting dressed for a date was work, not fun, and a source of anxiety. Kim's auric field was always broadcasting to men.

Kim is not aware that men are subliminally picking up on her vibe. And so all during her thirties Kim met different men and attempted to engage each one in a long term relationship.   And each of these relationships in turn seemed to become tainted with the same poison.

These relationship attempts all crashed and burned in a short time. It was insidious. There seemed to be an invisible wall between her and males her age. The men had different personalities, and different backgrounds, and each relationship attempt started from a different place. And then each relationship steered somehow to a similar set of problems. It would hang on for weeks in a limbo, as Kim desperately tried to breathe new life into it. And then some seemingly minor event would push the man over the edge, and he would end it. Let us take a look at one of these relationships, and see what caused its demise!

Kim versus Edward

It was a car break down that brought Edward into Kim's life. Kim was with one of her girlfriends when the car would not start. The battery they thought. Her girlfriend called a male friend to come get them and he in turn called one of his male friends, and the two of them came to rescue the girls. The four of them ended up going to a café for coffee. Edward, a single man, had just moved into the area. He was tall, manly, and spoke in a deep sexy voice. Kim thought Edward was very attractive. Edward immediately showed some interest in Kim. Soon the two of them were dating. Kim was excited about the potential of this encounter, and especially anxious. On their first date Kim discovered that Edward drove a delivery truck for a beverage company. She found out things about his past relationships and what his life goals were. Edward did not ask Kim where she worked or what her political views were. He wanted to know what Kim's favorite song was, and what she did to celebrate her birthdays and holidays. Edward was obviously seeking to be romantic. But Kim was conservative, and did not respond directly to Edwards's attempts to be romantic.

On their third date Edward finally saw Kim's expensive Condo. His reaction was not positive. It reinforced a vibe he had already picked up from Kim which indicated that she did not really need a man. Edward found out that Kim was a manager at her company and figured that her salary was at least twice as much as his. Right then, Edward begun to have reservations about the potential of this relationship. He had dated successful women before and it always ended badly. He did not like the emasculation and demeaning attitude that often came with this territory. And Edward was attracted to heavier women. He thought that in many ways, he and Kim had a lot in common.

In the beginning Kim tried to avoid the situations which had torpedoed her relationship attempts before. She resisted smothering Edward, and gave him space. She resisted talking about the frustrations on her job, something she had the habit of doing. She did not introduce him to her mother. But Kim did not realize she was still falling into the old traps. She was constantly broadcasting the non-feminine messages. And men respond to these signals with uncertainty, emotional apathy, and caution. Kim was broadcasting several negative messages:

- That she was not nurturing to males.
- That she was adverse to giving and receiving pleasure.
- That she did not regard males as her social equal, unless they were her financial equal first.

Edward pressed forward with the relationship, hoping to see evidence that Kim could still play the role in his life, that he thought a woman should play. Edward hoped that if he got closer to Kim, he might see a softer side of her underneath the corporate veneer.

For Edward, the first major red flag for him came up when he met Kim's daughter. Michelle was very yang, and very down on men. Michelle showed no respect or regard for Edward as an adult at all. This reinforced for Edward the notion that Kim was not nurturing toward men. If she was, her daughter would have a different attitude toward him. And then there was the annual sorority dance. It was a semi-formal event, attended by many local business leaders and persons of note in the city. Kim called Edward each day in the week leading up to the big dance, reminding him how important the event was, and making a number of suggestions she thought was subtle. Kim asked several times to see what Edward was going to wear to the dance, and after seeing the proposed outfit she strongly suggested that he upgrade. Edward drove a nice pick up truck only one year old. Kim wanted him to rent a car for the dance, or drive hers. Kim injected political topics into their conversation all week long. She wanted to make sure that Edward was up on current events in the city. She thought she was being very clever, but Edward made note of the change in conversation and felt she did not think he was up to conversing with her friends. He was deeply offended. On the night of the event Kim was dressed very conservatively. Edward was hoping to finally see a more feminine side to Kim but was again disappointed. It seemed to Edward that Kim was not seeking to seduce him. Her outfit was stylist but safe. She was obviously dressing for the benefit of the other women there.

At the event the couple mingled with people of all classes and backgrounds. But Edward noted that Kim consistently talked over him, and cut him off before he could make his points. When men or women addressed questions or comments to him, Kim let him start to respond, and then tried to finish his sentences for him. He gave her a couple of sharp looks but she did not get the hint. At one point in the evening Kim and Edward were sitting at the table with several of Kim's sorority sisters and their dates. It was mentioned that one of the men at the table was a single father, and what a fine job he was doing with his children. Another man at the table was lauded for cutting the grass of the single women on his block, and consistently helping them out with small maintenance tasks. Kim was aware that Edward was always helping people, and had even received an award at his church for community service. They had met when he came to help her friend who had car trouble that day. But to his surprise, while the other men at the table were being praised, Kim was conspicuously silent about him. It was a red flag.

Kim thought the sorority dance was a big success. The evening ended late, and Edward made the excuse that he was tired and went to his own house. He gave Kim a polite kiss but did not seek to be more affectionate with her. He was not feeling it. It was an issue with Kim's feminine energy. From the standpoint of her relationship, the dance was not a success at all. And a truly feminine woman would pick up on that.

Crossroads Point-   The Dance

After the dance event, Edward was not feeling very masculine, or appreciated as a man. And in fact he was trying to figure out where exactly he fit in to Kim's life. It was not feeling natural to him. Kim failed to take note of what had transpired. Edward was calling Kim less and less. Kim was seeing things just the opposite. She had never had so much fun at the annual dance before. Kim was the envy of many of her female associates. She was actually dating the man who went to the dance with her. Most of her peers were escorted to the dance by men who were just friends. Edward was attractive as a man. At the table the other women took note of his deep voice and were impressed. As Kim is advancing forward, Edward is feeling cautious. And then one night in the bedroom, Edward failed to get an erection. There was a sickly silence for 15 minutes. And in this silence, the bell tolling the end of the relationship begins to peel. Even then, Kim could have stopped the slide, but did not see the importance of femininity.

And then the nail in the coffin of the relationship came. Four months into their relationship, Edward was invited to a family event by one of his relatives. He invited Kim to go with him. It started with Sunday brunch. There were 40 of Edward's relatives gathered in a few rooms and on the deck. For many of them they were meeting Kim for the first time. Kim was trying to bond with Edward's sister and female cousins.

Finally brunch was served, and it certainly looked delicious. Part of Edward's family was from the south, and it is tradition for many southern families that at public events, the women served the men. The food was placed on a long buffet style table. But none of the older men went to the buffet table. Their wives or mates prepared them a plate and served it to them. Then the women got themselves a plate, and sat down in the big room to eat. The men had been served, and the women had their plates and had sat down. Kim got herself a plate, but did not offer to get Edward one. When Kim sat down and started to eat, and Edward still did not have a plate, Edward's friends took notice. They each gave Edward a look to see how he was taking this. Edward just looked down at the floor, feeling that he had been dismissed by Kim. Finally, seeing that Kim was not going to get him a plate, Edward got up and slowly went into the dining room to fix himself a plate. When he sat down there was an immediate look from his uncle. His uncle asked Edward, "How long have you known Kim?" He inquired about her family history. But the uncle was not really asking a question. Only the old school people in the room picked up on the uncle's meaning. The uncle was basically saying that Edward was too much of a man to accept second rate treatment from a woman just because she had a good job. The ending of the brunch coincided with the end of the relationship between Kim and Edward.

Edward started an argument with Kim about some other minor issue and in anger broke off the relationship. Kim was stunned. She had felt that he had pulled back a little, but was not expecting this at all!

Erica versus Darren
Remember Erica? Erica is a reformed Amazon woman. Erica is a creative and receptive woman approaching forty, who is working in the production department for a local theatrical company. She is doing what she loves each day. While Erica has never been married, she is finally in a serious relationship with a man she believes she could stay with for the rest of her life. This relationship is different from any previous relationship, because she has taken a very different approach to it. For the last four years Erica has been engaged in a transition from Amazon woman to fully feminine female. Erica has been cancer free for almost five years now. On the anniversary when Erica was cancer free for one year, she had a major epiphany and a major change in the course of her life. Changing her approach to relationships was not easy. Even after she begins to infuse a more feminine persona into her conduct with men, they did not always respond to her as she wished them to.

In her early thirties Erica was an Amazon woman. At this time she worked for the federal government in a job she hated, around people she disliked. The entire building she worked in was filled with human vipers and parasites. Erica was surrounded all day by women seeking to undermine her or men seeking to take advantage of her. It was a toxic environment. Then came the cancer, and her awakening to life. After she recovered from the cancer she went back to work. And she found that with her new found desire to get more out of life, she found her workplace atmosphere almost intolerable. But she needed the health insurance in case something happened. So day in and day out she lived in fear. A few months after she went back to work her grandmother died, and left her a house and some money. On the one year anniversary of being cancer free the tension and the fear had built up so high in Erica. And she exploded in a rage at herself. Why was she wasting her life? The doctors said she was completely cancer free and would probably live for fifty more years. So why was she still subjecting herself to torture at her job every day? Why was she still so all alone at night? And that night she tore through her house in a rage, throwing the symbols of her past life into the trash, rearranging her house to somehow find a way to rearrange her life. Shortly thereafter she quit her job with the government, and sold her big expensive house. Erica weighted about 135 and had a great figure. She had been a dancer in college. She had been sleeping in the tiny guest room, because her bedroom felt so big and lonely without a man. That night she stripped down to her panties and looked at her body in the mirror. She still had it going on she thought. She looked fabulous! Why was she still alone? Whatever the reason, just as she got over the cancer, she was going to put an end to this pattern of negative relationships. The answer to Erica's relationship prayers came from a very unlikely source. What tipped the scales for Erica was the input from an old woman named Ananda, an old friend of her grandmother's. Erica had known Ananda all her life. She was one of her grandmother's closest friends.

Ananda was exotic. Some people thought she was somewhat of a psychic, or medium or something. She just seemed to know things. Ananda was very mysterious. Erica's mom had once gone to Ananda for a "reading" and admitted that it had been very helpful. But her friends at the church frowned on such things and her mother never went back. Sitting out on the patio, Ananda begin to tell Erica very specific things about Erica's life. It was a bit eerie. How did Ananda know? Ananda told Erica that both her grandmother and Ananda had "seen" things around Erica all her life. Most curious of all Ananda knew about Darren, Erica's current boyfriend. She did not know Darren's name but she knew his personality. And then Ananda told Erica that she was aware that Erica was having problems in the relationship, the same problems she had always had. She went on to say that Erica was sending him one message with her mouth, and a completely different message (broadcast) with her spirit. Ananda was able to know all of this because her Seated Hawk faculty was active. She was in touch with her right brain in such a way, that Ananda could intuit all sorts of information about the people she loved. Erica asked Ananda for help. She was tired of this relationship yo-yo. Erica wanted to break out of the negative cycle of relationship failure once and for all.

Ananda and Erica went back to Erica's new house, (her grandmother's house) to begin the first lesson in the "art" as Ananda called it. Ananda told Erica that if a woman practiced the "art" she could influence any man to act in a certain way. This was intriguing. Erica began to learn this art from Ananda. She told Erica all she had to do was build the right "nest" and sing the "hummingbird song", and Darren would come running. By "nest" she meant Erica's personality, and by extension her home. And by hummingbird song she meant the siren song, the call of the wood nymph. They went into the largest bedroom and Ananda said to Erica, "this room is symbolic of your womb, and we are going to make it inviting. We are going to change the colors and scents and feeling of your bedroom and you must also change your body scents, colors and body language to reflect the room." Ananda said the colors, scents and body language of the woman was part of her "broadcast". They hired help, and set out to remodel the room. At the same time, Erica was to make similar changes to her personality.

Ananda told Erica that they were going to use the bedroom/ womb/ nest to imprint Darren. In the south they called it rooting him. They painted the room a sensuous pleasing pastel yellow color. No bright lights. No food smells or bad odors. They installed an aromatherapy kit and burned the same pure citrus oil in the room that Erica chooses to wear. This was Erica's "I am available oil, and I am willing to please you". The scent of the sweet citrus enveloped the room day and night. And soon every time Erica went into her bedroom she was uplifted. Ananda instructed Erica that every woman practicing the "art" should hang a special picture of herself in her bedroom near the bed. This picture should show her entire body, not just the face. The picture should be a large one, such that it can easily be seen as soon as one enters the room. There should be no other picture of a woman in the room. Her dress in the picture should be seductive. Erica decided to start imprinting Darren at his favorite nightclub, and end up in the bedroom. This was going to be fun she thought. She purchased a very short, tight fitting orange dress. It was the same color as the bedroom. Then Ananda took a picture of Darren from Erica, and placed it under a clear bowl of clean water, and put the whole thing on top of a dresser out of sight in the bedroom. She told Erica to change the water over the picture once a week. They were ready!

Erica put on the oil, and the orange dress, and took Darren out to the club. Erica paid for everything, and made sure Darren had a drink in front of him all the time. She told Darren straight up that she was about to rock his world, and all he had to do was sit back and enjoy it. It took the pressure off of Darren and started building up the anticipation of what was coming. The other men at the club envied him. Erica was hanging all over him like he was the man. This had never happened to him before. Darren wondered what had come over conservative Erica. He could hardly believe what was happening, it was like it was his birthday. They left the club early, and went up to put the bedroom and the 'art' to the test. The room smelled sweet, like orange blossoms in spring, the same aroma Erica was wearing. There was music playing, and immediately Darren went almost into a trance from the effect of the room. Erica immediately undressed Darren, and then slowly undressed herself. Then Erica "entertained" Darren until he could not take the arousal any more, and then she finally gave in to him. The imprint went in deep. Darren woke up a changed man. Ananda smiled. Erica had changed one of her broadcasts successfully.

Now the relationship between Erica and Darren lasted almost 18 months, three times longer than any of her previous encounters. And she was happy most of that time. But the relationship still had some problems. There was a big difference in the outlook on life between Erica and Darren. The main problem involved the influence of their friends. Erica still had many friends who were in the Amazon phase. Her friends did not rate Darren as being a member of the "select" group. And they tried their best to break the couple up. Darren's friends were just as bad. They did not like the hold Erica seemed to have over their friend. So they did their best to plant negative thoughts in his mind, and to break the couple up. After the cancer Erica wanted to be fully present in life, and have some of the exciting experiences that she had denied herself in past years. But Darren's friends did not validate Erica. And Erica's friends did not validate Darren. She became impatient with Darren and after 18 months she terminated the relationship. But they parted as friends. This was the first time Erica had remained on good terms with her ex. And though their relationship did not last, Erica counted it as a bright success, her best relationship ever. The cycle had been broken. She felt she was on her way to becoming the highest and best version of herself possible.

Awakening the Master Feminine

Opening the Treasure Chest

Chapter 11 Opening the Treasure Chest

Icon:
The icon of the Treasure Chest is a decorative chest, made of fine wood, with gold trim and hinges.

Image:
For the purposes of visualization, the image is a large wooden chest trimmed in gold. The chest sits in the middle of a large altar. To the left of the chest are symbols of abundance, gold coins, title deeds of property, ancient books, sacks of grain, a harvest of fruits, gems, and fabrics. To the right of the chest is a likeness of the goddess with her wings outstretched. The goddess holds in her hand the key to the chest.

So the Treasure Chest energy is the <u>nesting</u> instinct of a woman, seeking to bring about sustainable domestic prosperity.

The earth is constantly renewing all life. All life seeks to survive. Nature is a model of abundance. The Treasure Chest is talking about the inner desire every woman has to be prosperous, and the way she goes about obtaining prosperity. This instinct instills in the woman both a drive to have abundance, and the model through which she attains it. The treasure chest is speaking to the means via which a woman collects and gathers abundance. To understand this energy we must take note of the two key words in the definition above. Those two key words are sustainable and prosperity. Sustainable is talking about a condition that remains through the cycles. Prosperity speaks to general well being, not just wealth. So this energy is driving the woman to extract stuff from her environment, but to do it in such a way that nothing is reduced. In other words the woman takes as much as she can from the environment but never at a rate faster than nature can replace the stuff. A balance of ecology is maintained. Because nature produces abundantly, she is guaranteed prosperity. Then we go back to the theme of sustainability. How then is her general welfare made secure? How do we ensure that the woman can enjoy her abundance after she gets it? This is only possible in a climate of peace and wellbeing of everyone in her vicinity. Otherwise, another woman is going to try and take her abundance from her. A theme of unity is implied here. The theme of sustainability implies unity.

- The way to best harvest abundance is through joint effort. Different tasks, but common purpose. It is a theme of unity.
- The way to best enjoy abundance after harvest is to share. Different contributions, but common sharing. It is a theme of unity

The gold and grain and fruits on the altar represent the abundance in nature. The Treasure Chest represents the natural way we harvest this abundance. As we have been saying all through this book, the natural model is a model of abundance. But the average person may say, so what? Yes there are billions of dollars in the economy and tons of food on farms and tons of fish in the sea and all manner of stuff in stores and warehouses, but it is not mine. The individual person cries out, where is my abundance? Of course the masses of people have given away their abundance by virtue of their participation daily in the system of scarcity. At least that is partly true, there is always a struggle going on. The image talks about the abundance of nature, and the feminine energy used to harvest it. So basically we are recognizing that Mother Nature has made a provision for the mother of a family to be able to obtain the resources she needs to provide for her family and enjoy the experience of life. The golden chest represents this harvesting and collecting energy. How do we take the potential that exists "out there" and make that something we have personally. The goddess holds in her hand the key to the chest. In other words, the key to material prosperity is represented by a spiritual image. The key is unity.

It says first that when seeking to obtain a domestic goal women must ban together to approach it. When ever a woman gets to the place where she is ready to harvest, collect or gather something, she should avoid doing this by herself.   And then it says that if you want to accumulate a lot of stuff, if you desire prosperity, then share equally with those who helped you harvest, in spite of what each adult put into the basket. So right now a lot of people are reading this and saying wait a darn minute there, that is not how we do things in Kansas. In fact we do things exactly the opposite. And of course that is one way we can confirm we are in the scarcity model.

The Harvest Circle

These two unity themes seem simple and straight forward at first, but you had better look a little closer. Within these two unity themes are centuries of indigenous wisdom. When a woman becomes yin and feminine she changes the way she goes about seeking prosperity. Basically she lets go of the yang urges that insist that in order for us to have more, we need to deny our neighbors their share of abundance. The concept of unity implies a circle. Group effort implies a circle of people bound by some common denominator.

Down through the ages men have been thought of as hunters and women as gatherers. Hunting is yang. Gathering is yin. Can you see that? Hunting implies that you are going to kill and violate what you hunt. It is blood. This is not feminine. Hunting implies scarcity that is why you got to go out and chase after it. Gathering is yin. Vegetables do not run away from you. There is abundance, plenty for everybody. You just calmly walk up and harvest it. You do not hunt rice, berries or mangos; you just pick or cut it. Hunting is about scarcity, gathering is about abundance. Now these same principles apply to harvesting men, money, property and intangible corporate assets. The Amazon women today hunt men in an aggressive way, instead of gently gathering them in. They are aggressively on the prowl to snag a "good" one. But we must understand that whenever a woman hunts something she pretty much is sure to damage it.

Down through the ages men have been thought of as hunters and women as gatherers. Hunting is yang. Gathering is yin. From this treasure chest instinct women get their desire to shop and buy stuff. There is the whole shopping thing in there, this gathering and collecting instinct. The unity thing is the key to successful gathering/shopping. Do not go and try to pick enough nuts just for your family. You may meet a wild dog under the nut tree. No, go with a group, and pick nuts for the whole harvest circle. Take the young girls with you. Pick enough nuts for Audrey, who is pregnant. And pick enough nuts for old lady Ellen, who doesn't walk so well any more. The Treasure Chest energy says the best way to pick nuts is to take a big group of folks and pick a lot of nuts for everybody. So let's find out more about the component of the feminine energy we call the Treasure Chest. What is the role of the goddess in the feminine energy? How do these two unity themes allow a woman to "harvest" the things she needs in life, such as a man or enough money to pay her bills? Let's look at four women we will transplant from previous case histories. We are going to change them slightly. In the first episode these four unique women are going back in time 500 years to a small village. Then in the second episode we will bring these same four women back into modern times and show how the unity themes are relevant to today's scenarios.

Life Episode - Kim, Erica, Jennifer and Audrey

All through the book each woman represents one of the four archetypes of feminine energy.
Kim = Treasure Chest
Erica = Seated Hawk
Jennifer = Elegant Rose
Audrey = Moon

In the past episodes Kim is the Amazon woman with the six figure salary. Kim is overweight, single and has one daughter. Remember Erica, the earth conscious woman who is a little bossy. Erica is in good health and shape and is recovering her feminine nature. Remember Jennifer, the woman with ample bosoms who likes to stroll from one metro stop to another. Jennifer is a gorgeous young single woman who is trying to come to grips with the power of her rose. And Audrey is an industrious married woman of thirty who is pregnant in this episode. We have transported them all back in time to an indigenous village. We have gone back in time now 500 years, to a make believe village in a lush river basin. Kim, Erica, and Jennifer are single women in this village of Evolutia. Audrey is married in this episode.

This episode takes place in the 1500's. There are no grocery stores. To get food, the women go into the forests and fields to gather produce and nuts. The men hunt for game. The animals migrate, and so for half the year animals are abundant and easy to kill. But during the other half of the year the men do not find much on their hunts. During those months the village depends on the women to eat and survive. Kim is the star nut picker. Of all the women in the village Kim knows all about nuts, berries, grains and such. She knows when they all get ripe, and where the best nut groves and vines are. Kim will climb trees, wade through creeks and fight bees to get the best produce. By the time most women have collected one basket of fruit and nuts, Kim has gathered three. Erica is the seer and wise woman of the village. When there are bad omens, or the people are faced with some crossroads situation, everyone turns to Erica. She throws her "bones" and goes into trance, and like magic, Erica just intuits the answer. Jennifer is the entertainer for the village. She sings and leads all the dances. She is a seductress, the most attractive and alluring female in the village. Her hands have healing powers. And sometimes Jennifer likes to be the matchmaker. Audrey is the mother figure and mid-wife in the village. Although she is still young, the other women look up to her, even Erica. Hers is the voice of compassion. She is the nurse who looks after the sick. She is the best cook around. And her hut is always filled with children. The men like her the most, for she pampers them. She is the chief's wife. These four women represent:

Kim = Treasure Chest
Erica = Seated Hawk
Jennifer = Elegant Rose
Audrey = Moon

These four women are the leaders of the women in the village, and each of them has a following, a clique. The women of the village go out gathering food during the week. Audrey stays behind. They gather nuts, roots and berries. All week long the women gather. And Kim gathers more than twice as much as the next best woman. Kim gathers three times as much as Jennifer, who is usually the least energetic about gathering. It seems hard for Jennifer to remain focused. She is distracted by flowers and herbs. And sometimes Jennifer just spaces out for ten or fifteen minutes, off into a world all her own. At these times Jennifer is having a right brain experience, almost like Erica, except Jennifer is seeing the social life of the village in the future. Two or three times each day the other women have to remind Jennifer to get back to collecting. Kim notices how much less Jennifer collects next to her, and talks about it out loud. It annoys her that Jennifer will not pay attention to the most important task. The nuts and berries and roots will only be ripe a short time before the animals and insects get them. There is plenty now, but they need to also think about the winter. Jennifer, because of her lapses, gathers just a little less than the other women. But unknown to Kim, Jennifer also gathers a few special healing herbs, and plants that make oils.

At the end of the week all the produce that has been gathered is brought out to be distributed to the families in the village. The baskets and bags are filled over. There is plenty of food and stuff for all and then some. As the wife of the chief, Audrey is asked to decide who will get what. Now here is where the yin thing is different from the yang thing. Remember that second theme of unity; the ways to best enjoy abundance after harvest is to share. Different contributions, but common sharing. It is a theme of unity. If this were a yang thing, there might be fighting over who gets what. In a yang scenario each person might keep what they picked, and then many people in the village would be lacking. But the women operate on the treasure chest principle of common sharing. But in the village of Evolutia, this week there is conflict.

Audrey divides the bounty into equal amounts and gives each eligible woman in the village harvest circle an equal share. Kim and Jennifer stand next to each other and Kim looks over to see that Jennifer got just as much as her, and did less work. Kim is bitter. She complains to Audrey but Audrey is adamant that the tradition of equal sharing, over a century old, not be broken now. Then the situation is made worse. Jennifer did a healing on an older woman a few weeks back. To repay Jennifer for the health, the older woman gives Jennifer a full basket of the finest produce from her share. Now Jennifer has even more than Kim! And Kim has a daughter to feed, and Jennifer has no children. Kim is filled with rage, she grabs Jennifer hard, shaking her, and pushes delicate Jennifer down to the ground. Her words to Jennifer are not nice. The other women have to pull Kim off. Jennifer dares not fight Kim, who is bigger and much more aggressive. Jennifer gets up and backs away, her face fallen, her garments torn, and feeling bad.

The next day three new men join the village. It is rare for a single man to join their village. The oldest of these single men is Ben, and Ben is old enough for Kim. But it was Jennifer that made the men consider this village. They saw Jennifer and heard her sing last season. Her beauty and charm drew the men there. Ben remembers Jennifer and desires her. He sets his sights on obtaining her. No one in the village is surprised; all the men always want Jennifer. Kim is older than Jennifer, and fears that she has become too old to get a husband. None of the men seem impressed that she is the best gatherer. First the incident with Jennifer, and now the only man old enough for her wants Jennifer. Compared to the natural allure of Jennifer, Kim feels plain and unattractive. And there are many young girls just coming of age even more attractive and inviting than Jennifer, all looking for husbands. That night Kim cries herself to sleep. Who knows how long it will be before another single man joins the village. But Erica rejoices that night. She has been expecting these men to come. Her right brain ability gave her an insight that these men will play an important role in defending the village. And Erica has seen the disaster to follow, if Ben does not remain with the village. Jennifer also knows that Ben is meant to mate with Kim. Ben does not know either Jennifer or Kim but Jennifer presents well. Kim is the most compatible to Ben. If Ben gets to know Kim, he will see this. Erica approaches Jennifer with a plan. Both Jennifer and Erica must assist Kim to attract Ben to her. There is no woman in the village who has mastered the art of looking good, and getting a man more than Jennifer. She knows all the tricks. Jennifer even has special oils to make a woman smell good and compel a man. Only Jennifer can give Kim the makeover that will make Ben take notice of her. Erica asks Jennifer to please forgive Kim for the sake of the unity. Audrey also asks Jennifer to assist. Jennifer knows all about how to attract and please a man. Erica and Jennifer, being truly feminine, do not fight over a man. Jennifer agrees to forgive Kim and help her to spruce up. The next day Jennifer tells Ben plainly that she is not available. The decks are now clear for Kim.

Jennifer teaches Kim all about the rose power. She makes Kim a special oil, which gives off a scent. And she gives Kim some special roots to feed Ben to help things along. The women fix Kim's hair and make Kim a new outfit. And most of all Jennifer teaches Kim how to be receptive to Ben, how to broadcast her rose to Ben so that he sees her as being a woman who is pleasing to be with. Kim comes out into the village with a new attitude and a fresh new look. All the men take note of Kim, including Ben. Erica convinces the other women not to compete with Kim. Kim is able to win the affections of Ben. And after Ben discovers how industrious and prosperous Kim is, the deal is sealed. Ben and Kim get married.

One common unity is the key to abundance. Each person needs the others. If the village is attacked their life may depend on the fierce warrior nature of Ben. Jennifer wants a man, but she knows she can get one anytime. But she is not right for Ben, and if Ben gets mad at her, and leaves, everyone will suffer. She knows that Kim can make Ben happy. She helps because she knows it is the best thing for the village. On her wedding night Audrey comes to Kim and reminds her of the first theme of unity. "The way to best harvest abundance is through joint effort." Kim learns a valuable lesson, for Kim now realizes that this applies to finding a mate as well as finding food. The joint effort is required so that women with special talents can focus on what they do best. The oil that Jennifer made for Kim helped her to attract Ben's attention. She was so glad Jennifer knew how to do this. Kim remembers that day when she pushed Jennifer down and yelled at her. And then Kim began to get it. She remembered that Jennifer attracted all the men to her village in the first place. They came looking for that thing that Jennifer symbolized. But it ended up that Kim had this quality too. Jennifer was an icon. She symbolized what all women in the village had inside, which was attractive and pleasing to men. And Kim saw Jennifer now as an asset not as competition. Not only did the village need Jennifer to sing and dance and bring joy, but also to bring this quality out in the younger women. Jennifer was their best ally to help them keep their men. And Kim then understood that she too was an icon. Kim symbolized what all women in the village had inside, which was industrious, clever and able to get the most from nature to supply daily needs. The young women were always learning from her. And at Kim's wedding many men came to her expressing thanks. They gave Kim great gifts. Each man remembered last winter when game became rare, and most times they returned from their hunts empty handed. But the families still had food stored up, and got through the winter okay. The men knew it was largely because of Kim.

We leave the old village of Evolutia and return to the present time. The modern woman is likely to say, "how is hooking up with a bunch of women going to help me get a man. I am trying to keep my men away from those man stealing vultures." But this view is looking at things from the scarcity place, instead of from the view of abundance. There will always be enough men. There are plenty of men. What makes one woman steal another woman's man is not the lack of men. That is an illusion. One woman steals another woman's man because she is not able to generate one of the four archetypes of feminine energy. She has not become the rose, so she can not generate enough pleasure for herself and her man. She goes after another woman's man because she can not give or receive enough pleasure to keep men around. She has not become the treasure chest. Therefore she is living in poverty. She steals another woman's man because of the money. She has not become the hawk. Therefore men do not take her seriously, and look at her as a long term mate. She has a selfish worldview, not a community worldview. Thus she tries to steal another woman's man, because he shows respect to the first woman, and she wants it.

Often one will hear an attractive woman say that she went out with a male but he was not right for her. He would be perfect for such and such female however, she goes on to say. And you ask her, why she doesn't introduce him to the other woman that he would be good for. And often the response is something like, "well she will get mad at me if I do." These two women are not part of a harvest circle. And this is what needs to change. Women can be very smart about their jobs and education but very dumb about relationships. If a group of women formed a business concern they would have no problem with the concept of joint effort to harvest. A certain type of woman is assigned the operations function, another the shipping function, another production, another customer service, and finally one woman is assigned the marketing role. Everybody can not perform the marketing role. The marketing woman gets all dressed up and goes out and convinces people to buy the company's products. She is pleasing. She takes clients to lunch, laughs at their jokes and maybe even flirts a little. She gets them into the door and then all the other people in the firm take over, and complete the sale. It is no different in the arena of relationships; women have to work together in unity to harvest men. Each woman in society can manifest the hawk, the rose, the moon and the treasure chest. But they will not all manifest each energy to the same level of intensity. The treasure chest is the most complex feminine energy. And while one could say that the rose energy has the greatest impact on our daily life, we could also say that perhaps the treasure chest is the most important energy of all. Without resources nothing in life will further. And without the unity themes in the community the possession of resources will bring wealth but not prosperity. Nor will it be sustainable. To be sustainable, wealth must be guided by spiritual themes, the themes of unity. This is the road to sustainable domestic prosperity.

Awakening Circle Exercise

> But you will see in life that just like our story, the women in real life who develop their treasure chest energy before they develop their rose energy **will have a negative disposition against pleasure**. In the same way, women in real life who develop their seated hawk energy before they develop their moon energy **will have a negative disposition against nurturing men, and being submissive to men**.

To prepare for this awakening circle exercise each man and woman in the circle needs to reread the past episode. In the episode Kim, Erica, Jennifer and Audrey represent the four archetypes.
Kim = Treasure Chest
Erica = Seated Hawk
Jennifer = Elegant Rose
Audrey = Moon

This entire exercise session is devoted to a discussion of the conflict that exists between the four different archetypes of women. The group should also discuss how this conflict influences the relationships women have with men. In the session each woman in the awakening circle shall choose a point of view based on one archetype only. In other words as you read the story pick one of the four women, someone you can identify with. Pay attention to her role in the story, for you will have to defend her positions and actions in the circle exercise.

"In modern society there is always this conflict between the women who represent the different archetypes of the house of the woman. On one side we have the rose women and the moon women. And they offer men pleasure and nurturing. On the other side of the house we have the hawk women and the treasure chest women. These women make demands of men. They require men to follow the plan and go out and get resources for the home. And the moon and rose women are always in conflict with the hawk and treasure chest women. And kept apart this way neither side can harvest effectively. The harvest circle needs females from all four corners of the house of the woman."

The treasure chest faculty knits women together. That is part of its role. That is the role of the goddess. The image of the goddess speaks to the gradual steering of mankind away from the inferior state of life to a superior state of life. These themes of unity are speaking about personal evolution. At the crossroads, you must choose to abandon the selfish way, and learn to be inclusive. In this way the treasure chest faculty knits women together. There is great power in this, it is called SPIRALING!! **In spiraling, we take the four corners of the house of the woman, and form them into a working circle.** So when a woman is trying to bring forth her treasure chest energy, she has to evolve to get over her petty personal issues that keep her from working with other women.

In the development of your sexual power, no other lesson is more important. Women need to unite around common causes.

If you are a woman like Jennifer, who is relatively more attractive physically than most women, resist looking down on other women who do not have a figure like you. You can not harvest men with looks alone. Your job in nature is to bring the men to the table, not just for you, but for all the women in your circle. You have that Marilyn Monroe thing going on. Then help the other women show men their pleasing side.

If you are a moon woman like Audrey, you know how to keep men after the rose gets their attention. You know how to cook and nurture and make a home feel like a home. You have that Martha Stewart/ Rachel Ray/ B Smith thing going on. Your job in nature is to make the group feel connected together, to instill the spirit of family into the harvest circle. You are the hub around which the circle revolves. Your womb is fertile. Show the other women how to nurture men. Show the other women how to heal their womb.

If you are a hawk woman, you know how to choose the men, and which way to go at the crossroads. You have to develop your intuition. Your job in nature is to counsel the women when to press ahead in a relationship and when to pull back. You know how to keep the women safe. You are the females who can read the signals of men. Help the other women to develop their right brain abilities and to stop living in a left brain trance.

If you are a treasure chest woman you are the most important of all. You must bring forth the goddess first. You know how to get resources and turn these into sustainable prosperity. But do it for all the women in your harvest circle. You have the Oprah thing going on. Your job in nature is to instill the two unity themes into your circle. It is a difficult task. Often the women we love to hate the most are the ones who are the key to making our dreams come true. The reality is, that each woman has all four types within.

As you awaken into the fullness of your feminine nature, I believe the full truth of how much you are a part of other women will reveal itself to you. Stand in integrity. Know that each woman can only achieve a partial healing, until all women in the group are included at the table. If you find mister right, do not sail away into a cloud of bliss and leave your sister behind to whither and wait in solitude. With all force the sisterhood must muster its legions, and cast its nets into the waters of men, until a suitable mate is found for every sister in your group. Her pain is your pain; your joy is her joy. These are not idle words. My words are words of truth. My words are words of power. It would be ashamed to fumble the ball seconds before crossing the goal line, all because of one bitter lonely sister who was left, behind!

Beware of Jealousy

When you awaken your master feminine faculty and become a more feminine woman it opens up new possibilities for you. But do not expect your peers to be happy for you. Of course, if you are the dingy daffy Dorothy type, who wears rose colored glasses and ruby red slippers, then you probably think your girlfriends are going to stand up and cheer when you tell them about all the good things happening for you. But trust me daffy Dorothy, some of them will truly be happy for you, and some of them will not. Some of your Amazon women friends will be circling your house, yelling curses, wearing war paint, with thoughts of torture on their mind. They will be afraid that if you start acting feminine, you will raise the bar. Then their men will start expecting them to act feminine. This is when you really need a support group around you. For the vast majority of people in society are deeply invested in a scarcity culture. For we live in a time of serious choices and many crossroads. And whether they realize it or not, people are being forced to make a choice. They will change to embrace a sustainable way of life, remain in the scarcity model and face the dire effects brought on by this cause. It will not be pretty. Our world can not go on as it is. We use too much oil, too much wood, too much food, too much land, and too much water. And in the process of our consumption, we infuse too many toxins into the environment. It is the same in relationships.

Awakening the Master Feminine

About Men

Everything You Wanted To Know

Chapter 13 About Men

In This Chapter:
1. The Male Persona & Boundaries
2. The House of the Man.
3. Monogamy and Infidelity
4. Single Parent Mothers
5. Forgiving Our Fathers
6. Female Selection Criteria
7. The Basis For Hope

The Male Persona and Boundaries

In this chapter I hope to give women a sense of what men are thinking and what their motivations are. When possible I have attempted to capture their voice, and not present my opinion of them. I expect the typical female will find the worldview surprising. The section about Forgiving Our Fathers is of special note. Every woman should pay attention to this one. The original article was inspired by a powerful series of seminars done around this theme. These workshops were for adult men. Many males grew up without fathers and some of them are dead set against the whole notion of forgiving their fathers. It was a serious sore spot for them. No doubt stuff can get pretty intense out there on the front lines of life. All of the topics are challenging. So we are going to explore things from the male prospective.

In their heart of hearts men do desire to love and cherish women. At least most men had this desire at some time in their past. It gets twisted out of them sometimes. Men are just not allowed to express pure masculinity like they once did. If they do they get pounded by the forces in society that demand they conform. And in the face of this pounding some men become bitter, cynical, selfish, hurtful and disillusioned. I imagine that this man was once a boy, innocent and pure of heart. What happened to him?

The modern woman suffers from a general lack of natural knowledge about the male. To understand why the male is the way he is she must grasp the make up of his energy. Its attributes are his attributes. Its boundaries are his boundaries. He likes what the energy likes. Masculine energy is elemental. It is always the same energy no matter what container or vessel you put it in. In a male termite the energy can only express a part of its nature. In a male human it can express a lot more of its nature. The energy did not change, you are just seeing more of its characteristics. The characteristics were always there. But the other vessels were not capable of that level of expression. There are four categories to male energy; the eagle, hunter, warrior and healer. The male energy is a broad bandwidth of attributes. The four categories are a way to measure what he is expressing at this stage in his development. Each archetype of energy is equal to a small spectrum of the masculine bandwidth. And so some elements of masculinity are stuff you can measure and categorize. To the extent that you can accurately know what categories a man fits into, you can accurately predict how he will respond in a given situation. But this is not the only dimension to the male energy.

There are three basic stages to human evolution itself. This is the Tree of Life. There is the inferior man (Sahu), the superior man (Ab), and the divine man (Ba). At each stage of evolution a male is a different species of being. The dynamic of masculine energy flows through him in different way. The man with the healer archetype active will behave very different at the inferior stage, superior stage and the divine stage of his development. It is easy to determine what level of evolution a man has reached. There are probably less than 1,000 men on the divine level in the world. Your chance of meeting one is slim. The superior man is mature. The inferior man is immature. We will make the distinctions very clear as the chapter progresses. In all its aspects, we hinder men from expressing their natural masculine energy.

The modern male also has a certain mode of expressing his masculinity that is in harmony with his natural inner nature. But few men live this way. The modern machine world hampers the male in his masculine development. Many men today seem confused as to their role in the relationship. There is no blame. Society has changed so dramatically in the last few decades that the adult men of this generation can not necessarily follow the generation of their fathers. Many men today never really knew their fathers that well. For most of his life, the modern man is made to suppress his masculine nature. Men do not hunt in the wild forest anymore. Young boys are not allowed to fight on the playground anymore. Everything is controlled. If a man disciplines a boy or holds him to a standard of conduct, the women around want to put him in jail. Men have very little time to be men. Men can be men on the football field. But most men only watch and do not have time to play. Even in the army, once a bastion of maleness, the role of the male has been reduced. For even in the act of killing, he is now removed from his adversary. He kills from a radar screen or from inside a tank. He does not come face to face with his opponent. A gun stands in the way. This reduces him. The military soldier has been replaced by intellectuals and technicians that destroy "efficiently". War is now a matter of covert intelligence and high-tech weapons. There is no honor in it.

There is no place for a real man in our society. Disciplined aggression and strength of character should be a part of the male persona, even if he wears a suit to work. But we have stamped out this part of the man from most men. We have replaced it with gross competition. There is a difference. There is no place for the truly "male" man in court, in the office, in school, or at home. He must watch actors portray "real men" on T V while he sits on the couch and dreams. Because of this, so many young men abandon the desire to achieve honor, and instead seek the raw power and crude advantages that give them the advantage in a competitive jungle.

Western style societies have no empathy for the spirit of the male in the man today. And while we idealize the masculine persona in movie's we will not tolerant him in real life. Today he is considered crude. He will find himself out of a job if he dares to stand up on principle or buck the system. Even worse, he may land in prison if he can not conform. Too many boys grow up in homes filled with women. They are spoiled by middle class parents. Or the demands of suburban family life kill the male, in a slow death of cutting grass, and commuting. The modern machine world of the fire culture is devastating to the inner masculine nature of men. In the bedroom males wear armor over their masculinity like the condom over their penis.

Boundaries

Men live within an imaginary circle. The circle is their boundary. An important aspect of male energy is its relationship to boundaries. Men have a relationship to boundaries. There is no equivalent in females. Males have a linear, left-brain posture that attaches relevance or lack of relevance to an action, based on its position in respect to their boundaries. Things are either inside the boundary, outside the boundary or they remain hidden from him. Outside the boundary is bad. Inside the boundary is good. The male will act friendly and supportive to things inside the boundary. He is either indifferent or antagonistic to things outside the boundary. At puberty each male begins to enforce his first primary boundary, his personal security space. This is a physical circle about three feet out from him. When other males enter this sacred space, he will push them out, or relocate. From this point, the male begins to construct more boundaries. These boundaries are not physical, but mental. Most men are walking around supporting seven or eight of these imaginary circles, their boundaries.

The things to appreciate about boundaries are these.
- What happens to create these boundaries in the man's mind?
- What is the policy for allowing the boundary to be crossed?

The stronger and more evolved a man is the more rigid are his boundaries. Women by nature are boundary violators. But each man resists allowing his boundary to be violated if he can resist. In many cases this is a matter of life or death. He will seek to kill you or hurt you for crossing his boundary without permission. Crossing the boundary with permission is a non-event. In other words it is okay and there is no reaction from the male. Women are often guilty of boundary violation without knowing that they have done so.

Boundaries are created, they were not there before. Boundaries are almost always created by some agency outside of the man. Few individual men are evolved enough to create their own boundaries. All boundaries are created from a simple idea.
- The idea says that if we separate some element from its whole a great good will come from this.
- Or the idea is that if we do not separate some element from its whole something very bad will come from this.

Common boundaries involve personal property such as land or a car. The mental image of the boundary is stated outside the mind of the man so that others can know the boundary and respect it. This is a deed or title. The deed to the property says this is my boundary, the imaginary line around this property map. Do not cross it without my permission. I love everything inside this line. I hate everything outside this line. Then there are tribal type boundaries. The idea that creates these boundaries is still very simple, but is made formal by incorporation. This incorporation is the formal statement of the boundary so that all the men inside the boundary know who they are, and so that all the men inside the boundary can recognize all the other people who remain outside the boundary. There is usually a ritual to go along with a tribal incorporation. Examples of the creation of these boundaries are the street gang, a sports team, a business firm which sells stock, a church, a franchise business, etc. To be considered a boundary, the protocols of the boundary need to be enforceable by law. In the case of a street gang, if the state will not honor its laws, it will make up its own and enforce them.

Women think they know men, but most really do not. In the case of the inferior man, the only things that are really important to him are the things inside his boundaries. Even food, sex and money are not as important to him as the things inside of his boundaries. Money does not become critical to him until it is one of the activities of a corporation boundary. Only when it becomes important to his corporation does it take on extraordinary significance to him.   A boy does not really care about grades in school unless and until the school is incorporated and he adapts this boundary. In other words, unless the school becomes a tribal institution and admits him formally into its boundary, he will not be overly concerned with grades. If he is smart he might make good grades, but it is not a priority. But the coach knows how to motivate a boy. The sports team is a formal tribal intuition for which he must try out and be accepted. It has a well defined boundary. In the games each team has a territory and rules of engagement. There are uniforms to better establish the boundary. He loves everyone on his team and hates everyone on other teams. Most women think that by virtue of being in his family or being married to a man that you are within one of his boundaries. And they would be wrong. If families today operated like a farm or business then the male might consider it a boundary. But most families today are not formal tribes. They are just people living in the same space. There is no mental boundary for the child to observe. There is no formal process of being received into a family such as a rites of passage. Therefore when men grow up they just move away, there is no psychic connection to a boundary. In the old days some men looked at marriage as a boundary. But that is no longer the case. When the no-fault divorce laws and the family court system went into law the institution of marriage changed for males. Understand that from a pure left brain male perspective you can not just dissolve a boundary by a petition to a lawyer. A contract is a contract. The boundary is sacred. A man will defend a rigid boundary to the death. With the onset of common divorce the common boundary that did exist around marriage as an institution was dissolved. In fact many men see the woman coming into their home as an intrusion on their boundary. For about half the men today, the female mate is just a person who has permission to cross his physical boundary, nothing more. She is not inside one of his mental boundaries unless she is part of his gang, church, business or team, etc. If women were inside male boundaries in the home men would never hit or abuse them. That is against the code. Most men do not want to spend time with their wives to have fun. They want to spend time with the other men who are within their boundary. The male has real allegiance and integrity only to people who are within his boundary with him. Are you starting to understand? So the question the woman must ask is, which side of the circle does he see you on, the inside or the outside? Most females would be surprised to know. The man brings things inside his boundary to fill his needs such as food, water and sex. But only the members of his tribe have a special place in his heart. And a woman really does not wish to be within the boundary of a man, especially a rigid boundary, unless she is willing to play by the rules. For if a woman enters the boundary as a wife, if that becomes a sacred contract to the man, know that she can never break it.   There is no divorce. Women do not respect boundaries, but men sure do. He will never divorce you under those conditions. He will try to kill you, hurt you bad, or kill himself. In the army a man will often risk death rather than see the boundary of his unit violated. A man will risk death to defend his property. A member of a gang will kill to protect the gang.

The great male societies of the past were simple male boundaries connected to a religious theme. Some of the well known societies included the Gestapo (SS) of the Nazi, the Samurai Warriors of Japan, the Braves of the Lakota Sioux war clan, the Asanteman Warriors of the Asante Empire, the Knights Templar of Europe, the brutal Mau Mau revolutionaries of the Congo, or the Order of the Jesuits of the 1600's. They all had a code of service based on incorporation within a strict boundary. Some of these orders of men had high ideals. Others had no sense of honor or shame, and held nothing sacred except power. We may hate them or admire them, but we must recognize the value of their boundary system. The blueprint of these boundaries was shear genius. In each case a diverse group of men were transformed to be focused on the achievement of a singular purpose.   Some of these male societies were famous, others were equally infamous. I am not glorifying some of the men who rose to power with in these groups. Often their creation was more due to the times than the wisdom of the leaders. It is always easy to separate men and turn them against something. True greatness is the act of uniting men, and turning them for something. This is a lot harder to do.

The House of the Man

What is masculinity?   Masculinity is an energy.   As with the feminine energy, we divide the masculine energy into four archetypes, the cornerstones of the house of the man. The male spirit contains the potential to tap into the masculine attributes of all male ancestors by blood or race going back 10,000 years. These male energies equip the male to carry out the roles required by his gender. This is what makes a male a man. You can not train a boy to be a man. Education only is not enough.   He has to do something to change his energy. He will not be able to be taught properly until his masculine energy is awakened in all four categories. Until masculine energy changes the programs in his subconscious mind, reproductive system and auric field, you can teach him all you want to but it will have little impact on his behavior. His father and other men in the culture naturally draw out his masculine energy. And so a man is born with the instincts to be a man firmly embedded into his DNA. Every male has a complete set of these masculine traits. But for these dormant traits to play any role in his life, they must be awakened, cultivated and brought on line in his mind, body and auric field. In most men today, only a few of these traits have been brought to the surface. In most men, their natural masculine attributes and power lies dormant, unused, untapped, because we fail to cultivate them.

The Four Masculine Archetypes
The Way of Warrior
The Way of the Hunter
The Way of the Eagle
The Way of the Healer

The Warrior	The Eagle
Protective, rigid, paternal, aggressive.\n\nThe act and the art of engagement. The capacity to confront the obstructions in life, based on a set of codes and boundaries.	Logical Left Brain Thinking. Deductive, intellectual, segregative, critical.\n\nSeeing the steps to make a plan happen. Having a vision beyond the present, a worldview.
The Healer	The Hunter
Holistic, balanced, sociable, artistic, romantic.\n\nThe ability to restore a thing to a sound original condition.	Predatory, Disciplined, Persevering, Paternal.\n\nThe ability to be accountable for and responsible for, the welfare of others.

The Way of the Hunter
The ability to be accountable for and responsible for, the welfare of others. The word husband is derived from a word for farmer. A steward of the land. The hunter is the steward of the family. He produces the things the family needs through agriculture, or the capture of wild animals. In modern times he gets a job. At the core, the yang masculine energy is always looking for something to do. While the woman is looking at how the world is and what it takes to get what she needs, the man on the other hand is always looking at how he can change the world. That Is his dream.

The Way of the Eagle.
Looking down the road to anticipate. The necessity of planning to enable forward progress. The structure of a natural plan. The need for vision, and the expansion of the male worldview. The role of male vision in the ascension and development of mate and children.

The Way of the Healer.
The restorer. Healing is about natural alignment. To heal is to return to one's natural and original state from a state of abnormality. To heal, a male must know what the original and natural state is.

The Way of the Warrior
        The energy of the warrior brings into the personality of the male an inclination for engagement. He is willing and even anxious to confront others. We see this energy in the white blood cell of the immune system. Engagement may involve physical confrontation, or legal, economic, political or verbal confrontation. Of course when we think of a warrior we think of a soldier. But a soldier fights because it is his job. A warrior fights because it is his nature to fight. His heart is the heart of a champion. He is looking for a cause. This energy of the warrior is not just the disposition for fighting, but more so an inclination to do battle for a just cause. He wants to correct something. His inner desire is to return the corrupt thing back to its original pure state. At the heart of his desire to engage is a sense of justice. And it is not his strength or drive that makes him a hero to us. It is his unbending sense of justice that makes our hearts go out to him. He is the theme of every cosmic book hero. He is the spirit of Archangel Michael, who when called by God, challenges the evil Lucifer and throws down the one they said could not be overcome. He is the hero Hercules, the son of the deity Zeus. He is Heru, the son of the deity Auset, who avenges the death of his father, and throws down the evil Set of ancient Kemit. The theme is universal, and yet it is very often misunderstood by women.
        The essence of the energy of the warrior is the capacity to defend others, without concern for the harm that may come to oneself. THIS ENERGY IS NOT OFFENSIVE IN NATURE! It will only defend; it does not attack without cause. The warrior fights because it is necessary to restore the natural balance. The soldier fights because he is told to, and

he is paid to. The warrior fights with honor. The soldier knows no honor. His motto is, "All is fair in war." This is the saying of an animal, not a god. And so often today we portray men as warriors who are something less. The soldier, the cowboy, the pro athlete are held up as warriors, when they are only imitations. There are few warriors today, and a lot of imitations. It is necessary for the woman to recognize the difference.

A man needs to possess his warrior energy if he is going to be a husband, father, or play any role in the community. It is absolutely critical. And women still want and need the warrior, but can not find him, because they have forgotten what he looks like. Their image of the warrior male is crafted by the movies. But in real life he seldom looks or acts like that. Most often he is not rich, exceptionally handsome or famous. He looks ordinary, and acts ordinary, until he is faced with the crossroads. When the dodo hits the fan he heads for the eye of the storm while other men are running away. He shoulders his responsibilities while other men abandon theirs. He stands up for the underdog. He takes on the unpopular causes in society because they matter to people. Often today he loses his fights. And this is what the female does not understand. In the movies the hero always wins. But most of the true warriors today are losers. Their causes did not prevail. If they had won, our world would be better. And because they are not celebrated, she does not recognize him. We think the hero is always going to be 6' 4" tall, handsome, and action oriented. But the warrior may be short, ugly, poorly dressed and shy. He is a warrior by his heart and energy.

Standing up straight is the ideal of masculine energy. It is not about posture. It means to stand firm about an ideal. To keep one's word. In the face of adverse situations, to nonetheless remain in male integrity. It is this energy of the warrior that makes a male "stand up straight". But the modern woman does not place a high value on the warrior energy. She is more impressed by the money of the hunter, or the charm of the healer.

The Master Masculine Faculty

Within the DNA and spirit of each man resides the full compliment of the attributes of masculinity. This bank or store of attributes contains all male traits that any man in his bloodline has ever had, going back 10,000 years. Any man can bring forth any male trait that any of his ancestors possessed since the dawn of time. But these traits are only dormant possibilities. He is not born with the actual use of any of these traits. At birth a male child is not much different from a female child. For any one of these male traits or attributes to play any role in his life, they must first be awakened, cultivated and brought on line in his mind, body and auric field.

Each male human contains within himself an internal faculty for becoming a man. The internal mechanism that brings his particular bank of masculine attributes into manifestation in his person we call the master masculine faculty. His master masculine faculty is the intelligence within a man's subliminal program that chooses from this vast bank of potential male attributes, selects some, and takes these attributes out of their dormant state in the DNA storehouse and activates them. The master masculine faculty takes a sleeping trait in his DNA and brings it on line. The master masculine faculty first springs into action when the boy enters the stage we call puberty. In fact, the onset of the master masculine faculty is what brings on puberty.

But the master masculine faculty of each man encounters many obstructions as it tries to develop him into the highest and most natural version of a male that it can. Year after year it recedes further into the background as he replaces natural traits and natural lifestyles with artificial replacements. And in most men today, before they reach the age of 25, the master masculine faculty shuts down prematurely, goes into remission, and becomes inert and inactive. In most men today, only a few of these traits have been brought to the surface. In most men, their natural masculine attributes and power lies dormant, unused, untapped, because we fail to cultivate them. Out of the four archetypes of masculine energy, most males enter adulthood with the use of only one archetype out of the four. But the typical male does not comprehend this. He believes this is just an aspect of his personality. But having only limited use of his male energy, he takes on a limited, narrow and dysfunctional worldview. His outlook on relationships is impaired in accordance with the archetype that is dominant in his spirit. As a young male, he attempts to relate to females based on whatever archetype he is. If he is the eagle type, he tries to be logical, looking ahead, scheming, etc. If the healer type he uses romance, charm, wants to 'remake' her, etc. But by definition he is not able to conduct a successful relationship. He is not capable of this as a young man. Some of them realize their short-coming and struggle to evolve in a short time. Others stay in the same dysfunctional state for years.

Each man is born with the potential to be a great father, a great provider, a super warrior and a super stud in bed. To become the highest and best version of a man possible, he must bring forward all his potential. But most men today do not. In the male, the master masculine faculty awakens at puberty and brings on one or two attribute sets on line. And even if the man makes the most of the archetype he has, it is not enough. Such a man can be a champion in one arena, and still fail at life. This is the situation most men find themselves in. He is a good warrior, but a poor healer. He is a good hunter, but a poor eagle. The man does his best to impress women and find a mate. Therefore he wears a mask. The mask is there to play up his good side. And more importantly, the mask serves to hide his imperfections due to the missing archetypes. And men are becoming more yin. And they do not know why. For the female seeking a relationship and family, this presents some pretty critical challenges.

Each female starts her adult life with a built in attraction to one of the four male archetypes. It is based on her father, and her womb imprint. In other words each female is more attracted to the warrior type, eagle type, hunter type or healer type, based on what her father was, and or which archetype the men who first imprinted her were. But she is never satisfied with him. Because what she really needs is a fully developed man, with all four archetypes active in his energy field. Also most women bring a lot of fear or anger into their sexual life that further complicates their ability to see men clearly. There is no blame in this. Men are even more in the dark. In our society men and women are under many illusions and false beliefs from the influence of money, power and religion. We struggle under the burden of the scarcity model. It is cause and effect. In the incomplete development stage that most men are in, they are not capable of providing the female with the relationship experience she so desires. Now, for the most part, men want to love women, and women want to love men. How do we stop getting in the way of that?

Infidelity and Monogamy

The Male View of Sustainable Relationships

There is currently no working system of monogamy in the west. What we have in our society is the façade of monogamy. Not the real thing. Most people who think they are in monogamous relationships are in fact sharing their mate. Infidelity is common with both males and females committing the offense. Over the long term of a relationship both men and women are more likely to be guilty of infidelity than to remain true to their partners. There is the added dynamic of bi-sexuality today. Not only do women cheat with men, but they cheat with other females. Not only do men cheat on their mate with other women, but they cheat with other males as well. In this environment, a person should consider than their mate has indeed cheated on them, unless they have investigated and obtained evidence to the contrary.

For the most part women seem to embrace the concept of monogamy as an imperative. Without a contract of monogamy women feel it is impossible for them to fully invest in a relationship, or obtain the full measure of what life with a man has to offer. Most females maintain the position that it must be monogamy or no relationship at all. There is no training ground. There is no in between. Men are forced to choose. If they fall in love with a woman, they must concede to a long term relationship, or hit the bricks. Women force men into monogamous relationships rather they are ready or not. And the fact of the matter is, the majority of young adult men are no where near ready for a long term relationship.

Men crave stimulation. The yang male is always looking out, seeking new interaction and adventure. He thrives off of arousal and change. Males crave stimulation and are very intolerant of things which remain static. The male worldview on monogamy is negative. He sees the long term relationship as a trap, a prison. This is because it often becomes a prison for his spirit when he is dealing with the underdeveloped female. Males like risk. Females are naturally risk adverse, especially when they have children. Women want security. Men seek just the opposite. Males seek to be challenged, and like to chase stuff. At their core, they are predators. They do not stop being a predator until they enter the superior man stage we talked about. In the same way a lion, wolf, dog or hawk is a predator, the male is a predator. He is a wild thing from his teen years into early adulthood, and our attempts to tame and domesticate him are only partly successful.

Male patterns of infidelity start in childhood. He enters puberty with the disposition toward infidelity because he is copying the model he sees in outer society and his own family. If as a boy, his mother divorced his father then this sets the stage for his subliminal programs in support of infidelity. You may tell a child it is bad to cheat on your mate, but they follow the models they see out in the neighborhood. In the male, the pattern of infidelity may start as early as the age of two. Later as a teen, his master masculine faulty awakens, and the juvenile boy is imprinted as a male. When his master masculine faculty awakens, it brings on puberty.

It looks out to identify the alpha females in his vicinity. These are his peers or older. These are usually the most attractive females with the most fully developed yin, feminine energy. The boy then seeks to become an 'Alpha' male to the dominant females. His imprint is determined by the rejection or acceptance of the alpha females. This imprint is further formed by the energy signature of the first female he makes love to. So his iconic female is a composite of the dominant diva of his peer group, and his first sexual conquest. Often the woman is the hunter and he is the prey. Refer to the book, <u>Awakening the Master Masculine</u>, to read the full discussion of the male imprinting process. A pattern of infidelity may be inserted into his subconscious during this period.

The Most Common Pattern of Infidelity

Most males never reach the point where monogamy is the active program. In males who attempt monogamy, it is forced over an underlying pattern of infidelity programmed into the template during puberty. After a period of resistance, the adult male succumbs to the attractive force of the female and enters into a long term relationship. At the point where the male enters the relationship, he is not fully mature. His masculine energy is still in a developmental stage. In these situations, the female in question has some significant Amazon attributes. In other words, her yang energy is highly cultivated, while her yin energy is less developed. In the early phase of the relationship her yang take charge posture may be a plus. But she wants to wear the pants in the household. She insists on playing the role normally intended for the male. She will of course run into increasing conflict with the male in this regard. As his masculine energy matures he becomes increasingly less tolerate of any other male energy in the household. It is like having two men in the house. In the sexual sense, her excess yang energy becomes increasingly less attractive.

One day the male finds that he feels an irresistible attraction to another woman. It is not that she is more attractive than his mate, but her energy magnetizes him. She is a yin feminine female. He may resist her, but in a few weeks or months he meets another. On the other side, he is no longer fully aroused by the mate. There may be some residual attraction there, but not much. He feels like he has been going to bed with a male in a woman's body. And then one day when he gets the opportunity to be with a woman, who is more yin than his mate, he goes for it. It happens fast and without warning. The next thing he realizes, he is sneaking around with a yin female. He finds these episodes very compelling and hard to resist. He is not thinking straight. And then of course he is caught. Of course things go down hill from there. He will get caught sooner or later, and the discovery of his infidelity will injure his mate and shatter his image of himself. He will begin to see himself more clearly, and understand better that he is immature.

Infidelity Pattern Number Two

The second most common pattern of male infidelity involves money. Most men can not indulge themselves in infidelity as they desire to because the women they desire are not available to them. To take this chance, a man is looking for a woman who is somewhat attractive, and she needs to be more yin and feminine than the first woman. But the reality is that most attractive women have options. And there are not a lot of feminine yin women out there anymore. So money becomes a factor. The men with the money have the most options. The pattern involves a married man who begins an affair with a single, never married female who has at least one child. The female got pregnant early, probably during her teen years, and as a consequence, has financial issues. The father of her baby is not supporting her. Often the young woman is out on her own, or living with her mother in a strained relationship. After the young single mother endures three or four years of this, she is looking for financial relief. The woman is looking for a male sponsor.

The married man now approaches her and finds she is more receptive than he might have supposed. Maybe in a normal situation she might have been out of his league. But due to his financial standing, she gives him some of her time. If she likes him, and he is generous with her, she decides to become his silent mistress. He helped her with money issues and a shoulder to lean on, and she provides him with the sexual favors he so desires. Often these women prefer married men because they are not yet ready to marry. And they choose men who might not otherwise be eligible because it gives the woman more leverage. If the man is equal to the woman in attraction, she does not have much leverage. Also once the affair is over, it is easier for her to leave.

The primary motivation for the male in this situation is to have intimate access to an exciting attractive woman that normally might not give him the time of day. This is a dream come true. Not only is she perhaps more attractive than his wife, but more importantly, she is attentive to his needs. His contributions to her count and she shows appreciation for him. He feels her genuine appreciation. This probably improves his sexual performance in bed immensely.

Third Common Pattern of Infidelity

The third common pattern of infidelity involves an older man and a younger woman. The male is 35 years plus. The female is at least 10 years younger than him. Most men make mistakes, and regret many of the decisions made in the early part of their adult life. They reach a place in their life that is unexpected. It may not be bad or good, just not where they thought they would be. The woman they are with is on one course. And the man is on the same course. And then one of them changes course. And the other partner does not. They start to grow apart. But because of kids or other reasons he does not seek to end the primary relationship. But this man yearns to redo his life.

Into the scenario comes a younger woman. She may not be more attractive than his wife. In fact, he is probably looking for a copy of his wife, but younger. The younger woman may possess the positive attributes his likes in his wife, but lacks the negative attributes he associated with his shortcomings. He pursues the younger woman as a metaphor for attempting to redirect the course of his life. The younger woman is receptive to the new concept he has of himself. His wife is not. He wants to reshape and remake himself. His wife will not or can not divorce herself from his past mistakes and the image of that. He can not change or revise himself in her eyes until he undoes the mistakes of his past and shows he is capable of better behavior. And so the man withdraws emotionally. He just goes through the motions of it. Often the wife does not even notice, so fixed is she on her own course. And he begins a hot passionate affair with the younger woman.

Of course there are numerous patterns of infidelity. Whenever the relationship reaches the crossroads, you must beware. If the woman becomes pregnant there is an added risk of infidelity. The possibility of a child does funny things to the mind of the male. He wonders if he can shoulder the great responsibility of a family. He believes these are his last few months of freedom.   There is pressure on him. He has established a pattern of regular sex. Now his mate is no longer able to make love to him. The pressure builds and he may seek a release outside the marriage. It is not really a sexual thing but a safety valve. The same holds for a death in the family. There is a loss. There is grief. The burden of sadness weighs heavy on him. It is a marker that shows life is not forever. He looks around to see where he is on the journey of life. And he may seek to have an affair at this time. The male spirit is strong in some ways and weak in others. Men fear death. They can face death easy in battle or in a fight. A man would die gladly to protect his wife or children. But he fears the slow loss of life. He fears losing his chance to live life fully. These are the signs that a woman should beware of. That he is growing older, and his dreams seem to be slipping away. At these times he can grow closer to his mate. Or he can seek consolation in the arms of another woman.

If you have had an affair and he discovered it this is another issue. Men do not handle this very well at all. The thought of another male between his woman's silky thighs, pleasing her, pressing into her, can torment a man. This is especially so if he thinks his woman really enjoyed it. The visual of another man in hot embrace with his woman will play over and over again in his mind. If this happens, the couple should get immediate therapy and counseling. Otherwise he may become a powder keg waiting to explode. And if he seeks to have a revenge affair, it will probably be with one of your close friends.

Monogamy is not the province of the spiritually immature. A man should have well developed masculine energies **in place** before they can really work that monogamy thing for real. Of course if you just want to pretend then go on. But you need to really have your ducks in a row before you can vow to love the same person for the entire rest of your life. Before you jump up and vow to love someone forever you need to make the investment so that you can back that vow up. What makes you think that you are not going to make any of the major personal mistakes that terminate relationships? For a man to be able to live up to his vows, he must have a level of spiritual maturity. His full masculine energy needs to be on line. A lot of men are writing those monogamy checks, and a bunch of those checks are gonna bounce. It does not matter if he went to college or not. It does not matter what church he belongs to. It does not matter what his corporate title is, he can not back up such a vow, unless his masculine energy is there.

Men have generally loss the respect for the feelings of women. And men have pulled back emotionally from relationships, dating and marriage. This is especially true of young men. Many young men would prefer to play video games on a date with a young girl than to try and work through complex personality issues. The female side of the relationship dynamic has become a complex minefield. Typically, the modern young male is not even remotely interested in going there. The tactic and motif of today's young man is to look for the lowest hanging fruit to pick. He is not trying to climb any trees. If the woman presents any serious psychological challenge, their most likely response is just to move on to the next case. If she is very feminine and supportive, they may just overlook any issues and try to just push ahead. The maturity level of males is dropping rapidly every decade. As this happens they must pull back for they do not have the traits and skills to deal. So a young female today looking for a real old fashioned relationship is in for a shock. Sorry Daffy Dorothy, you came to the wrong time period. In the European and Asian communities there are still pockets in society clinging to the old values. Some religious institutions and isolated communities cling to the old ways. But in the Native American, African American and mixed race communities the pockets are small or non existent. Young African American females have almost no market for monogamous relationships. If they force marriage, and many do, there is an 80% to 90% certainty of divorce in seven years. And while they are married, they are almost certain to be sharing their man, rather they know this or not.

Monogamy may appeal to women because it implies a guarantee. It implies stability and children need stability. But I think before we get back to a time when we will see men really stand and be men, and the institution of marriage becomes honorable again, both men and women will have to give up some of these absolute demands they cling to so violently.

What is the reason and purpose for a woman to enter into a relationship? What is the underlying motivation for monogamy? Is monogamy about a sustainable relationship? Or is monogamy really about personal economic advantage? In my opinion, it is more important that the relationship have the quality of being sustainable, than that it just meet a requirement of being monogamous. I do not believe that all sustainable relationships absolutely must be a situation of monogamy. When females force the construct of monogamy on the relationship, often it has the net effect of hurting, destroying trust, and making new wounds. The males are not ready. And society seems unwilling to invest funds in programs that will mature men. Nor are women currently funding these types of ventures. It seems most men and women these days choose personal economic advantage over sustainability any day. Sustainability means your relationship is still going strong 20 years from now. Personal economic advantage means that you are doing better than your neighbors and friends at any specific time. There is a big difference.

It seems that most women who are heavily invested in monogamy are invested out of a quest for personal advantage, and not for the sake of sustainability. Why does a wealthy woman buy a Lexus, instead of a Toyota Avalon? They are almost the same car. They are made by the same company. They are often built on the same assembly lines. Except the Lexus is a luxury brand, and costs up to $20,000 more. Both cars give you an excellent ride. The reason that woman will spend the $20,000 extra is because she is seeking a personal advantage, not prosperity. Purchase of the more expensive car reduces her net worth. It is the brand she is paying for, the luxury brand. It is because other people can not own one easily. There is a value attached to that. People spend $80,000 on a car mainly because other people can not. The illusion is it sets you apart, gives you a special quality. It is personal economic advantage.

In relationships, men feel cheated when their woman has an affair, because their personal advantage has been taken away. The man feels violated in the innermost part of himself, because his woman was penetrated by another man. She had to take him inside her, it is a deep violation. The illusion was that she set him apart from other men; he thought he held some special quality in her eyes. He looked for his validation inside her womb. It was an illusion. Personal advantage means that you are doing better than your neighbors and friends. If you fall behind for even one day, it is a disaster. If all of your neighbors and friends are millionaires, then you have not achieved personal advantage until you are a multi-millionaire. You see, if you live in West Pohick Junction, and every body in West Pohick Junction got gravel driveways, well you done did something when you go and get your driveway paved with asphalt. You a big man and you got personal economic advantage. You come home, and your wife got on a French maid outfit, hair up in a bun, and she smiling like, the freaky freaky about to happen. It is because you guys got the personal advantage over those hick neighbors. But if you live in West Malibu your neighbors got those long curving driveways, paved with the imported granite inserts from Europe, in fancy designs. They look too nice to drive a car on. You got your nice paved driveway in the best asphalt money can buy, but guess what? Next to your neighbor's, your driveway looks plain and cheap. It is the same driveway, your car rolls on it nice. But you are not satisfied. Why? Because they got the personal economic advantage over you. Therefore many women are heavily invested in monogamy, as a means to personal economic advantage.

Female Selection Criteria for Mates

As we have stated before, there are three events that shape the image of what a female desires in a male.

1. She wants a man like her father if her relationship with dad was good. If the relationship with dad was bad, she wants a man who is what her father was not.
2. She is imprinted by the first two or three men she has sex with. Based on his energy, she desires a man who is similar.
3. Her master feminine faculty awakens and brings on puberty. During the early stages of puberty she forms an image of the alpha male based on the men in her environment who make a positive impression on her.

In all three instances above, there is a good chance that the male role models involved are negative in character. Thus the icon she shapes of an ideal male is one who has a negative character. If she were in fact to enter into a relationship with this 'ideal' male the experience that would result would be a negative one for her. In other words females are looking for a mate who is essentially dysfunctional.

Select versus Non-Select

Females who are sexually viable are constantly grading and evaluating males as to their sexual worthiness. It does not matter if they are 13 or 60, married or single, a stripper or a nun. There are exceptionally few exceptions. It is common for young adult females to compare their abilities to sum a man up quickly and accurately. They call this female radar. And women are very good at it. Most women decide in the first five minutes whether a man is to be placed in the "select" or "non-select" category. It is then based on this initial determination that a male is included into a woman's sphere of activity, or he is excluded from contact with her. Some women will maintain minimal communication with a few men from their non-select category for either friendship purposes or to support some special interest they may have. But mates are chosen exclusively from the "select" category. And most women even restrict their male platonic friends to men from their select category. As a consequence of this practice, women typically have a circle of male friends who represent an exceptionally small bandwidth on the spectrum of possible males out there.

Women tend to place men in one of four basic categories when it comes to dating. Two of these categories are deemed "select" categories, and these men are sought after and given special treatment in relationships. The other two categories are the men who do not make the first cut. These are the "non-select" men. They are not sought after. The non-select group represents two-thirds to three-fifths of the total male population. It is a larger group than the select group. Refer to the chart that follows...

The model in the table is peer driven. It does not seem to be devised to achieve any objective other than simply a means to obtain desires. Many women I interviewed told me that they decide in the first five minutes whether a man is to be placed in **the "select" or "non-select" category**. If they decide you are select, you still have to pursue them, but it is a formality only. She has already decided that you can get some. It is mainly necessary not to do anything stupid or rash. The man makes the first move, and the woman will guide the rest of the process from there on out. "Players" will tell you, chasing after a woman who has not already chosen you is a waste of time. Real men do not bother. My advice to men is **never** to chase after some woman who is not actively seeking to seduce you. Single females who are not seeking to seduce a man are either dysfunctional, or still in their "little girl" phase. You do not want to get caught up with that at all. The worse thing that can happen is that the man will obtain her. He will indeed be sorry he did. When a woman is healthy, mature and feminine she is always in an auto-seduction mode. She is attractive and alluring by definition. She does not have to try, or put any effort into it. She is born as a man magnet. To be anything else is a sign of unnatural development!!

When it comes to mate selection, nine times out of ten it is the females who choose. Most playboys, players, pimps, and skirt chasers will tell you straight up, that chasing after a woman who has not chosen you is a fruitless exercise. Most women decide in the first five minutes whether a man is to be placed in the "select" or "non-select" category. And if they decide you are non-select, no amount of persistence or charm or gifts will sway her.

The four categories are named allegorically: 1.)Mr.Goodbars,   2.) The Masked Men,   3.) The Nice Guys,   4.) The Gamesmen.

Category of Eligibility	Description
Mr. Goodbar (Select)	Exciting, Charming, Appealing. He satisfies a desire for passion and romance. Like rich chocolate, she wants to indulge as much as possible. But these men tend to be Self Centered. Women serve at their pleasure. They relate to women on their terms.
The "Masked" Men (Select)	Successful, Handsome. He satisfies a desire for money and power. He has become that thing that women want on the surface by wearing a mask. But he is Non-Committal. And these men bear emotional scars beneath the mask.
The "Nice" Guys Non-Select	Bland, Reliable, Not Exciting. Nice Guys are too yin. They may have good intentions, but nice guys always lose out. She welcomes platonic relations with him, but flatly rejects his romantic advances. Nice guys get no panties.
The Gamesmen Non-Select	Persistent, Phony, A Facade of Macho. He lacks substance. He wants to get his, "by any means necessary."

Today the selection criteria have shifted away from character issues and compatibility to material issues. Men are judged today based strictly on what is on the surface. The criteria include; looks, money, power, sex, religious affiliation, peer appraisal, etc. Being judged as part of the select group does not guarantee the women will choose you, but being classed into the non-select group guarantees that they will not.

This is how the westernized woman gives away good men. She rejects men who have not reached a level of surface appeal or material achievement. Men of honor, dignity, good intentions, and high moral value and etc and kicked aside if they do not meet the strict criteria. The young woman wants men to "already be there", instead of choosing the most compatible males, and "helping him get there". If the army used her model and refused to accept soldiers who were not already trained, few men would make the armed forces. Her selection criteria are based on a scarcity model. And this scarcity model is where all of the problems start. Perhaps women as a group recognize that male adults are lacking in some of the development needed to become a good mate. But there does not appear to be any overall understanding of what it would take to get males to finish their development. Nor does there seem to be an appreciation for what that would really entail.

Often today men from the non-select group are just pushed aside. They are trampled over in the rush to get to the men of the elite aristocracy. When women "settle", even for a "good" man or a "nice" guy, they often treat him in an inferior way. He does not get her best effort. The nice guys do not get the midnight booty calls, his wife does not shop at Victoria's secret, and he will never come home to find that his mate has run his bath, put flower petals on the bed, and is waiting for him with that see-through lace bodice and G-string thing on. She is not broadcasting the elegant rose. The male response to this is a gangster mentality. Men will do just about anything to be in the select category. This includes selling drugs, buying a big car, getting the best job and hanging out only with other select men.

In the second place, she forms a lasting attachment to men who resemble the first boys she had sex with. The womb of the teen female is IMPRINTED by the first few men who enter her vagina. If you look at the first two or three men that she has sex with, and sum up a composite of their traits, you will see the type of man she has attracted all her life. If these first sexual episodes were less than wholesome, her selection criteria will be severely flawed. She will have a strange attraction to, and a sexual appetite for, males who are dysfunctional and impaired. The result is that men are very confused about what their role in a relationship is. To attract a woman you have to project this image of being a 'bad boy'. But once in a relationship, the woman becomes upset if you act like a bad boy. Bad boys are just that, bad. They have many girlfriends and tell lies when it suits them. But what gets them into the woman's bedroom, will not keep them into a relationship or marriage. She will thus attract to herself men who will not satisfy her, and in fact may harm her. It explains why she has blocked part of her feminine energy, and continues to engage in behavior that has shown historically to be unproductive for her. Now if you want to know why some women enjoy being tied up by men, and others always want to "save" a man who needs help, and some women want a rich man, and still others only get turned on by the dominant type, you need only look back at their father, and the first men they had sex with, and evaluate what was going on in her life at that time. You will have the answer to your question. And you will have a preview as to why her feminine energy is blocked to the extent that it is. For the master feminine faculty simply follows the recipe or program. It has to work with what is there.

Nature is based on a model of abundance. There are enough people that everyone can have an attractive, healthy, loving mate. Scarcity is created by man due to the greed of a few, and the ignorance of the many. It is war, political oppression, racial oppression and governments that create scarcity. It does not exist naturally, you have to make it. The fashion industry thrives off vanity, low-self esteem, and romance. The car industry designs cars to break down and burn a lot of fuel. It sells parts, and promotes the oil business. They spend millions to change the style of cars every year so that you will spend billions because your two -year old car is obsolete. The planned life span of a personal computer series, software, video device (DVD) or electronic entertainment device is no more than two years. Business people actually sit down in a room and try to figure out how to make their products obsolete in the desired time span. Women promote the scarcity model by creating a class of men who are non-select. The proper action is to identify a class of men who are underdeveloped. Work on ways to encourage these men to finish their development. Do this in a way that validates the male, instead of destroying his self esteem.

Today many older women feel lost. They feel out of place and disconnected. They have lived the life that society has crafted for them. They dressed the way they were supposed to, acted the way they thought was proper, tried to do the right thing, and sought with great effort to share love with the men in their lives. But through all of it they were not completely present. It was not the real them. They lived for their parents, their children, their husband, their job or their church. Because they agreed to support the scarcity model, there was no room in their life for themselves. This is the counterfeit life, lived by the counterfeit persona of people who are not fully present. The main portion of their lives was lived to support the elite, not themselves. And just as women currently have issues with their feminine energy, so do modern men have issues with their masculine energy.

Some men play relationship games, as part of their strategy to get what they want. They see the emotional baggage many women carry more than they see the potential that is there. And in the quest to complete their strategy there is often a good deal of lies told, masks worn and promises broken.

Infidelity, abuse, being alone, experiencing the rejection and frustration of dating, and not having sex on a regular basis, are outcomes most people wish to avoid. A monogamous relationship with a faithful mate is seen as a solution. The natural outcome when women seek natural prosperity, personal evolution (men and women), and natural pleasure, is that they achieve sustainable relationships. For as we have said, these are the common denominators that men want. This is the natural sexual model of a relationship, and it tends to be sustainable. Prosperity, personal evolution and pleasure all add value to the relationship. The outcome when women seek personal economic advantage, promises based on moral codes and regulations, and strategies based on avoiding the risk of pain, is to remain alone, through divorce, rejection or infidelity.

In regard to men, know that males are becoming more yin. White men are becoming more feminine, but at a slow rate. Black men, Asian men and Native American men are becoming more feminine and yin. And they are doing so at a faster rate. Women must quickly gain an understanding of why!! And learn how to combat and counter this.

Forgiving Our Fathers

Father Son Relationship.

The foundation upon which a man's manhood is built is the proper relationship with his own father. Today, men suffer because there is no generational continuity from grandfather to father to son. Even if the father was present, but did not mentor his son properly, there is a fault. The male experiences this break in continuity as an emotional trauma. Once the adult man clears up the issues with his own father, then he can cultivate the attributes that make him an above average father to his son or daughter.

When you are a child, your parents are all you have. When one of them dies or leaves you it is a trauma. Perhaps the worse trauma of traumas because as a child you do not understand. Many men grow up without the father present on a daily basis. This absence adds a special challenge when they attempt to make the transition from boyhood to manhood. As adults these men often form a male to female relationship strategy that is based on an imbalanced model. They observed their mother interact with men and come to certain conclusions as a result. But it is not the same as if the man was their father. There is a certain part of the communication between man and woman that is missing for them. Their opinion of themselves is based in part on their opinion of the father and in general of all men. This is shaped by the opinion of the mother and sisters toward men in general. And if the father was absent it makes a negative statement about men on its face. If the mother remarried the step father may have helped the situation. But even so, it will not blunt the anger these men feel at being abandoned.

I have attended or been the speaker at many workshops and retreats. At the all male sessions it is usually a challenge just to keep the men's attention. There are usually three or four guys nodding off in the back, and others looking anxious for the session to be over. But the workshops on the theme of forgiving the fathers are never dull. The room is filled with tension. You can read the stress on the faces of the grown men who did not have a father present growing up. You have to be careful about what you say. To a man who was abandoned by his father, the very idea of forgiveness brings up a deep rage. There is normally some yelling, crying and often the possibility of physical confrontation. That is how strongly men feel about this. They may hide their full feelings from a woman, but they are there.

In respect to men who were abandoned by their fathers, there are two conditions. The first is when they have reconnected with the father and maintain some level of commerce with him, even if just to visit on the holidays. The second condition is when they refuse to speak to the father, or do not know his whereabouts. It is the second condition that is the problem. If a woman is in a relationship with a man who is still angry with his father, there are certain things she needs to know. Such a man can be fine as a mate and may treat you as good as gold. In fact he may even try to compensate for the wrongs other men have done. But the woman would do well to keep her eyes open. There are some minefields there, and she would do better not to accidentally set one off. Of course we all have our private issues and minefields. And these men are no worse or no better than others. However, men who grow up angry with their fathers have a particular issue or hindrance. As a boy growing up they learned to obey and respect women but not men to the same degree. Information and wisdom that normally passes from male from male does not get to them as easily. This may not sound like much, but take my word It is a very significant thing. This hampers them in some strange ways. Some men are naturally very resistant to male authority figures. It is just their personality. Others resist other males as a result of a psychosis, a belief that all men are inherently flawed. If they become policemen they believe certain types of men are evil, and can not be reformed. If teachers they believe some male students can not learn no matter what. They are often suspicious of the motives of other men. Even so, this does not stop them from making friends or having a normal relationship. There are so many ways that this may present itself in a relationship that we can not characterize it in one model. But I would advise any female in this situation to look into the dynamic of this father issue. If he ever gets the opportunity to patch things up with his father do encourage it. In family issues be careful not to side with members of his family against him, not even as a joke. The father issue will probably come up in your relationship indirectly. It will not show up as a conflict between you and him. Do not place yourself in between him and the object of his anger. Stay out of the way. And if you can, try to get close enough to him that he may one day feel safe to talk to you about it.

The Basis For Hope

When I speak at events the most common question on the lips of women is; "is there any real reason why I should believe that my aspirations for a soul-mate relationship will come to be?" "Tell me why I should get my hopes up!" When one considers the attitudes men and women bring with them to the table it can make one pause. Of course most women look around them and see nothing but relationship failure. And for many devoted women the nights and weekends hold little promise of satisfaction, or relief from tension. Many women are so busy trying not to let the children down, trying not to let their husbands down, that their own future no longer looks bright. Often she is the last defense against collapse of the family unit. And I can tell you with assurance that no one in their right mind on earth or in heaven wants to see her fail. Her daily routine sometimes consists of unfulfilling work, in a company run by people who have clearly lost their minds. And she may come home to ungrateful kids and a husband who falls asleep watching the late show.

The fact is that nature has empowered woman so much. She has no idea just how powerful a being she is. The only way that women can fail, is if they stop following the natural plan. A woman can not fail unless she intentionally abandons her feminine gifts. And for some reason, that is exactly what some women are doing. And if women continue to go through life without using all the tools nature gave her, the outcome will not change.   First women as a group should start to take some responsibility for how things got this way. When they do that hope starts. And then we must recognize that the wisdom to set things right is here. It has always been here waiting for people to use it. And then she needs to look around and see that many men want to love her. That is their intention. Hope lies in finding those men, and surrounding herself with them. Sooner or later one of those men will notice her, and turn intention into reality.

There is hope when she considers the law. The law of attraction says that if she broadcasts the right energy out, the right energy will come back to her. This is the law. It has always worked, and it will work for her. There is also the law of manifestation. In a nut shell the law of manifestation says that each of us is always in the process of creating our future based on the beliefs that we hold in our consciousness today. What we visualize and think and imagine and anticipate tends to shape our future reality. These visions and beliefs seep into our subconscious mind. There they are broadcast into the "matrix". Our planetary matrix is the sum or composite of all these dreams, thoughts, visions and belief systems. The powers of nature use this matrix as the template, or model in designing what the future reality of man will be like. This is the really short explanation. But it is saying that a woman or man can shape and influence their own destiny. There are limitations of course. There are other people around us who help to shape out reality. But more and more people are shifting to a mindset of harmony on this earth. The green movement is rising. The organic movement is coming on strong. The people are waking up. We have seen an era of civil rights, and an era of spiritual rights is coming. There is more to it of course. Karma is a vital component. And the degree to which your vision or thought matches the divine plan has a bearing on how it shapes the matrix.   Your sexual energy determines the power your vision has to change the matrix. And this is the woman's trump card. For the sexual energy which is often the source of so much trouble, is also the force that can heal and change. We have been in a sexual dark age, but that veil is lifted for anyone who has the wisdom to look beyond. We have placed our faith in money and material things but many now see that we must move beyond that. The solutions are at our fingertips. We just need to grasp them and go to work. There is more than just hope. People are finding their way to happiness everyday. It is an extraordinary time we live in. Join an awakening circle or some group, and start to make this your reality.

Talk to men in college and see how fast their eyes glaze over once you start to talk about the serious side of relationships. So many men have put up the old male force field. No real emotions come through. No real investments in females are allowed. Men make the best compromise they can without bringing down the force field. No Jedi mind-trick of the female can disable his force field. You can have that coke bottle shape and wear tight jeans all you want to, but it still will not penetrate into his heart. So many men have pulled back and are hiding behind an emotional shield. If a woman is thinking about breaking through the male force field she really needs to really understand that table of validation. Give out the validation, and demand it in return. The relationship battle is not hopeless. Most men recognize that they are not naturally among the group of "select men" as defined by the majority of women. To be included, they need to wear a mask. Most men recognize that they fall short of the abstract standard of manhood. Each man has a vision of this in his mind. And they say they do not care. But on some level they really do. In the back of our minds remember that the opposite sex wants what we want underneath all the facades and masks. When you plumb through to the rock bottom of a man's soul he wants more than anything to love you.

Life Episode The Anguish of Non- Select Men

Audrey, Kim, Erica and Jennifer met in college, and remained in contact for some years through the college alumni association. Audrey married William shortly after college and is still married. Erica married after college and later got a divorce. Now in her thirties, she is in a relationship with Kenneth that she believes will result in marriage. Jennifer has never been married. She has lived a little in the fast lane, and admits that she has made mostly bad choices when it comes to picking a mate. Her relationships have been for the most part short, unpleasant and filled with disappointment. Now in her thirties she does not trust men easily, and has very low expectations of men. Her financial situation is poor. And for the most part her encounters with men now are about sexual gratification and gaining access to the good life through the men she dates. Kim never married after college, but she wants to get married more than anything. But of all four women she has had the worst experience with men. She was in one long term relationship in her twenties that ended very badly. After being together for over one year he ended their relationship over what she thought was a small argument. He never came back. And she discovered that the whole time he was with her, he was also seeing one of her female acquaintances. And there were signs that there were other women. This one experience was a severe blow to Kim, and in the months after she gained forty pounds. For almost five years Kim had almost no sexual activity. The bright spot in Kim's life has been her career. She is now the head of her department in a mid-sized retail company and makes a good six-figure income.

Over the years these four women have come in to contact with many men. Women routinely rate men and assign them into two categories, the "select men" and the "non-select men" according to criteria. Audrey is still married to William. He is considered select. Erica is dating Kenneth, considered by most women as non- select. And there are also Charles, Andrew and Marvin. Charles is by most accounts considered one of the select men. He drove a new Mercedes and lived in a very large house on the good side of town. Charles was an old associate of Jennifer's. Andrew and Marvin were considered by most women as being in the non-select category. They were regular guys, and each had pulled back emotionally from women. Normally the select men and the non-select men do not socialize together.

When Charles first met Jennifer he thought she was attractive and wished to have sex with her. But after getting to know her, he decided against this. Jennifer also thought that Charles was okay as a friend, but did not wish to be intimate with him. They remained as friends, but did not communicate much. Andrew is divorced. Andrew had some sexual issues and has trouble keeping a good job. He went from one job to another and could not find where he belonged. Marvin lacked self confidence and had esteem issues. He was a nice guy, but not very aggressive when it came to women. Andrew and Marvin were associates of Audrey and Kenneth. For the last seven years Audrey, Kim, Erica and Jennifer have only seen each other twice each year at alumni events. But this is all about to change because of a chance meeting, a charity event.

It was an event to raise money for Audrey's favorite charity. At the event Audrey and William ran into two old friends, Marvin and Andrew. William was surprised to see them there. This event was a little above their pay grade. As it happened, Charles and Kenneth were also at the same event. The event was being held in a reserved area of a private club. In one room off from the main event was a large screen television and the game was playing. Some of the men gathered there to watch the game. And soon many men had gathered there, including William,

Kenneth, Charles, Marvin and Andrew. It was one of those rare times when the select men and the non-select men were hanging out together. When the game ended, a general conversation started amongst the men present. At first the talk was about sports, but soon it switched to the single women at the event. And then a very interesting thing happened. Charles, a man from the select group, started to relate a story about a woman who had recently come to see him. She showed up at his door late at night with a fur coat on, and only panties underneath.   She proceeded to provide Charles with an evening of provocative entertainment. Kenneth heard the story but did not believe it. Kenneth felt that Charles made the whole story up, to pump himself up. So Kenneth, a man from the non-select group, challenged the authenticity of Charles's story. Kenneth, who was dating Erica, did not believe anything like that had ever happened to Charles, because it had never happened to him.

An intense argument followed that soon engulfed all the men in the room. The men from the non-select group sided with Kenneth; they refused to believe a woman would just show up at some man's door with only panties on. It was something that only happened in the movies they said. But the men from the select group sided with Charles. These men insisted that women did risqué stuff like this all the time.   Basically Kenneth and Marvin challenged Charles and other men about the account.   It was the select men against the non-select men. Finally Charles became fed up. He excused himself and went out into the main room. In a few minutes Charles returned with two attractive women by his side. After an introduction and some background conversation, Charles proceeded to tell the same story he had told the men, to the two ladies. When he finished he asked the ladies if they had ever done anything like that, and why. The first lady told all the men in the room of an almost identical account. She said she always did something risqué at the beginning of all her relationships to set the tone. The second lady would not talk about her own personal stories, but she did tell the men something one of her girlfriends had done. The episodes were steamy and hot. Charles was vindicated. Marvin and Kenneth had to concede. Then the men from the select group begin to make fun of the men there from the non-select group who had doubted the story. Smiling, they asked Kenneth why no woman had ever done anything "special" to him. They asked if he was very religious or conservative, basically making fun of him. And they joked about Kenneth, basically saying that the reason no woman had ever showed up half naked at his door was because he did not know what to do with it if they did. The jokes started to fly between the men. At first it was just fun and even Marvin laughed.   But this changed when one of the ladies slipped and made the wrong comment. She said jokingly, her friends only did things like that to certain men, not all men. Her comment was intended to defend her friends, it was not directed at Kenneth, but as soon as she said it all the men looked at Kenneth and his face said it all. She tried to clean it up but it did not help. Kenneth was cut deeply, but he had always known that women treated him differently than most men. He was just a nice guy, not sexy or rich like some other men. It was a sore spot and the lady had opened the wound up wide. Kenneth stood up, and without comment just walked out of the room. Marvin followed Kenneth to the bar. The two men sat at the bar and talked about how regular guys get treated by women. How unfair they thought that players get all the excitement, while nice guys like them were lucky to get any action at all. Kenneth said, "what really bothers me is my woman does not think I am worthy of a little special treatment. I feel second class man!" Kenneth confided to Marvin that Erica never even wore any sexy underwear or did anything adventurous. Erica had never really done anything exciting in their relationship. When Kenneth made discreet hints to Erica she accused him of not being "spiritual". She made Kenneth feel perverted for just wanting a little erotic play. Kenneth got into trouble yesterday for being late from the market.

The repercussions of this incident would spread beyond this event. The men in the room retold the whole incident involving Kenneth to their dates. Everyone was laughing at Kenneth. The story reached the ears of Audrey. She was furious. Audrey turned to William and asked him why he had done nothing to stop this from happening. The relationship between Kenneth and Erica was shaky right now, and Erica was stressed to the maximum about it. The timing could not be worse. Audrey feared that Kenneth would blame Erica and pull back. William had not thought about that. Audrey was right. The impact from this chance incident between Kenneth and Charles did not end when the event was over. Kenneth pulled back from Erica and did not call her for a week. After seven days and no contact with Kenneth Erica was a powder keg ready to explode. When she finally reached Kenneth's friend Marvin, he did not have anything good to say. Marvin had never seen Kenneth so depressed. Erica had invested so much in this thing with Kenneth and if it went sour she was not sure how she could go forward. In gross desperation she turned her wrath on Audrey and Jennifer. Erica believed that Jennifer was the woman Charles was talking about, who had showed up with only panties and a fur coat on. Jennifer was known to do stuff like that. Erica blamed Audrey just for hosting the event. Erica's friends were gathered at her house to support her. She would not eat, and could not sleep. There was concern that she might do something to herself.

William and Audrey argued about the incident all week. When Kim heard about the drama she was upset at Audrey, because Audrey had not invited her. Kim was taken off the list automatically by the computer because she had not attended in the last three years. But Kim felt it was personal. Kim felt it was because she made more in salary than the three women put together. Maybe it was because she had refused to loan money to Audrey a few years back. Audrey and Jennifer were always meeting new men, and they always had plenty of male friends. They claimed to be Kim's friend, but they always had an excuse why they never introduced Kim to any of their male friends. Kim wondered if it was because of her weight. It was not like this in college. Kim wished they could go back to the college days.

Jennifer was going through a very tough time. Why now she thought? Erica was one of the few friends Jennifer could count on, why this drama now? It was so unfair. Erica was her life line. Erica had been there for her in the last few weeks. Without Erica she did not know if she would have made it. "Why did that fool Charles have to tell that old story," she thought. Jennifer and Charles had never even slept together! It was about another woman, not her. Erica was crazy about Kenneth. In fact Erica was so crazy about Kenneth, that Jennifer avoided even meeting him. She did not want to even take the chance that Kenneth might look at her the wrong way and make Erica jealous. Erica was too sensitive and jealous. It had to do with her brush with death, and the fear that Kenneth might be the last opportunity for Erica to find happiness. It was just a feeling Erica had. Now Jennifer was being blamed, and she was not even at the charity event! Jennifer felt that if Kenneth pulled back it would devastate Erica. And Erica would take it out on Jennifer. Everyone always took it out on Jennifer. That is how Jennifer felt.

A joking comment made at a charity event now threatened the friendship of four women. Every day that Kenneth did not call, the tension built up between Audrey, Erica, Jennifer and Kim. In the hard times it was Erica who always held them down. But now Erica was at the crossroads. Kim was the only one removed enough from the incident to pull the group back together. Kenneth was plain on the outside, but had a heart of gold. He made Erica laugh, and he was always helping people. Erica thought the world of him. How could this have happened? How could it be fixed?

End of Episode ....